PITT'S GALLANT CONQUEROR

To Anne
for waiting so long

PITT'S GALLANT CONQUEROR

THE TURBULENT LIFE OF LIEUTENANT-GENERAL SIR WILLIAM DRAPER K.B.

JAMES DREAPER

I.B. TAURIS

LONDON · NEW YORK

Published in 2006 by I.B.Tauris & Co Ltd
6 Salem Road, London W2 4BU
175 Fifth Avenue, New York NY 10010
www.ibtauris.com

In the United States of America and in Canada distributed by
Palgrave Macmillan, a division of St Martin's Press
175 Fifth Avenue, New York NY 10010

ISBN 10: 1 84511 177 X
ISBN 13: 978 1 84511 177 9

A full CIP record for this book is available from the British Library
A full CIP record for this book is available from the Library of Congress

Library of Congress catalog card: available

Typeset in Sabon by Steve Tribe, Andover
Printed and bound in Great Britain by TJ International, Padstow

CONTENTS

ILLUSTRATIONS

PREFACE

In 1966 I was crewing on a yacht sailing in the Hong Kong to Manila race. As we coasted by the Bataan peninsula and swung past Corregidor to enter the Bay of Manila, talking about General MacArthur and the Japanese invasion of 1942, our American skipper asked, 'Did you know that the Brits once came here and captured the place?' None of us knew – and his remark went unexplained as we changed sails to cross the huge sweep of the bay.

Years later, involved in research in London, I came across a small copy of the Gainsborough portrait of Lieutenant-General Sir William Draper, with a laconic description on an accompanying card: 'Believed knighted for the conquest of Manila 1762'. In exploring the accuracy of the inscription I discovered details of a life and its setting which seemed to deserve a wider audience.

Within the period broadly covering the long span between the triumphs of Marlborough and the future greatness of Wellington, only one soldier, Wolfe, was accorded the posthumous rank of national hero, with Clive of India as a comparable figure from the East India Company's service. Yet the record of achievement which contributed so much to the expansion of British influence during that period, particularly during the Seven Years War of 1756–1763, was a tribute to the ability of commanders to overcome the hazards of systems without safety nets.

The idea of the 'simple soldier' unquestioningly building the Empire in distant lands was more a product of the historical retrospect of the nineteenth century than the reality of the eighteenth. Commanders then often needed to, and did, act with the spirit of independent entrepreneurs; and they had no inhibitions about acknowledging that the prospect of booty was a spur to action.

This spirit of aggressive resourcefulness was necessary within situations where systems and logistics were inadequate and at the mercy of distance and time. The machinery of government and administration, dependent on small cadres of overworked individuals, was usually far behind the pace of events. Precedent and tradition were in the process of being formed rather than followed. Ad hoc answers to local problems were often the only realistic option.

Subsequent difficulties multiplied when these ad hoc solutions failed to fit within the framework of distant systems. The classic dilemma of the period was that faced by the British government and the East India Company which, via the local victories of Robert Clive, almost by accident acquired the responsibilities of a sovereign power, governing and exercising fiscal powers over enormous territories.

On a much smaller scale, the capture of Manila, capital of the Philippine Islands, from the Spanish in October 1762 presented a similar dilemma to the government in London. It was one of the more improbable victories of the Seven Years War, remaining the most easterly battle ever fought by the British army, on the edge of the known world, at a time even before Cook had discovered the coast of Australia. It also was the only occasion when forces of the East India Company fought alongside royal troops outside India. It was unique not least because it depended entirely on the presence of the soldier who planned and commanded it, Brigadier William Draper.

William Draper was one of that small group of officers who, through their record of courage and merit, came to be entrusted with commands demanding imagination and initiative. The coup de main at Manila, a successful combined operation with a naval squadron commanded by Rear-Admiral Samuel Cornish, was without doubt a military victory. Yet its aftermath, hinging round the legitimacy of the ransom agreement between the British victors and the Governor of Manila, involved the British and Spanish governments in more than a decade of tortuous diplomatic jousting, the Madrid government choosing to regard the Manila coup as akin to piracy rather than a legitimate act of war. Draper's continuing readiness to involve himself in subsequent public controversy for a cause he believed worth defending led him a few years later, in 1769, into the disastrous confrontation through which he became best known to the British public, that of adversary and victim of the political satirist Junius. His more congenial links with the sporting world were marked by his eventual chairmanship of a committee in 1774 which revised the Laws of Cricket that have formed the basis of the game ever since. In that capacity, he arguably had more influence on the wider public than through any of the achievements of his turbulent military life.

The example of his achievement at Manila outlived him. Plans for a subsequent expedition in 1797, ten years after his death, included the possibility that command of the troops be given to Colonel Arthur Wellesley, the future Duke of Wellington. Wellesley too shared the chimera that this command would make his fortune, but the expedition got no further than Penang before being recalled. Manila remained dormant in its isolation until being seized by the Americans a century later. The conquest of 1762 receded into history as a military eccentricity, an ironic success brought to nothing by the force majeure of time and distance, politics and diplomacy.

James Dreaper, Shaftesbury

ACKNOWLEDGEMENTS

In the lengthy process of research for this study I have benefited greatly from the assistance of others usually more knowledgeable than myself and who have been invaluable in pointing me in fruitful directions. I particularly valued the help and patience of the staff of the Reading Rooms, the Manuscript Department, and the Oriental and India Office Collections of the British Library; the Department of Prints and Drawings of the British Museum; the National Archives; Public Record Office; the Bodleian Library; the Guildhall Library; the London Library; the National Portrait Gallery; the Courtauld Institute; Bristol Central Library and Bristol Record Office; the County Records Offices of Dorset, East Sussex, East Yorkshire, Hampshire, and Somerset; the Brynmor Jones Library, University of Hull; the University of Southampton; the Royal Historical Society; and the Fitzwilliam Museum. I acknowledge the permission of Her Majesty Queen Elizabeth II to make use of material from the Cumberland Papers in the Royal Archives.

In the United States of America, the staff of the National Portrait Gallery; the Fine Arts Museums of San Francisco; the Henry Morrison Flagler Museum; the Frick Art Reference Library; the Huntington Library; the William L. Clements Library of the University of Michigan; the New York Public Library, and the Philadelphia Museum of Art have all been most helpful.

Many individuals have been encouraging in their advice and suggestions over an extended period and among these I should like to thank Professor Ian Beckett, University of Luton; Mr Hugh Belsey, Curator, Gainsborough's House; Mr Peter Beauclerk-Dewar; Dr John Booker, Head of Archives, Lloyds Bank; Ms Jacqueline Cox, Archivist, King's College Cambridge; Mr Joe Darracott; Professor Martin Daunton, University College London; Lady de Bellaigue, Registrar of the Royal Archives; M. Pierre de Longuemar; Mr Donald Dougherty; Mr Stephen Green, Curator MCC; Mr John Goulstone; Dr Alan Guy, National Army Museum; Mrs Penelope Hatfield, Archivist of Eton College; Colonel Malcolm Havergal; Dr Tony Hayter; Mrs Victoria Hutchings, Museum Curator, C. Hoare & Co.; Mr Donald Jones; Mr Michael

Jones, Royal Historical Society; Major P. A. Lewis, Regimental Archivist, Grenadier Guards; Ms Fiona MacColl, Archivist, National Westminster Bank Group; Mr Michael Purcell; Mr Stanley Rosenthal; Mrs Marjorie Salkeld, East Yorkshire Local History Society; The Secretary, Society of Merchant Venturers of Bristol; Ms Susan Skata, Librarian, Trinity Church, New York; Ms Alison Turton, Head of Archives, Royal Bank of Scotland; Mr Philip Winterbottom, Archivist, Drummonds Bank; and above all my wife Anne without whose continuous encouragement and research assistance this work would never have been completed.

'Manila's gallant conqueror, basely traduced into a mean plunderer, a gentleman whose noble and generous spirit would do honour to the proudest grandee of this country.'
William Pitt the Elder,
House of Commons, January 1766

'Take care Sir William how you indulge this unruly temper, lest the world should suspect that conscience has some share in your resentments. You have more to fear from the treachery of your own passions than from the malevolence of mine.'
Junius to Sir William Draper,
Public Advertiser, 25 September 1769

I

FORMING CLAIMS
TO AUTHORITY

1

UNCERTAIN
OPPORTUNITIES

On Clifton Down above Bristol stand two monuments, an obelisk and a cenotaph. In their isolation amidst the trees they seem to embody the expression of some private and distant tribute. They, and the nearby sign still marking Manila Road, are residual ghosts of men and events which in their time commanded global attention.

Both monuments were gestures of loyalty from the man who originally commissioned them, Lieutenant-General Sir William Draper. They were intended only for the garden of Manila Hall which he had built on Clifton Down following his return from successful command of the expedition which captured Manila, capital of the Philippine Islands, from Spain in 1762.

The obelisk, dedicated to William Pitt the Elder, Earl of Chatham, and the cenotaph dedicated to the 79th Regiment of Foot, Draper's Regiment, were both crucially relevant to his achievements. Their presence in Clifton was itself an expression of loyalty to the city in which Sir William had been born in 1721.

His family's presence in Bristol was a typical result of the incessant need in the eighteenth century for the younger sons of minor gentry to search for patronage and place. His young father, Ingleby Draper, had been found a place in the Customs and Excise in Bristol through the influence of his own father and had come to live in Bristol only a few years before his son, the future general, was born there.

The family from which Ingleby Draper sprang had, like hundreds of similar families over the centuries, progressed from yeomen farmers to merchants

3

and landowners, producing successive generations of minor gentry playing a useful role at county or national level. The staying-power required for such continuity depended on an amalgam of robust health, watchfulness, and familial self-interest. All these qualities were present in Draper's immediate line of descent.

His branch of the family had been based in the Oxfordshire village of Nether Worton where the house built by his ancestors still stands close to the village church. Ingleby's own father, William, had in 1694 married Anne Daniell, sole surviving child and heiress of Ingleby Daniell of Beswick in the East Riding of Yorkshire. Her estates were the platform on which William Draper earned his reputation as Squire Draper, one of the greatest of early masters of hounds.[1]

The Squire's reputation around Yorkshire, particularly in the East Riding, placed him at the centre of a wide and influential network of friends, acquaintances and alliances. Within this amiable society he never lost sight of the need to provide opportunities for the seven of his eight sons who were not in line to inherit the Beswick or Nether Worton estates. In keeping with the accepted patterns of their times they were found places in the navy, the army, the church, and where possible among the fortunate few in the jostling crowd of place seekers on the Government's payroll.

One of Squire William's younger sons, William Henry, joined that growing source of opportunity for the landless sons of minor gentry, the Honourable East India Company. When he first went to India as a 'writer' in 1715, the days of the great fortunes of the nabobs still lay ahead, but the trading life in India offered prospects which could hardly be matched in England. William Henry, whose career included the curious distinction of being appointed the first Mayor of Bombay, in 1726, created for the family an Indian connection which was to last well into the next century.

The Squire's second son, Ingleby, named after his maternal grandfather, was found a 'place' in Customs and Excise. The Customs Service had long been regarded as one of the most lucrative sources of employment on the Government payroll, and its senior positions as useful sinecures for supporters of the Government. Ingleby Draper was first appointed as 'King's Waiter in Bristol Port' in October 1715, when he would have been no more than eighteen.[2] 'King's Waiter' was a quaint title for a junior manager, but it gave him a tiny income and, more important, a clear line of opportunity.

Bristol was then the second largest city in England, its port at the height of its commercial importance with a population of around 80,000. Contemporary prints, especially those depicting the view from the heights of Clifton, convey an astonishing spectacle of a city threaded together by the masts and spars of the ships moored along the arms of the rivers Avon and Frome.

The wealth of Bristol had grown through its seaborne connections with the expanding colonies of North America, the sugar trade with the West Indies, and participation in the slave trade from Africa to the Caribbean and America.

The commercial importance of Bristol gave the city a corresponding political importance with Parliament and the King's government.

Bristol was thus a place of opportunity for a young man. Unfortunately for his young wife and four surviving children, Ingleby Draper did not live long enough to make any lasting mark. He died suddenly in 1722, aged only 25, a month or two before the birth of his younger son William, the future general.[3] He thus left a widow Mary, with two sons and two daughters all below the age of eight. She, the daughter of Alexander Harrison an alderman of York, was herself still only in her mid-twenties at the time of her husband's untimely death, and was thrown immediately into the unenviable position of having to depend on her own or her late husband's families. Their financial support must have come to her help, but it says much for her own resilience that she was able to bring all four of her children to maturity in defiance of such a devastating loss. She never married again and yet lived long enough to enjoy some of the fruits of her son William's triumph at Manila some forty years later.

William was found a place at the Cathedral School in Bristol which provided the basics of a classical education under the guidance of the Reverend George Bryan, headmaster from 1709 to 1743, a length of service which says as much for his powers of endurance as for the undemanding pressures of the time.

During the years when the schoolboy was absorbing this classical grounding his mother was coping with the problems of arranging for the futures of her older children. In 1729, when William was about eight, Mary Draper was recorded in the Court Minutes of the East India Company as 'praying leave to send her daughter Anna, together with a maid servant, to take care of her uncle Mr William Henry Draper at Bombay'.[4] Permission was granted the following month, and Anna, then aged about thirteen, would have departed on one of the East Indiamen, even at that age considered mature enough to undergo the hazards of the long voyage to India.

The family connection with the East India Company was again used a year or two later to provide a position for William's elder brother, named Ingleby after his father, who joined the Company's Maritime Service. His career, however, did not last long enough to provide anything other than a distant sorrow for his family as he was drowned at sea off Canton, on the China coast, aged only twenty-one, when serving on one of the Company's ships, the *Cowan*, in 1735. In the Bombay Mayor's Court in 1736, administration of his effects was granted to Thomas Moore, a surgeon in the Company's service, 'one of his creditors, whereas the said Ingleby died some time ago in Canton in the Empire of China, intestate as well as insolvent ... '[5]

The only consolation to the widowed Mary Draper for the loss of her elder son was that by then the Company surgeon, Thomas Moore, had become her son-in-law, having married the young Anna two years after her arrival in Bombay.[6] Moore, with his wife and their three surviving children, returned to Bristol a few years later, he to establish himself as a prosperous apothecary.

By then William was showing early promise. From the Cathedral School he was accepted by Eton in 1733, 'on the Foundation', that is as a King's Scholar, or Colleger. Eton during that period mirrored the indiscipline and violence of the society whose future leaders it was producing. Though it may have produced gentlemen, it was no place for the gentle. The life of the Collegers was notoriously tough, living as they all did in the Long Chamber for the whole of their time at Eton, unlike the richer Oppidans who lodged more freely in the town. The Sixth Form ruled the Chamber as it chose, imposing its arbitrary rule on the younger boys who accepted their lot, knowing that their turn would come.

The core of the education remained the study of the Latin and Greek classics, much of it laboriously committed to memory. Games were organised informally but there was opportunity to engage in a whole range of active sports including rowing, cricket, fives, and real tennis, as well as all the country pursuits in the amiable countryside which then surrounded Eton. Etonians also enjoyed the privilege of joining in the regular meets of the Royal Buckhounds in nearby Windsor Great Park.

Eton's powers of refinement somehow managed to transcend the brutality of its system and traditions. The whole ethos of the college was based on an unquestioned acceptance that it existed to perpetuate a ruling class capable of excellence in every field. Beneath the façade of effortless superiority lay both the self-assurance of being a born, or chosen, member of the elite, and the toughness of the survivor. The assumed right to leadership may have produced intolerable arrogance but it was equally often justified by subsequent achievement. Scholarship was always deemed to be of less importance than worldliness in eighteenth-century society, though it provided a shared set of values among the educated. Access to wider society via the route of the Eton scholar was no guarantee of future success in itself but it opened the way to early acquaintance with the leaders of the future.

From his time at Eton, William Draper counted among his lifelong friends Christopher Anstey, the irreverent scholar who went on to become celebrated as a minor poet and author of the *New Bath Guide*, which many years later made him a literary celebrity. The fact that Anstey was an Oppidan seems to have been no bar to their friendship. Both of them matched their potential by gaining scholarships in the same year to King's College, Cambridge, Draper going up in 1740 at the comparatively late age of eighteen.

At that age many of their contemporaries would already have gained military experience, as the long years of peace under Sir Robert Walpole's successive ministries had finally been shattered by the outbreak of the War of Jenkins' Ear between England and Spain, a conflict which was soon to be absorbed into the wider War of the Austrian Succession.

Growing up in Bristol, and at Eton, William Draper would have been well aware of the clamour which had been mounting for more than a decade against the 'depredations' inflicted on British shipping by the Spaniards, particularly in the Caribbean. The Peace of Utrecht which had ended the War of the Spanish Succession as far back as 1714 had supposedly clarified points of demarcation between British, Spanish, and other European powers relating to trade around the Americas. The reality was much less clear, and much more contentious.

In an age of commercial expansion there could be no set of rules to which any, let alone all, of the parties would strictly adhere. Self-interest, so easily masked and glorified as national interest, was the order of the day. British merchants looked upon it as a matter of principle and fact, to be supported by the Government of the day, that trade with British colonies should be exclusively reserved to themselves. The fact that Spain should understandably have a similar attitude to its own sphere of influence, particularly South America, was looked upon by British traders as an intolerable presumption which needed to be, and frequently was, challenged.

Attrition continued throughout the 1720s and 1730s, each of the nations allowing their merchants and mariners to act as surrogates for their trading interests. The merchants in turn came increasingly to feel that they were bearing the brunt of the action; the merchants of Bristol, for example, forwarding in 1731 petitions to Westminster complaining of the 'harassing interruptions to trade, and the heavy losses to which they were subjected'. Throughout the decade a feeling of national indignation, stirring folk memories, gradually created a head of steam which finally vented through the bizarre conduit of Jenkins' Ear.

Captain Robert Jenkins was a hardened privateer who also happened to be a skilful self-publicist. His ill-treatment at the hands of the Spanish *guarda-costas* in Cuba some years earlier had hardly been more than expected by either side when privateers were intercepted; but he had been presented with a great opportunity when the *guarda-costas* cut off one of his ears, telling him to take it home and present it to his King. Jenkins did exactly that, preserving it in a bottle of spirit and presenting it, not personally to his sovereign George II, but more effectively before a committee of the House of Commons. Jenkins' reply to the question as to what he thought about his ordeal – 'I recommended my soul to God and my cause to my country' – was shrewdly calculated to trigger exactly the sort of public reaction against which Robert Walpole's cautious policy of sustaining peace was no longer effective.

War on Spain was declared in October 1739 to great public acclamation. Walpole's prediction that bell-ringing would soon be followed by hand-wringing was accurate, but counted for little against the ebullience of a national mood which believed that there was more to be gained from a short conclusive war than from an uneasy and protracted peace. The war unfortunately proved to be neither short nor conclusive.

The excitement and domestic political turmoil which followed the outbreak of war dominated the national scene throughout the time that William Draper was at King's. The pace of events as the war progressed must have seemed more compellingly interesting to any lively undergraduate than the pattern of life in a Cambridge college during those years. Under a succession of undistinguished Provosts, King's had lost much of its previous repute, reflecting the intellectual and academic torpor of the times.

The lethargic tempo of Cambridge life allowed plenty of time and opportunity for sport, and the Etonians at King's played a significant role in the growth of cricket at the university, usually fielding a side in an annual match against the Rest of the University which they habitually won. William Draper's enthusiasm for cricket which lasted throughout his life was nurtured at King's and brought him the additional benefit of entree to a wider circle of contacts than would have been possible for a scholar devoted only to his studies.

During his four years at King's, at the end of which he graduated with a BA in 1744, the reverberations of the outside world had been growing more insistent. Robert Walpole's predicted hand-wringing had begun as war with Spain revealed the lamentable state of the country's military readiness. Worries about setbacks against the Spanish soon began to appear minor in comparison with the commitments which would be needed as Britain gradually became more involved in the War of the Austrian Succession.

The war against Spain was essentially maritime, with Britain's campaigning efforts dependent almost entirely on the strength and expertise of the Royal Navy. Initial plans for an offensive effort against the Spanish were breathtaking in both their strategic vision and bold absurdity. These envisaged simultaneous pincer attacks in the Pacific and the Caribbean, totally disregarding the reality that half the Navy's establishment of eighty-four ships was unfit for service, only 21,000 seamen could be mustered from an establishment of 28,000, and logistics pointed to the impossibility of mounting simultaneous expeditions over such vast distances.

An alternative plan, hardly less feasible, presumed a combined naval and military expedition to the Caribbean and a small harassing force to the Pacific around Cape Horn. The disasters suffered by the large expedition despatched to the Caribbean shattered the national mood of complacency. The only victor in the protracted agony of the siege of Cartagena in Colombia was the tropical climate, whose main weapon, yellow fever, was Spain's most effective and least costly response to the stubborn bravery of the British expeditionary forces. The reverses suffered by the expedition led to its eventual recall at the end of 1742, by which time Robert Walpole had resigned from office.

The task force sent to the Pacific under Commodore George Anson to 'annoy and distress the Spanish on the Pacific coast of America' turned into an epic circumnavigation lasting four years. Anson departed on his voyage with a tiny force of six men-of-war and two victuallers, his ships overloaded with 250 unfortunate Chelsea pensioners who had been cynically contributed by the army as 'the military force' in the almost certain knowledge that few would ever return to be a further burden on the army vote. Anson's protest about the inhumanity of this deployment was ignored, and in fact none of the veterans returned.

Anson's successful circumnavigation, and his capture of the Manila galleon, elevated him deservedly to the status of national hero. The thirty-six wagons of booty from the Spanish galleon, paraded through London, were celebrated as a national triumph on Anson's return in 1744. The euphoria of this triumph tended to obscure the harsh truth that only one of Anson's ships, the *Centurion*, finished the voyage, and that while four men had been killed in action more than 1,300 had died of scurvy and other diseases.

Anson survived to become First Lord of the Admiralty during the Seven Years War, and his enthusiasm for a fresh expedition against the Spanish in the Pacific was to be the most influential voice in the decision to mount the expedition against Manila in 1762, twenty years later, when command was to be given to William Draper.

While Anson was engaged on his unreported voyage, England was being drawn reluctantly into the wider European conflict which came to be known as the War of the Austrian Succession. The byzantine manoeuvring among the European powers to fill the vacuum created by the death of the Emperor Charles VI of Austria in 1740 led to England championing the cause of his daughter Marie-Therese of Austria, but refraining from declaring war on any of the other powers pushing rival claimants. The consequence of this limited commitment was the despatch to Flanders of yet another British army destined for the sort of drawn-out and inconclusive campaigns which tended to reinforce the aversion of the British public to continental involvement.

The Battle of Dettingen in 1743, memorable chiefly because it was the last occasion on which a British sovereign, George II, personally led his troops in battle, was an encounter between two armies of countries still posing as auxiliaries of the different claimants to the Austrian throne. The outcome of the battle was hailed in England as a victory though in reality it was more a fortunate escape.

William Pitt, then a rising political force, used the occasion of Parliament's Address of Congratulation to George II on his leadership at Dettingen to suggest that England's involvement in Europe was distorting national priorities in favour of those of the House of Hanover. This not surprisingly infuriated his Sovereign, both on a personal level and also because George II could never detach himself from his simultaneous responsibilities on the continent as Elector of Hanover.

Pitt was then beginning to promote the ideas which were to influence his policies during the rest of his life; the underlying belief that Britain's long-term interests would best be served by avoiding commitments on continental Europe in favour of maritime expansion on a global scale. His strategic thinking arose naturally from the history and ambitions of an aggressive island people. Its historical and political importance was that it was being propounded by a potential leader sensing the national mood of the time.

In the aftermath of the Battle of Dettingen the French, believing that they had exposed the weakness of the British army, planned an invasion of England, urged on by the Young Pretender, Prince Charles Edward, who saw in Britain's distractions in Flanders the opportunity for a possible restoration of the exiled Stuart dynasty. The invasion project was eventually aborted, and its only important outcome was that England and France formally declared war in the spring of 1744, thus setting the scene for a further four years of conflict.

The national mood in England was still in favour of war, and the army was beginning to expand to meet its greater commitments. It was not surprising that William Draper, having attained his Cambridge degree, would opt to lay aside the prospect of further studies in favour of joining a suitable regiment. One of his uncles, Edward Draper, a senior lieutenant in Honeywood's Horse, had been killed at Dettingen, another, Charles, was serving in Lord Charles Churchill's Regiment of Dragoons, while a third, John, a Royal Navy captain, had died on service a year or two earlier. There were sufficient service connections to influence him towards the career which he was to follow for the rest of his life. He sought, and received, a Commission as an Ensign in Lord Henry Beauclerk's Regiment, the 48th Regiment of Foot, in March 1744.[7]

The career on which he was embarking was to be exposed in full measure to all the uncertainties of eighteenth-century life.

2

STEPS TOWARDS VISIBILITY

In the middle of the eighteenth century the British army was the product of a collective and magnificent denial of the logic implicit in Britain's hatred of standing armies. Its growth was a typically British solution to a dilemma facing a nation unwilling to admit the need for, or pay for, a large permanent army, while acknowledging its necessity in times of war. It was a curious coincidence that the British troops fighting in Flanders and Germany should have been part of an Allied army named the Pragmatic Army. If anything was pragmatic it was the British army.

The army had grown as an appendage to the Crown, with the Sovereign wielding direct control over its structure, command, and deployment. The vital purse strings were, however, under the control of Parliament, via annual votes for the maintenance of the army. This repetitive ritual inevitably reflected current political attitudes, as well as a permanent reluctance to burden the taxpayer. Since the taxpayers were primarily the landowners and merchant classes who provided Parliament with many of its members there was a considerable element of self-interest in opting for parsimony. In times of peace there was always pressure to reduce the level of manning found necessary in the previous war. It followed that the royal forces were always below the required strength at the outbreak of the next conflict. This unsettling process of expansion and contraction was not unique to Britain, or to that century.

Parliament's broad consensus was that the peacetime army should be limited to guards and garrisons, expansion only being approved when specific emergencies arose. By 1739, at the outbreak of the War of Jenkins' Ear, the army establishment had been allowed to drift down to only 18,000, in comparison with the French standing army of 300,000. The puny figure of 18,000 was not even a firm indicator of the actual strength of fighting units. Hence the miserable tale of the Chelsea Pensioners being drafted to form the 'military support' for Anson's expedition to the Pacific.

Parliament's attitude towards the peacetime army was a faithful reflection of that of the general population: simple hostility. The public wished that the army did not need to exist, or if it had to, could be somewhere else, preferably abroad. The consequence of this attitude had resulted in the gradual development of a complex network of ad hoc arrangements between the King, Parliament and the people, through which the army was raised, supplied and maintained without any of the parties being charged with sole responsibility.

The traditional method of raising regiments had remained largely unchanged since Charles II's day, being a direct contract between the Sovereign and a nobleman or gentleman to provide troops in return for their pay which was voted by Parliament and channelled through the offices of the Paymaster General and the Secretary at War. The individual commissioned to raise a regiment as colonel was customarily allowed to name it after himself. The money voted by Parliament was entrusted to the colonel, who was also entitled to receive the sums paid by the regiment's first complement of officers for their commissions. Most of the colonel's personal income was therefore derived legitimately from what he was able to save in the running of his regiment. This opportunity in turn created the system of regimental agents, men of business, who handled the regiment's financial affairs on behalf of their employer the colonel.

Day-to-day responsibility for handling regimental duties was entrusted to a lieutenant-colonel, and in peacetime the colonel would only occasionally feel obliged to acknowledge his direct involvement with the regiment bearing his name. Most regimental officers formed a self-perpetuating brotherhood within which promotion was largely achieved through purchase from fellow officers. A commission was therefore as much an investment as a call to arms. Yet it also inspired officers to a sense of honour because it was still a direct contract between themselves and their Sovereign, and raised them, in their own estimation, above the clergy or the professions.

Both Parliament and regimental officers were in favour of the purchase system, the former because it saved money, the latter because it was a form of investment. The blatant flaw underpinning the whole system, that it produced an army dependent on financial bargaining and patronage rather than professional merit, was apparent to all, not least to successive sovereigns. The sale of commissions was declared illegal early in the eighteenth century, but the ban was totally ignored. George I thought it wiser to regulate what he could not abolish, and in 1720 issued the first of the tariffs for the sale of commissions, a practice which defied all attempts at reform for the next century.

A young man such as William Draper, intent on a career as an officer in an infantry regiment in the 1740s, had to find about £400, the official price of an ensign's commission. Uniform would cost a further £200, so this initial outlay of a minimum £600 represented a heavy commitment even for families of considerable means.

If the system for recruiting and retaining officers had its defenders there was almost nothing to be said in defence of the way in which the rank and file were treated. Army service was regarded as a barely preferable alternative to vagrancy, debtor's prison, or transportation. The army's ranks were filled with men often lured into taking the King's shilling by the offer of bounty to their recruiters, and held there usually by fear of retribution which followed unsuccessful desertion.

The Red Coat received scant respect; an unwelcome presence in England, and a forgotten one when posted abroad. At home the lack of any formal structure for provisioning the army meant that regiments had to make their own arrangements for billeting and feeding when posted to duty in a particular district. Innkeepers were obliged by law to provide accommodation, and the prospect of having to wait for eventual payment while feeding and sheltering turbulent soldiery made the hosts understandably sullen towards their unwanted guests.

The situation for regiments posted abroad to British colonies or outposts was even more haphazard and usually deadly. It was simply assumed that the same arrangements, or lack of them, as in Britain would apply in places as varied as Jamaica, Minorca, or North America in the winter. Since most regiments, once posted abroad, remained there unrelieved until a particular need arose to move them elsewhere, overseas service was regarded almost as a sentence of transportation for life, for officers and men alike.

Any attempts to rectify the more blatant scandals of army inefficiency were bedevilled by the ramshackle structure of command and control at the most senior level. The Sovereign, as Commander-in-Chief, was aided directly by the Secretary at War, who played a crucial role in day-to-day administration, but lacked any great political authority. The headquarters staff of the army was extraordinarily small, consisting only of the staff of the Commander-in-Chief, the Adjutant-General, and the Quartermaster-General.

To compound this complexity, and in line with the historical insistence that no one group should ever be in a position to seize military power, the Master General of the Ordnance had completely separate responsibility for the issuing of all military equipment. Being responsible for the artillery he also commanded all the gunners and engineers who, when stationed in Britain, were deemed not to be part of the army at all. The Master General's responsibility for issuing all equipment included accounting for, and negotiating for, the supply of all *materiel*. It followed almost inevitably, with so many lucrative contracts at stake, that the post would be given by the Sovereign to a powerful political appointee who would profit greatly from his tenure of office.

Given the inadequacies of this whole arcane structure, it was almost miraculous that the army performed so well in times of crisis. The key to its continuing reliability, and renowned steadiness on the field of battle, lay in its sensible dependence on the basic strength of the regimental system, with each regiment of cavalry or infantry representing a cohesive entity held together by shared experience and common loyalties. Within these small 'families' personal and regimental honour was the glue which overcame all the other weaknesses of the system. The evident merit of the regimental system over any other enabled the army to contract or expand, according to need, in a routine which was broadly based on the principle that the youngest regiments raised in wartime would be the first to be disbanded when peace returned.

The process of rapid expansion which began in 1741 when the demands of the war with Spain became evident, and gathered pace into the War of the Austrian Succession. Among the regiments freshly raised in 1741 was the 48th Foot, under the colonelcy of the Hon. James Cholmondley, based in Norwich.[1]

William Draper, in joining this regiment as an ensign in March 1744, would have needed the recommendation of a sponsor, as well as funding for the purchase of his commission. Oblique references made by him years later suggest that he somehow had gained the patronage of the powerful Townshend family based on Raynham in Norfolk. Whether this Townshend connection arose via the Harrison family of William's mother,[2] or more directly through George Townshend, a contemporary of his at Eton, Cambridge, and the army, remains unclear; but the friendship of the Townshend family was a sub-theme which ran beneficially through most of William Draper's life.

Within two months of his joining Cholmondley's regiment, the 48th, it was despatched for service in Flanders where the Allied army was engaged in an inconclusive summer campaign against the French. By then the colonelcy of the 48th had passed from James Cholmondley to Lord Henry Beauclerk, one of the five sons of the first Duke of St Albans and grandson of King Charles II and Nell Gwynn. A veteran with almost thirty years service Lord Harry brought the experience required for leadership of a regiment as yet untried in battle. As it turned out, his leadership qualities were hardly needed, as the 48th had the easy task for more than a year of being part of the garrison of Ostend, then the main base for the British forces.

The lull of 1744 was broken in the following year when the new ministry in England under the Duke of Newcastle and his brother Henry Pelham pressed for more aggressive pursuit of the war. George II's favoured son, William Augustus, Duke of Cumberland, who had shown great personal bravery at the Battle of Dettingen, was given command of the Allied army, though still only twenty-three years old.

It is debatable whether so young a man should have been entrusted with command of a disparate army of 45,000 British, Dutch, Hanoverians, Hessians, and Austrians ranged against the 80,000-strong French army led by the veteran Marechal de Saxe. To endorse the young Duke's authority, George II appointed him Captain-General, a rank last held by the great Duke of Marlborough forty years earlier. The challenge of meeting expectations aroused by so splendid a title and so enormous a responsibility might have daunted the most self-confident of young men, but if Cumberland had any doubts he had little time to brood. Within two months of his arrival in Flanders the two armies met on 11 May 1745, at Fontenoy, close to the city of Tournai.

The Battle of Fontenoy, which might have earned the young Cumberland a reputation alongside that of the great commanders, ended inconclusively with each army losing no less than 8,000 men, and the Allied army withdrawing to regroup. The 48th, still in garrison at Ostend, took no part in the battle but was deployed within days to remain with the army during that summer's campaign. By then the colonelcy had yet again changed hands, from Henry Beauclerk to Francis Ligonier, a younger brother of the redoubtable Jean-

1. *William Augustus, Duke of Cumberland (1721–1765), favourite son of King George II and Captain-General until 1757. He was colonel of the 1st Foot Guards, and was personally responsible for William Draper being transferred from the 48th Foot to be adjutant of the 2nd Battalion of the 1st Guards in 1746 and considered as one of the Duke's 'family' of favoured officers.*

*2. General Jean-Louis (later Field-Marshal Earl)
Ligonier (1680–1770), the only French-born soldier
ever to become Commander in Chief of the British
army. He succeeded Cumberland as Colonel of the
1ˢᵗ Foot Guards in 1757 and was instrumental in
approving the choice of William Draper to form a
regiment for service in India in the same year.*

Louis Ligonier who rose from being a young Huguenot refugee to become
eventually Field-Marshal and Commander-in-Chief of the British army.

To add to the concerns facing Cumberland, news of his setback at Fontenoy
had finally convinced both Louis XV of France and Prince Charles Edward Stuart
that the Young Pretender's moment had arrived. The distractions of a British
army battered in Flanders, and the woeful state of the defences in England,
presented the Young Pretender with perhaps his last and greatest opportunity
of restoring the Stuart dynasty to the throne. By the middle of 1745, only three
months after Fontenoy, he had raised his standard in the Highlands.

Cumberland immediately despatched ten battalions home from Flanders,
but the defeat of the English by the Scots at Prestonpans in September magnified
the crisis. A further eight battalions, including the 48ᵗʰ, were ordered direct
from Flanders to Newcastle. The battalion embarked from Williamstadt in late
October, but the usual North Sea autumnal gales scattered the ships widely
and the 48ᵗʰ only reached Berwick in the last days of the month.

As Prince Charles's troops headed south towards Derby, the veteran General Wade despatched two regiments of dragoons and two of infantry, including the 48th, to reoccupy Edinburgh. The regiment stayed there until early in 1746, during which time Cumberland had taken the bulk of his forces back to the south of England in anticipation of a French invasion.

At the same time the ailing General Wade had been replaced by the abrasive Lieutenant-General Henry Hawley, a veteran known to his troops as 'Hangman Hawley' from his liberal use of the gallows. He quickly assembled his force of 8,000 men with the intention of breaking the Jacobite siege of Stirling Castle, but on 17 January 1746 the Jacobites almost outflanked the royal forces, and were only contained when the two opposing armies met on a rain-swept ridge of Falkirk Muir in late afternoon. As a gloomy dusk began to fall, Hawley ordered his cavalry to attack the Jacobite right wing. This proved a costly error. A volley from the Scots dispersed two of the cavalry regiments, and the remaining English cavalry retreated from a wild charge of the Scottish infantry. The sight of their cavalry being routed spread alarm among the infantry on the left of the King's army, who began to retreat in rain-soaked disorder. Only two regiments, the 4th and the 48th, held their ground, preventing a rout by their steadiness, and eventually enabling the royal troops to leave the field in some semblance of cohesion.

James Cholmondley, the first colonel of the 48th and by then a brigadier, was present at the Battle of Falkirk and wrote afterwards:

> The 4th kept their ground, and I got my late regiment to form on their right. In this situation we kept our ground and with the assistance of the officers, who deserve the greatest credit for the spirit they showed, I got the men to be cool, as cool as ever I saw men at exercise and when the rebels were down upon us we not only repulsed them but advanced and put them to flight. My chief inducement in giving this account is to do justice to the officers of those two battalions who behaved so well that their stand stopped the rebels from pursuing our troops, which else would have been cut to pieces ... [3]

The losses at Falkirk were less important than the fact that the battle was seen as a disgrace for the royal forces, redeemed only by the 4th and 48th who bathed in the temporary glory of having retrieved the royal army from disaster.

In the aftermath of Falkirk, Cumberland was again called upon to restore morale by assuming direct command. The three months between his return and the final encounter at Culloden testified to the rigours of waging a campaign in the Highlands at the end of winter. Following Francis Ligonier's death from pleurisy, Henry Seymour Conway was also appointed to his first colonelcy – to succeed Ligonier as colonel of the 48th, ten days before the Battle of Culloden. Conway was an exact contemporary of William Draper at Eton, though he had seen more military service. His command of the 48th, which changed its name from Ligonier's to Conway's, came in time for him to be present with his new regiment at the battle.

Culloden earned, and has retained, its melancholy place in British history less as a military engagement than as a last desperate charge of the Scottish clans against the final crushing of the Jacobite cause by the overwhelming strength of the English forces. The comparative figures of losses sustained in the battle on 16 April testified to the disparity between the two armies, the Scots losing almost 2,000 dead whereas the English losses came to just 350. The 48th, or Conway's, was deployed in the second line and suffered only slight losses.

The sequel to the battle added to that sense of dismay which has always deterred any English regiment from claiming Culloden as a battle honour. The repression of the clans and the subsequent months of brutality meted out to the population of the Highlands in the search for rebels stained for ever the reputation of the royal troops, equally with Cumberland's. Though he himself had left Scotland in July to return to London as a national hero, the myth makers in Scotland and England contrived within months to label the Duke as 'the Butcher', the nickname he has carried into history, overriding the memory of all his other achievements.

In the aftermath of Culloden, back in England preparing for the next campaign in Flanders, Cumberland concentrated on improving standards of discipline and training in the army. His belief that officers should be commissioned and promoted according to merit may now seem entirely self-evident, but was then encountering almost total resistance from the great majority of officers. Where he could, he singled out those with merit. This determination to recognise potential probably explains the transfer of William Draper to be Adjutant of the 2nd Battalion of the 1st Foot Guards on 21 May 1746, only a month after Culloden.[4]

The 1st Foot Guards, to become more widely known as the Grenadier Guards, ranked as the most senior line regiment in the army, and Cumberland took great pride in being colonel of the regiment. Because there is no record of the exact procedure by which a young officer with almost no 'influence' could be singled out for transfer from a new infantry regiment to one as distinguished as the 1st Foot Guards there were probably linked factors to explain William Draper's transfer; his bravery on the field at Falkirk, the recommendation of the Colonel of the 48th, Henry Seymour Conway, and Cumberland's own pinpointing of an officer who could be relied upon to undertake the responsibilities of being an adjutant as a crucial step in his career.

Adjutants have never been the most popular of regimental officers. Their role in assisting the commanding officer in maintaining standards of discipline and training, as well as correspondence and administration, immediately distances them from their brother officers. The period of duty as an adjutant has always been considered a bed of nails. In the turbulent regiments of the eighteenth century it was a position demanding extra qualities of firmness, patience, and resourcefulness. Yet for William Draper the potential hazards of accepting such a posting would have seemed small in comparison with the distinction of being singled out for transfer to a regiment as fashionable as the 1st Foot Guards, and, more importantly, being brought to the attention of the Captain-General himself.

The 1st Guards returned to Flanders in January 1747 as part of the British contribution to the Allied army, again under the command of Cumberland. The effort required to bring armies to battle was as protracted as usual, and it was not until 2 July that action was finally joined, as Cumberland's forces blocked the advance of Saxe's army towards the strategic stronghold of Maastricht.

The battle was fought around the village of Laffeldt, and involved more troops than were present at Waterloo. The Guards regiments were engaged in close combat around the village which changed hands three or four times with heavy casualties on both sides. Later in the day the French cavalry made so determined an attack upon the Dutch in the centre of the Allied line as almost to cut the army in two. The day was only saved by a brilliant counter-charge of the British cavalry under General Ligonier and Colonel Henry Conway which gave Cumberland's army sufficient breathing space to retreat in good order to defensive lines around Maastricht.

Ligonier, who had been taken prisoner at the end of his charge was brought before Louis XV of France who conveyed his dismay at the appalling human cost of the battle (total casualties being around 16,000) and French weariness with a war which had been dragging on for more than five years. Ligonier's release on parole, and his return to Cumberland's camp, gave momentum to the negotiations which were to lead to the Treaty of Aix-la-Chapelle in the following year.

During the winter, while the Guards were quartered at Eindhoven after the siege of Bergen-op-Zoom, the momentum towards peace quickened. Negotiations were complicated, not least by the need to await news from distant fields of conflict in North America, the Caribbean, and India. The Treaty was finally signed in October 1748, all the signatories recognising that the terms would simply give them time to recoup their strength. The continuous tensions around the overseas possessions of England, France, Spain, and Holland remained unresolved; and with the exception of the swapping of the British conquest of Cape Breton in Canada for the French seizure of Madras in India, nothing definitive was agreed. The French withdrew from Flanders, thus negating all Saxe's victories of the last four years, and also pledged final renunciation of support for the Jacobite cause. Though all the parties benefited from the end of hostilities, the peace was uneasy and partial. Future conflict had merely been deferred.

3

PLEASURES OF PEACE:
CALL TO COMMAND

With peace restored, the army resigned itself to the inevitable process of contraction. The Guards, despite their permanent role of providing protection for the Sovereign, shared in the losses. Officers numbers were reduced proportionately, and for the majority with other interests there was reduced need for regular attendance for regimental duties. Peacetime had more diversions to offer.

William Draper was missing from the lists of the Second Battalion in May 1749. By then he had been back at King's, Cambridge for almost a year, alternating his time there with service during the months when the war was winding down. He took his Master of Arts degree, and was at the same time elected a Fellow of King's, which did not prevent him being promoted to Captain-Lieutenant in April of the same year. This seemingly odd double-life was acceptable when the boundaries between being a full-time soldier and a permanent civilian were loosely defined.

With the prospect of peace stretching ahead he might have considered taking holy orders and settling for the life of a cleric, or equally an academic. Neither career was very demanding in the middle of the eighteenth century. The clue to his decision to pursue his career in the army is summarised in Anthony Allen's 'Skeleton' of King's College members, compiled in 1750, the year after Draper had been elected a Fellow:

> William Draper, grandson of William Draper of Beswick in
> Yorkshire, a famous fox hunter. A Lieutenant in Lord Henry
> Beauclerk's Regiment of Foot, 1744, and afterwards Ensign in the

Guards, and Adjutant and Lieutenant to the Duke of Cumberland's Regiment. He is a young officer of great courage and a great favorite [sic] of the Duke. He came back to college in March 1748 to commence Master of Arts which he could not do regularly at the commencement, before being detained abroad in the army.[1]

It would have needed a strong yearning for a religious or academic life to have tempted a young man of spirit from a career in which he had already proved his mettle, earned a reputation for great courage, and attracted the personal encouragement of his Sovereign's favourite son. Apart from all the military prospects which lay ahead, he was also ready to enjoy the pleasures which awaited a young Guards officer in time of peace, even one without much private income. As a member of White's club, to which he had been elected in 1745, he was at the centre of London's social scene at the time of life when options for pleasure were seemingly endless.

The end of the war had immediately allowed resumption of the fashionable coming and going between London and the rest of Europe, but particularly with the Court of Louis XV at Versailles, where Madame de Pompadour was then at the height of her influence. The gaiety and brilliance of Versailles, superficial as they were, made an attractive contrast to the dowdiness of the Court of St James under the ageing George II, and there was a constant stream of British visitors.

The British Ambassador, the Earl of Albemarle, acted as a conduit for visitors, among whom were many young British officers. James Wolfe, still unknown outside the army and seven years before he gained immortality at Quebec, wrote from Paris to his mother in 1752:

> Lord Albemarle has done me the favour to invite me to his house
> when he has had the foreign ambassadors and some considerable
> men of this country to dinner, but I have no great acquaintance with
> the French women, nor am likely to have – it is almost impossible to
> introduce oneself among them without losing a great deal of money,
> which you know I can't afford ... [2]

William Draper, who would have been equally short of funds, appears to have been among those who not only gained entry to the Court, but had considerably more success at making his mark. Many years later, *Town and Country Magazine*, in one of a series of 'Tête-à-Tête' sketches focusing on liaisons which were currently the talk of London, referred back to his earlier years:

> His personal merit and abilities, his extraordinary address united
> to a most elegant and athletic figure, could not fail attracting
> the attention of the opposite sex. Indeed he has from his youth
> been their professed votary, and he in return was one of their

greatest favourites, but he always conducted his amours with such judgement, honour and secrecy that scarce any have transpired to justify the charge ... When abroad, in France, where every married woman upon the *ton* considers it a necessary appendage to have a *cher ami*, he could not fail; being particularly distinguished by ladies of the first rank; and as they do not consider it necessary to make any deceit of their intrigues even to their husbands provided a proper degree of decency is preserved ... many countesses and women of rank were publicly talked of as having disposed of their favour in behalf of the captain ...

... The late King of France testified an uncommon predilection for him being invited to most of his hunting matches; and it was averred that he frequently assisted at the *petits soupers* of Madame Pompadour. Louis XV used to call him '*le beau garçon Anglais*' and said he was one of the most accomplished Englishmen he had seen at Versailles ...[3]

Even allowing for the hyperbole of the anonymous writer the sketch indicates that Draper must have had unusual personal qualities to have enabled him to become persona grata in such a demanding milieu, not least in his ability to converse fluently, or at least seductively, in French.

Though the range of his various liaisons at Versailles is now impossible to establish, it is possible to accept as accurate the remarks about his athletic figure. He had a lifelong enthusiasm for cricket and real tennis, particularly the latter which he continued to play into his later years. As for cricket, he had remained a competent batsman and bowler since his time at Eton and King's, and in June 1751 was in the Etonian side which played in the first series of one-day matches played successively over three days on Newmarket Heath.

A contemporary newspaper, announcing the event, wrote:

A great match at Cricket is made between the Rt Hon. The Earl of Sandwich and the Rt Hon. The Earl of March for £1500, to be played at Newmarket, on the 25th of this month and the following two days, the gainer of two games in three to be the winner ... The Earl of Sandwich and the Earl of March both play themselves. The Duke of Kingston and Lord Howe play in the Eton side for the Earl of Sandwich; the two bowlers on that side are Captain Draper and Mr Silk; the other gentlemen are not all fixed. They will be dressed in the handsomest manner, in silk jackets, trousers, velvet caps, etc. 'Tis said that near £20,000 is depending on this match ...[4]

The first match was declared a draw as Eton did not have time to complete a second innings. Eton won the second match, largely due to an innings of thirty-two by Draper, the highest score of the day. The match on the third day was won by the Rest of England. The papers reported: 'We hear the odds ran very high on the English side in the first and ensuing matches.' Turnover on the betting might well have been more than the forecast £20,000, already an enormous sum in contemporary terms.

A month later another 'great match' was played in memory of Frederick, Prince of Wales, heir to the throne, who had died in March 1751 following aggravation of a cricketing injury suffered the previous season. The respect shown by his fellow cricketers to their late royal patron was in contrast to the lifelong contempt expressed towards the prince by his father, George II. 'Poor Fred' caused almost as much trouble by dying prematurely as he had during his life. The new heir to the throne, Frederick's son, the future George III, was not yet thirteen. In the ensuing row as to whether the Duke of Cumberland, uncle to the future king, might become Regent during his nephew's minority, all the animosities against Cumberland suddenly resurfaced. The old King found it difficult to understand why his favourite son, so recently hailed as a national hero for saving the country from the combined threat of the Jacobites and the French, should now be the focus of so much factional animosity. He complained to Henry Fox, 'The English nation is so changeable. I don't know why they dislike him. It is brought about by the Scotch, the Jacobites, and the English that do not like discipline ...'[5]

On the last point he had perceptively touched upon the irritation caused by Cumberland's continuous efforts to reform the army and improve its professional standards. Many of his proposed reforms appeared to officers to be impinging on their traditions and privileges. The common sense which, for example, lay behind his order that regiments should be designated by numbers rather than named after their current colonels was interpreted as a Germanic attempt to turn the army into a body of anonymous cannon fodder. The Guards regiments, because of their permanent presence in the capital, found it less easy to escape from the watchful vigilance of Cumberland, who, as both Captain-General and Colonel of the 1st Guards, was constantly seeking to introduce new practices which he considered would improve regimental standards.

Other reforms jarred the sense of personal independence which was both the strength and weakness of the officer caste. Soldiering, especially in peacetime, was felt to be a matter of personal choice rather than dedication to a system imposed from above. The average officer, though willing to risk his life on the battlefield, saw no compelling reason why he should spend too much time enduring the tedium of peacetime soldiering.

Certainly the pursuit of pleasure was given high priority among Guards officers and they gave much time to the pleasures of the fashionable life of London, particularly in gambling and heiress-stalking. The clubs and chocolate houses of St James's, the drawing rooms of the great houses, the pleasure gardens of Ranelagh and Vauxhall, the theatres and taverns – all saw more of the officers than any parade ground.

It seems entirely in keeping with William Draper's current priorities as a Guards captain that when he opened his account at Drummond's Bank in 1751, his first payment should have been to Robert Arthur, owner of Arthur's chocolate house, to pay off existing debts and maintain his credit for further gambling.[6]

During those years he apparently shared accommodation around St James's with two of his brother officers, the Hon. Robert Brudenell and Richard Peirson. *The Times*, in a posthumous sketch of Draper in 1787, wrote that 'at this period he joined in a plan with two of his military colleagues to keep house together and by such an oeconomical junction they were all enabled to make a figure, which individually it would not have been in their power to support.'[7]

In this eighteenth-century equivalent of the bachelor pad, Draper at some time appeared to have been keeping as his mistress the young Maria, or Polly, Hart. She, daughter of a dancing master, went on to become mistress to Henry Thrale, a friend of Samuel Johnson. Polly Hart, a skilful horsewoman, was a high-spirited character who appeared occasionally on the stage as a member of Garrick's company, and even earned a mention from the minor poet Charles Churchill, who referred to her 'transient gleam of grace'.[8] She later became common-law wife of Samuel Reddish, one of Garrick's regular company. By then her liaison with William Draper had long been overtaken by events, but she was to appeal to him for funds many years later when they were both in financial straits.

The undemanding life of the Guards seems to have filled the years of peace between 1748 and 1756, but their passage must have reminded Draper that he was now into his thirties with little to show for ten years' service and with no great challenge foreseeable to enable him to prove his worth. Events were, however, moving to accelerate the renewal of war. The period of peace roughly corresponded in England with the years in which the Pelham brothers, Henry, and Thomas, Duke of Newcastle, exercised ministerial control. On Henry Pelham's sudden death in 1754, Newcastle was forced to confront the growing problems caused by the friction between British and French interests in North America and India. Newcastle found himself disconcerted by these colonial struggles which seemed distant in time and space, and far less familiar to him than the complexities of European power-balancing and English power-broking. It was also Newcastle's fate to have to share power shortly with that embodiment of the aggressive national spirit, William Pitt.

Throughout the eight years of peace in Europe the nations with overseas interests continued to press for territorial or trading advantage. While the constant friction in North America between the separate British colonies and the more cohesive French settlements was strategically of the greatest concern to the British government, the situation in India was equally worrying.

There, the jockeying between the East India Company and the French *Compagnie des Indes* had been in progress for decades. The settlements of each company, dotted along the enormous lengths of the coasts of India, were the bases from which they contrived to increase their power and trade through alliances with local Indian rulers. While the East India Company regarded trade as its crucial priority it nonetheless felt obliged to combat the growing influence of the French during the years when the energetic Marquis du Dupleix was intent upon territorial expansion.

In the nineteen years between 1735 and 1754, Dupleix showed a strategic and military grasp far beyond that of the counting house. Had his successors been of the same stature, it is arguable that India might have become a French rather than a British dominion. Only from 1748 onwards was French superiority seriously challenged, as the troops of the East India Company began to be shaped into an effective fighting force under the newly arrived veteran Major Stringer Lawrence, based in Madras.

The early success of the young Robert Clive at Arcot, south-west of Madras in 1752, under the command of Lawrence, was the first significant victory for the Company's troops; hailed as such in London despite the fact that it had taken place during a time of peace. The directors of the Company thereafter argued persuasively that royal forces were needed to support the Company's troops if Britain's interest were to be fully safeguarded.

Accordingly, and regarded only as a temporary measure, the first regular forces of the Crown were committed for service in India in 1754. Cumberland, as Captain-General, nominated the 39th Regiment, commanded by a veteran colonel John Adlercron. Those involved with this experiment were aware of the likely problems. Royal forces had never before fought alongside Company troops. All the questions of command and logistics would have to be worked out on the spot. Cumberland believed that the only way of overcoming the predictable squabbles would be to give Adlercron overall authority. He was therefore appointed Commander-in-Chief India before his departure, with authority over the East India Company troops as well as his own.

The wording of the King's Commission to Adlercron carried so many time bombs of interpretation that Adlercron was to suffer from them for the whole of his time in India. The regimental motto of the 39th Foot, later the Dorset Regiment, '*Primus in Indis*', was probably the only assertion not subject to argument or misinterpretation.

With royal ground forces committed to India for the first time, the drift towards war was reinforced by events in North America. In the following year, 1755, when the expedition under General Braddock, sent out to re-establish British rights beyond the Alleghenies, was routed in a French ambush, England belatedly woke to a real crisis.

In January 1756, London rejected a French ultimatum about hostile acts by British ships. Rumours flew of a pre-emptive invasion by the French to coincide with an assault on the island of Minorca, key to Britain's naval power in the Mediterranean. The invasion scare, as so often before and since, failed to materialise; but when the French landed in Minorca in April the two countries were once again at war. The Seven Years War, the first truly global war, was about to unfold.

The outbreak of war saw immediate attempts to remedy the sins of omission which had accumulated during the years of peace. The armed forces had once again to be built up at extraordinary speed. In this process of expanding the army, General Ligonier played a crucial role. As Lieutenant-General of the Ordnance he was more directly involved with administration than the Duke of Cumberland who as Captain-General was shortly to return to Germany to lead yet another allied army.

Ligonier was in effect Chief of Staff for the army, the parallel function in the Royal Navy being performed by the veteran Lord Anson as First Lord of the Admiralty. Between them they enabled William Pitt, the dominant figure in the Government nominally under the leadership of the Duke of Newcastle, to put the country onto a war footing.

Ligonier's nominal superior as Master General of the Ordnance was the third Duke of Marlborough, grandson of the great duke. An amiable and dutiful figure, a major-general at the age of fifty, he had gained his post as Master General more for political than military reasons. He nonetheless occupied a crucial position at the centre of the military and political nexus, and his closest staff would have been in frequent working contact with Ligonier, Cumberland, and the Secretaries of State.

It must therefore have been a great relief to William Draper when he was appointed an aide-de-camp to Marlborough early in 1756, along with the Hon. James Brudenell, younger brother of his friend Robert Brudenell.[9] The appointment was acknowledgement of a long-standing acquaintanceship on which *Town and Country Magazine* commented:

> This acquaintanceship first arose at the Tennis Court at Whitehall where the Duke constantly attended, being a great admirer of the game which he played very well. Draper was about His Grace's match and they frequently played together not for capital sums but for mere amusement. The Duke often invited him to be his guest and his engaging manners, mental abilities, and general knowledge recommended him to the Duke's patronage.[10]

This appointment to Marlborough's staff came at a pivotal point in Draper's career, and must have made him acknowledge that his patronage by Marlborough and Ligonier was likely to distance him further from his earlier patron, the Duke of Cumberland.

There had long been tension between Cumberland and Ligonier, as the Duke had heard the gossip around the army that he had been jealous that Ligonier's bravery at Laffeldt had saved his command from becoming a rout. It was thus not an easy decision for Draper to accept the posting to Marlborough's staff. Cumberland, as Captain-General and the King's son, carried immense authority. To risk forfeiting his good will was an unenviable choice for a junior officer. Yet the alternative, soldiering on at regimental level, made the risk worthwhile.

His acceptance of the post, in February 1756 also gave him the confidence to embark on marriage in the same month. His bride was Caroline Beauclerk, younger daughter of Lord William Beauclerk, brother of his old colonel in the 48th, Lord Henry Beauclerk. As a member of the family of the Dukes of St Albans, a great-granddaughter of King Charles II and Nell Gwynn, she was of a social rank far above that of her bridegroom and supposedly in a position to bring him great advantage.

At the time of her marriage she would have been at least twenty-four, almost eligible for the dispiriting title of 'old maid'. Her portrait by Gainsborough, painted some years later, conveys much of the melancholy sweetness of her nature. It endorses Horace Walpole's description of her in a letter to George Montagu a few years earlier when recounting an evening spent at Vauxhall with some rackety friends:

3. The 'sweet, spirit-lulling' Hon. Caroline Beauclerk,
who became William Draper's wife in 1756. She was
the youngest daughter of Lord William Beauclerk and
great-granddaughter of Charles II and Nell Gwynn.
Her portrait was painted by Gainsborough in the late
1760s, shortly before her early death.

> Here we picked up Lord Granby, arrived very drunk from Jenny's Whim, where instead of going to old Strafford's catacombs to make honourable love, he had dined with Lady Fitzroy and left her and eight other women and four other men playing at brag. He would have fain made over his honourable love at any terms to poor Miss Beauclerk, who is very modest, and did not know at all what to do with his whispers or his hands.[11]

The 'modest' Miss Beauclerk had, over this period, according to *The Times*, become 'sensible of Draper's merit, and though her relations rather opposed the connection was not to be turned from her purpose and at length married him. Nor had she any reason to repent the choice she had made.'[12] The marriage seems to have been founded upon deep affection rather than hopes of a shared fortune, and to have endured on that basis.

They were married on 21 February 1756. The Parish Register of St Martin-in-the-Fields contains a Special Licence from the Archbishop of Canterbury, noting their 'desire that their marriage be solemnised at all speed', and granting them the licence to marry at any convenient place. The ceremony took place at the nearby house of Andrew Drummond, the banker. Caroline's sister, Charlotte Beauclerk, had married John Drummond, Andrew's son, some years earlier and the two sisters were close. Charles Beauclerk, Caroline's brother, was also one of the witnesses to the marriage, so the opposition of the St Albans family had not gone any further than an understandable concern that Caroline could have made a grander match.[13]

Almost immediately after their marriage Caroline and William were separated by his call to duty as Marlborough's ADC. The outbreak of war, followed swiftly by the humiliating loss of Minorca, increased fears of a French invasion. Marlborough spent the summer of 1756 coordinating the movement of such artillery as could be mustered to oppose any landing of French troops in southern England.

The invasion crisis lasted until the autumn. By the end of the year William Pitt, as Secretary of State for the South, had become effective head of a new ministry. The military needs of the moment had reopened all the underlying tensions between the proponents of the 'blue water' strategy, and those still favouring Britain's commitment to a European solution. Cumberland departed to Germany in command of yet another bizarrely named allied army, the Army of Observation, while Pitt, realising that Britain could not spare a major body of troops for the continent, initiated his programme of diversionary raids upon the French coastline, which was to continue sporadically through the war. From the first raid on Rochefort in September 1757, a shambles of hesitation and muddle, he absorbed the lesson that successful combined operations demanded young leaders with resourcefulness and drive.

Meanwhile, the news from North America and Germany had been doubly depressing. Cumberland suffered reverses in North Germany, and, confusingly briefed from London, entered into the Convention of Klosterzeven with the French commander, the Duc de Richelieu, by which the French gained concessions without having to join battle.

Cumberland, believing that he had been acting on the King's instructions in signing the Convention, returned to London in October 1757 totally unprepared for his father's furious and unjustified comment on his arrival at Court: 'Here is my son who has ruined me and disgraced himself.'[14] Cumberland, in a fit of pique at the undeserved rebukes, immediately resigned his posts both as Captain-General, and Colonel of the 1st Guards, effectively terminating his active military career.

Pitt took the opportunity of Cumberland's resignation to have General Ligonier designated as Commander-in-Chief in England, the first professional soldier to be so appointed. Although the veteran Ligonier was then in his seventies, his vast experience qualified him admirably to be Pitt's adviser on all military affairs, particularly on the appointment and selection of officers. With Ligonier's experience matched by that of Anson at the Admiralty, Pitt now had in place two professional chiefs-of-staff with sufficient authority to make decisions based on military rather than political or factional priorities.

Their advice was needed on a global scale as Pitt sought to determine the balance of demands from distant theatres of war. Among these was the need to respond positively to the East India Company's call for more royal troops and greater naval protection in the face of resurgent French strength.

It was easier to deploy the Royal Navy than to reinforce the land commitment. In January 1757, Pitt instructed Vice-Admiral Watson, commanding the squadron in the Indies, to 'help the Company in the execution of any plan they may have for distressing the enemy' as long as it did not run counter to his principal duty of protecting the safe passage of Company ships.

The situation on land in India could not be resolved so directly. It pivoted around the uneasy relations between the royal troops and those of the Company. Colonel Adlercron's role as 'Commander-in-Chief' had been beset with quarrels and misunderstandings. He had arrived in India in 1754 with the mental baggage of a veteran soldier and none of the required talents of a diplomat. Stringer Lawrence, another veteran with a record of success in India, was himself a pugnacious figure disinclined to make things easier for the new arrival. After two years of unsatisfactory squabbling, George Pigot, as President of the Council in Madras, recommended in March 1756 to the Secret Committee of the Company in London that the field officers of the 39th should be withdrawn and the rest of the troops incorporated into the Company's forces 'as measures that may remove the inconveniences now laboured under'. In short, Adlercron could go, but his troops should stay.

The Government in London agreed to this plan, and orders recalling Adlercron and the 39th from India were sent early in the year. More than 450 officers and men thereafter elected to transfer from the 39th to the Company's service as preferable to anything awaiting them on their eventual return to Ireland.

In the interlude following despatch of the recall orders, Pitt, Ligonier and their advisers, including Cumberland who remained close to the king, weighed the options for the next stage of military support for the Company. If the right replacement for Adlercron were chosen the problems of the last three years might well disappear.

Fortuitously, at this juncture the Duke of Newcastle received a letter from William Draper, typical of the sort then received every day by senior politicians from supplicants wishing for any sign of ministerial goodwill. Newcastle, still nominally head of the ministry, would have felt no embarrassment at the frankness of an officer, now aged thirty-six, who could feel that he was in danger of slipping in the race for promotion despite his closeness to the centre of events. It read, after the usual ornate expressions of humility and courtesy:

> As Your Grace has been pleased to give me leave to imagine that
> I have some small share of your good wishes ... I take the liberty
> to beg your protection and patronage in securing me the rank of
> Lieutenant-Colonel at this juncture. Flattering myself that His
> Royal Highness's resentments towards me have not outlived his
> commission what I humbly request of Your Grace is to be made
> Deputy Quartermaster of England ... I do not presume to ask this
> favour of Your Grace from any consciousness of my own merit,
> but as a friend of Lord Lincoln; and as many gentlemen my juniors
> in the army have of late been honoured with that rank, I fear Your
> Grace may think me lost to all sense of ambition and spirit, not to
> say disgrace, were I wanting to myself on this occasion.[15]

The cryptic allusion to Cumberland's 'resentments' showed how aware he was that his distancing from Cumberland might have been fatal. The timing of the letter, and its style, throwing in the name of Newcastle's favoured nephew the Earl of Lincoln, an Eton contemporary of Draper's, suggest that he had no inkling that his name was already being given serious consideration for possible command in India.

Ligonier had simultaneously apparently decided on Draper to be selected for command, with a brother officer in the 1st Guards, Cholmondeley Brereton, to be his senior major. Newcastle, writing to Ligonier on 7 November responded to that news with the comment that:

> I am extremely glad that poor Draper is made so happy. The King
> speaks to me of both the officers with approbation – particularly
> Draper. Had I known of the design to send officers of that rank I
> should have recommended a very near relation of mine Captain
> Monson of the Guards who is a very pretty young man and only
> wishes to go abroad anywhere to serve. I have long recommended
> him to the Duke but without success.[16]

Newcastle's equally cryptic reference to 'poor Draper' seems to confirm that there had been some gossip in London that he was in danger of being bypassed in consequence of Cumberland's resentment. He must therefore have been as surprised as he was gratified when, on 11 November 1757, less than a month after his letter to Newcastle, he received a warrant from Lord Barrington, Secretary at War, commissioning him as Lieutenant-Colonel 'in the East Indies only' to raise a Battalion of Foot, 1000 strong, 'to embark for the East Indies to assist the forces of the United Company of Merchants trading to the East Indies in the vigorous prosecution of the war in those parts'.[17]

George Monson, another brother officer in the 1st Guards, must have been equally pleased to have been chosen, almost simultaneously, as Draper's second major. The seemingly curious designation of the new regiment, which came to be numbered as the 79th Foot, or Draper's Regiment,[18] was apparently an effort to forestall possible disagreement with the East India Company about the exact status of the royal force. The effort was only partly successful, and a letter from the directors in London to Fort St George in Madras, showed that

4. William Pitt the Elder, Earl of Chatham (1708–1778), whose leadership during the Seven Years War laid the foundation for Britain's victories. The 'Great Commoner' was decisive in his choice of selecting young commanders for projects demanding drive and imagination.

5. Major-General Stringer Lawrence (1697–1775), 'Father of the Indian Army', who commanded the East India Company's forces on the Coromandel coast during the vital years of conflict with the French. His relationship with royal forces sent to India was always uneasy and he remained particularly sceptical of any advantage that might be achieved by the Manila expedition in 1762.

there would still be plenty of opportunity for future quarrels:

> Under our difficulties of raising men for our own forces His Majesty was most graciously pleased to give orders for assisting the Company with about one thousand men to be draughted [sic] out of the new raised regiments. We were in hopes that these troops would be under the command of the Company's officers ... in order to prevent the like difficulties and inconveniences which have happened to Col. Adlercron's regiment; but ... His Majesty's ministers could not be prevailed upon to alter their own dispositions and method, which is that the body of forces instead of being a regiment under the command of a Colonel is called a battalion and is to be commanded by a Lieutenant-Colonel William Draper and the Majors Cholmondeley Brereton and George Monson. The assurances we have received

from the King's Ministers that it is recommended to these gentlemen in the strongest terms to avoid altercations and to contribute
everything in their power for the service of the Company, and the
great readiness which the Colonel expresses to cooperate with the
Company's officers in every measure tending thereto gives us great
hope that this body of forces will be of good service.[19]

The assumption underlying these words was to remain a source of tension
between the Crown and the Company not just for the next few years but
until well into the next century. The tensions revolved around the simple but
immensely important question; were the priorities of the East India Company
to take precedence over those of the King's government, or vice versa, or were
they to be considered identical? The letter to Fort St George encapsulates the
almost accidental way in which these crucial issues were raised without any
indication that their long-term implications had even been addressed, let alone
understood. As far as the directors perceived the immediate situation, royal
troops were being sent to protect and promote the interests of the Company.
Although the directors had not achieved their hope that the troops would
come under the direct command of Stringer Lawrence when they arrived in
Madras, they were nonetheless to be used for the Company's service.

Draper immediately went through the hustle of assembling his completely
new regiment, achieved by the drafting of whole companies from other young
regiments. They had to be brought together in time to embark on the East
Indiamen which would be sailing in convoy with their naval escort early in
the New Year.

As his regimental agent he chose the ubiquitous John Calcraft who already
had more than thirty regiments in his 'stable'. Calcraft, a financial and
political insider, was an incomparable source of gossip and correspondence
for all the colonels whose regimental affairs he handled. A few days after he
was appointed he was already passing on the news in a letter to Colonel Ralph
Burton in New York:

> This will give you the pleasure of hearing that Draper is made
> happy; a battalion is formed of 900 men from the nine youngest
> companies of the 2nd Battalions in England, and Draper has got it
> with the rank of Lieutenant-Colonel; Brereton is his major. No let is
> to be made to it as it goes to the East Indies that Lawrence and Clive
> may not be commanded. This is the only good news. Now for the
> bad. The Duke [Cumberland] resigned as soon as he came home.[20]

During the same weeks, Adlercron in Madras, ensuring that the 39th left India
on schedule, was writing a final justification of his conduct to his Captain-
General, Cumberland, unaware that the Duke had already resigned. His long
report enabled him to comment on some of the tensions awaiting his successor,

and he ended by getting in a final volley against his military colleague who had too often been his adversary:

> I can't help informing Your Royal Highness that I have but too much reason, as well as others, to believe that any little Jealousies, or Discontents, which may have subsisted between His Majesty's Troops and the Company have been under-hand greatly encouraged by Colonel Lawrence.[21]

This indictment had already been discounted in London in favour of leaving Lawrence in command on the Coromandel coast. The mistake of designating Adlercron's successor as Commander-in-Chief in India was not repeated. Indeed Draper, in the Instructions received from Barrington shortly before departure, was specifically ordered:

> ... to call together the officers under your command and recommend them in a particular manner the avoiding of all disputes with the officers of the East India Company, and that they use their utmost endeavours to live with them in the greatest harmony as the contrary behaviour will be very displeasing to us.[22]

The priorities expressed in these Instructions show that Ligonier must have given particular thought to the qualities needed by Adlercron's successor; and had opted for William Draper not just because of his proven courage but for his wider skills in handling situations requiring tact. Draper's frequent contacts with Ligonier, as ADC to Marlborough, had finally paid a dividend.

Ligonier himself, in recognition of his new pre-eminence in the wake of Cumberland's departure, was confirmed as Commander-in-Chief on 30 November 1757. He simultaneously replaced Cumberland as Colonel of the 1st Guards, a unique double achievement for one who had come to England as a Huguenot refugee sixty years earlier. To celebrate this event with his usual gusto Ligonier held 'a grand reception' at his London house in December.[23] His many guests included fellow-officers from the 1st Guards, among them William Draper accompanied by Caroline who after little more than a year of marriage was about to be left alone for a predictable minimum of two years.

By the date of Ligonier's party, the East Indiaman the *Pitt* awaited at Gravesend the embarkation of the troops on 21 January 1758.[24] They were to arrive in Madras eight months later, just ahead of the last French siege of the Company's most important base in India.

4

TO INDIA
AND A SIEGE

Seasons, winds, distances, and the pace of sailing ships dictated and explained both the strategy and tactics of all combatants involved in the overseas wars of the eighteenth century. Every plan was contingent upon the predictability of the seasonal trade winds, and equally upon the unpredictability of the local weather. It was difficult enough coordinating plans for action in Europe. Overseas, the dimension of uncertainty meant that only the most general instructions could have any chance of fulfilment.

The urgency apparent in the mustering of Draper's Regiment was needed to ensure that the troops would be ready for the next seasonal convoy to India. The departure season coincided with the late winter months in Europe so that ships arrived off the coast of South Africa six months later to be carried by the monsoon winds across the Indian Ocean.

The new regiment was assigned to a number of ships, Draper and Brereton with two companies being allocated to the *Pitt* and other ships, while the other companies under the command of George Monson were divided between five more, some scheduled to call in at Bombay on their way to Madras. The *Pitt*, a ship of 600 tons with a crew of 250 as well as fifty marines, was unusually large to be chartered by the East India Company. The normal size of an East Indiaman was an exact 499 tons, for the eminently sensible reason that ships of 500 tons or more were obliged by law to carry a chaplain on board.

The log of the *Pitt*, which the troops boarded at Gravesend in January 1758, records the usual delays in assembling the full convoy, providing a naval

6. Fort St George, Madras was the most important of the Company's settlements on the east coast of India and key to control of the Bay of Bengal. It had no port, and all disembarkations had to cope with the heavy surge of waves onto the beach.

escort, and waiting for favourable winds to carry the fleet down the Channel.[1] As early as 17 March, as the fleet finally got under way, the log noted 'that many of our ship's company and soldiers complain of pains in the head and bones which we find to be the first symptoms of putrid fever which many men are very ill with'. The first soldier was 'commended to the deep' two days later, and from then until the end of the voyage to Madras there is a doleful litany of the toll of 'putrid fever', now known to be typhus.

By April, when the *Pitt* was near the Equator, 'the malignant fever continues very violent among our people', the log adding almost superfluously 'our melancholy situation causes a general dejection among the ship's company and soldiers.' At the beginning of May, the voyage was broken for almost a fortnight on the island of Fernando Noronha off the coast of Brazil, when about a hundred of the most seriously ill troops and sailors were landed in the hope that they would recuperate in tents rigged on the beach. The log encapsulated the dilemma facing Captain Wilson, master of the *Pitt*, and Colonel Draper, noting, on 14 May, 'a consultation of the officers whether we should stay until the sick had recovered, which we do not see any likelihood of, or proceed as fast as possible to save the monsoons upon the coast ... it was agreed to proceed.'

Draper had time to report back in a letter to Barrington, the Secretary at War, from Fernando Noronha that 'contagious fever brought on board by one sailor from a privateer has made great havoc amongst us.' On a more cheerful note he finished his letter by regretting:

> I wish I had any opportunity of sending Your Lordship some
> most excellent turtle which this island abounds with; the ignorant
> inhabitants are unacquainted with their merit. They kill them only
> for the sake of the bill – what barbarians.[2]

Despite their best efforts, with constant references in the log to 'using our wind sails to throw fresh air into the lower gun decks ... burning tobacco between the decks ... burning gunpowder ... and washing with vinegar', the death toll was near a hundred, roughly split between the ship's crew, marines, and royal troops.

The *Pitt* finally reached Madras on 14 September, where news was awaiting of the growing threat posed by the successes of the enlarged French forces based on Pondicherry. The newly arrived troops, relieved at last to be disembarking, must have landed on the wave-swept beaches by Fort St George in the gloomy knowledge that they would very soon be under siege within the Fort where barrack conditions would be hardly better than those on board.

Madras at the time was the most important of the Company's settlements in India, the key base for any power wishing to dominate the east coast of India. It had no natural harbour, but the formidable ramparts of Fort St George were almost alongside the beach, protecting a small but prosperous trading town.

The current Governor of Madras, George Pigot, a spirited thirty-nine-year-old, worked closely with the military commander Stringer Lawrence in planning against the impending French campaign towards Madras. Pigot had appealed in August for reinforcements from Bengal, but Robert Clive in Calcutta had refused the appeal on the realistic grounds that a diversionary attack planned against the French in the Carnatic would prevent a pincer attack being mounted by them against Madras.

The town was thus on its own; and Pigot and Lawrence must have been heartened by the timely arrival of Draper's two companies, even if the rest of his battalion was still at sea and unlikely to arrive for a few more months. Lawrence and Draper had probably not met before Draper's arrival in Madras, their military careers having coincided only when both were on the battlefield of Culloden, but in the small community of the army they would both have been aware of the other's milestones. Lawrence by then was a portly sixty-one, courageous, accustomed to getting his own way, and devoted to the Company which he had served since his secondment in 1748, while remaining sceptical about the merits and motives of most of the men he served with or commanded.

As he took Draper on introductory visits to the local nawabs, he would have had time to brief him on the latest movements of the French forces and the predictable plans of their commander, Comte Thomas Arthur de Lally Tollendall. This sonorous name lightly masked the fact that Lally Tollendall was not French at all, but the son of one of the Irish 'Wild Geese', Sir Gerald O'Mulally of Tullendally, who had served the French army in the Irish Brigade since the days of James II and the Old Pretender. His son, Thomas Arthur, whose name had transmuted to French style, was by 1758 himself a veteran who had fully earned the distinction of commanding the French forces in India. Yet the fact that he should have been entrusted with such a command illustrates the uneasy priorities of the Court at Versailles: a 'desirable' command would have gone to a Frenchman with influence at Court rather than to a semi-foreign auxiliary. The generals of the beau monde in France would have looked upon command in India as tantamount to indefinite exile in a hostile climate; and if Lally Tollendall could achieve Versailles' objectives with limited resources, so much the better.

His force of 2,000 men had been despatched from Brest in May 1757, directed to strike first at the British settlement at Fort St David and thereafter at Madras. Had they made all haste to India these regiments could have landed late in 1757 in time for a campaign during the cool season. Instead, Lally had to accept the capricious timing of Admiral Comte D'Aché who commanded the French squadron transporting the troops. D'Aché delayed the progress of his small fleet in the hope of seizing any East Indiamen en route. The result of this loitering, added to adverse weather, meant that Lally's force took ten months to arrive from France. Almost 400 men had died of sickness on the voyage, and Lally's relations with D'Aché, so crucial to any successful campaign, were strained even before he set foot in India.

The French had lost time not only on land, but also more vitally at sea, where Admiral George Pocock's squadron had been reinforced by the arrival of a further squadron under Commodore Stevens which began harassing D'Aché's fleet in a series of actions which slowly undermined Lally's plans throughout the rest of the year.

Lally scored an initial success in June 1758 when Fort St David, a few miles south of Madras, capitulated after a short siege. But the *Te Deum* sung in triumph in Pondicherry Cathedral, followed by banquets and festivities, could not disguise the fact that the public treasury was empty, that Lally had upset various local sensitivities, and that he was already in a state of furious dismay with the whole local Council of the *Compagnie des Indes*.

Lally complained with good reason of the deplorable ignorance of Governor de Leyrit and his council about the territory over which they supposedly exercised some control. He was particularly irked by the lack of an effective intelligence system; but his ultimate irritation was the total absence of any arrangements to pay either his own troops or any locally recruited forces, be they Sepoys or European deserters.

Lack of funds delayed Lally's push after the fall of Fort St David. An overland march required money, and the *Compagnie* said the treasury was empty. Lally thereupon took his forces south to extort money from the Rajah of Tanjore. This foray was a shambles, ending in a retreat to Carical, south of Pondicherry, where Lally received the bad news that D'Aché, badly mauled in an engagement with Pocock, had decided to retire with the whole of his squadron to the safety of Mauritius, thus effectively conceding naval supremacy to the Royal Navy. Despite Lally's protestations that absence of naval support would jeopardise his campaign, D'Aché remained resolute, his only parting gift being treasure worth around £30,000 seized by the illegal capture of a Dutch ship which had ill-advisedly put into Pondicherry Roads.

Primed with these new funds, Lally concentrated his forces for the push on Madras, almost a year behind schedule. Stringer Lawrence, meanwhile, now reinforced by the arrival of Draper's companies, and aided by a good intelligence network, had concentrated his small resources by recalling to Madras as many of the Company's troops as could be spared.

William Draper, newly arrived into the claustrophobic and quarrelsome world of Madras, would have had an immediate introduction to the environment which had made Adlercron's service so difficult. Yet it seems that all parties were determined to avoid such a repetition, and the imminence of Lally's appearance before Madras concentrated their minds on the details of military defence.

Lally had meanwhile committed another error in insisting that the Comte de Bussy, the experienced commander of the French forces to the north, should move his troops southwards to rendezvous with Lally's, and hand over command to the inexperienced Conflans. De Bussy, surmising correctly that this would result in all his gains of the last year being lost to Clive, obeyed with extreme reluctance, smarting from the peremptory manner in which Lally overrode those who attempted to reason with him. All this ill-will further undermined the fragile unity of the French forces.

It was thus nearly the end of November 1758 before Lally finally marshalled his army for the move on Madras. Bypassing the fortified village of Chingleput he slowly drew his whole force onto the plain about a mile south-west of Fort St George into which the garrison had finally retired. Finding his direct route to the Fort blocked by inlets and small rivers, he moved to the northern flank of the Fort, occupying the Blacktown area of the town from which the local population had already fled into the Fort. This commercial quarter was an immediate target for plunder, and the French forces, undisciplined and unopposed, seized the opportunity with relish. By the following morning they were visible from the Fort as being in such a state of drunkenness and disorder as to present an easy target for a vigorous sortie by the defenders.

The sortie was proposed by Draper, who, according to Lawrence in his *Memoirs*, 'communicated his thoughts to the Governor and Col. Lawrence to whose superior authority and great judgement he paid the utmost deference'.[3] Draper assembled a force of around 500 men, mostly Company troops, and two field pieces. 'After a dram and a biscuit' they sallied from the Fort by the Western Gate, one hundred of them under Major Brereton following a route parallel to Draper's to cover his eventual withdrawal.

As the British column moved in to attack the disorderly French in the streets of Blacktown, the element of surprise was lost through the untimely beating of the 'Advance' by the drummers. The French formed up to repel the sudden attack but were taken in the flank with a volley from the British infantry and rounds of grapeshot from the field guns. The French took refuge in nearby houses and Draper, ordering his guns to cease firing, rushed forward with four of his grenadiers to secure some cannon which the French had left unsupported. To his dismay, he found that the rest of his troops, in action for the first time, were cowering around the other buildings.

Henry Vansittart, a member of the Council at Madras at the time, reporting the sally in a subsequent letter, wrote:

> The Regiment of Lorraine was surprised and a monstrous hot action ensued. Colonel Draper made such a rush as would astonish all who do not know him, and if he had been briskly followed by his two platoons of grenadiers he would have brought in eleven officers, fifty men, and four guns more. But they did not do justice to their leader who received the whole fire of two platoons to himself. He had several balls through his coat, but was not touched.[4]

In the confusion which followed, the French rallied, part of Draper's force was cut off, the Comte D'Estaing, one of Lally's brigadiers, was taken prisoner, and the British had to retreat along the prearranged route where Brereton's detachment covered their withdrawal. De Bussy could easily have cut off this line of retreat, but did nothing; either because he was still sulking with Lally or because his men were still too drunk to move. The British reached the safety of the Fort under the cover of the guns on the bastions without further mishap. The foray resulted in losses of almost 200 men killed, wounded, or taken prisoner, though the French suffered worse losses. Later Lawrence issued a cryptic Garrison Order of the Day:

> Colonel Lawrence thanks officers and men for their behaviour this morning, and recommends a greater coolness and attention to orders given them as their repulse and misfortune has been entirely due to that misfortune and not to any valour of the enemy.[5]

The inconclusive sally allowed both sides to settle down to the almost ritual procedures and conventions of a long siege. Lally began the laborious construction of artillery batteries while being forced to pay attention to his lines of supply through Chingleput where the resourceful Company officers, Captains Caillaud and Preston, were conducting damaging guerrilla attacks.

The French batteries finally opened up early in January 1759, but a month-long bombardment was unable to score any decisive effect against the defences of the Fort. Lally proposed a capitulation before the bombardment began, but this was firmly and unanimously rejected. The defenders were aware that despite the disparity of numbers, Lally's force of over 5,000 outnumbering

Lawrence's 3,500, the French general's resources were fully stretched and that time was probably on their side.

The disappearance of D'Aché's squadrons was now to prove crucial. News reached the Fort on 24 January that Admiral Pocock's squadron had arrived in Bombay on 10 December, made a rendezvous with the ships carrying the remainder of Draper's regiment, and that the whole force was now heading round the coast for Madras. On 16 February the sails of Pocock's squadron became visible on the horizon, and Lally ordered a withdrawal. Two days before the arrival of Pocock's ships, Lally had written to de Leyrit, the Governor of Pondicherry, in gloomy terms:

> I reckon we shall, at our arrival at Pondicherry, endeavour to learn
> some other trade, for this of war requires too much patience. I am
> taking my measures today to set fire to the Black Town and to blow
> up the powder mills ... PS. I think it necessary to apprise you that
> M. Soupire [his Chief of Staff] has refused to take upon him the
> command of this army which I have offered to him and which he is
> empowered to accept by having a duplicate of my commission. You
> must, of necessity, take it upon you, together with the Council. For
> my part I undertake only to bring it back. Send therefore your orders,
> or come yourselves to command it, for I shall quit on my arrival.[6]

Lally's threat of abandoning his command came to nothing, but his realistic assessment of the impossibility of long-term success in his command was to persist until his eventual defeat and departure two years later.

The timely arrival of the British squadron had been the final blow to Lally's siege of Madras, which was to prove the last major offensive of the French in India. Demoralised, his army began the retreat towards Pondicherry, Lally himself nursing a grievance that he had not received the support his command deserved. For his remaining time in India he was constantly on the defensive in the field, and in equally constant attack on the civil authorities of the *Compagnie*. As usual he considered everyone except himself out of step, and his behaviour became more erratic and intolerable with the decline in French fortunes. Whatever his undoubted qualities as a fighting soldier, India had found him wanting as a general; and he still had to face new adversaries when he returned to France. Sir John Fortescue accurately pinpointed the failings of an essentially warm-blooded emotional man:

> Violence without strength, energy without foresight, imperiousness
> without ascendancy – such are not the qualities that go to make a
> great leader in the field.[7]

In the wake of Lally's withdrawal Madras struggled to rally from the effects of three months of siege and bombardment.

5

OFFERS AND DEPARTURES

In the Hardwicke Papers in the British Library, almost hidden between official reports of military deployments in the 1750s, is a copy of a personal letter from William Draper to Colonel Richard Peirson, his brother-officer in the 1st Guards and friend since the days of their shared house in St James's.[1] It was written a few days after Madras had been relieved:

> From the shattered remains of Madras, Feb 18, 1759
>
> My dear Peirson,
>
> Mr Lally's disgrace before this town has outweighted his short-lived triumph over St David's. The facility with which he took that place, the strongest in the Indies, made him imagine he could carry Madras with the same rapidity but the bravery of our garrison has made amends for the weakness of the fortifications. After a long and bloody siege he decamped in the night of 17 February leaving behind thirty pieces of large cannon, vast quantities of ammunition, his hospital full of sick and wounded, and many other marks of fear and confusion.
>
> Brereton and myself have had a full share of the fatigue during this tedious business, being alternately field officers on duty from ll

December during which time I never had my clothes off except for
a change of raiment. We hope the Grenadiers of the 1st Regiment
will not be ashamed of us on our return. Poor Monson joined us on
the last day of the siege not a little mortified that their unlucky and
tedious passage prevented them from sharing with us the danger and
fatigues of this affair.

The constancy and perseverance of our people deserve the greatest
encomiums as we had no places of security from the enemy's shells
when off duty, so that many were killed in their sleep. The loss
of officers and men in the different attacks and sallies has been
very considerable; of the former we have fourteen killed, as many
wounded, the latter in proportion. The part of my battalion that
was here behaved incomparably well. If you are acquainted with
any officer of Duroure's, Kingsley's, or Napier's please inform them
it's for the credit of their several corps to have sent us such brave
fellows, though as M. Guise expresses it we have used most of them,
for there has been some warm work.

In the sally of 14 December I had four musket balls through my
uniform but providentially suffered no hurt. Our manner of fighting
is not quite so pleasant or profitable as Mr Clive's with the nabobs.
The brigades of Lorraine and Lally and the other Europeans are
as poor as ourselves; it's one shark devouring another, or Nugent
against Fitzgerald or Roache. Lally's behaviour has savoured more
of Galway than of Paris. He has detained women prisoners, his
messages were rude and ill-bred. He has basely burnt the Governor's
and Col. Lawrence's country houses, and sent the doors and
windows to Pondicherry; in short I can't pity them as one might a
generous enemy. They never had the courage to attack the breach
which was practicable for fifteen days together, expecting I suppose
that we should be contented to march out with honours of war
according to the usual customs of most garrisons. But the brave old
Colonel Lawrence, the Governor, Mr Pigot, Brereton and myself
determined from the commencement of the siege not to listen to any
terms of capitulation, for the loss of this place would have drawn
after it the loss of the whole country …

Enclosed I send you a list of the general and staff officers of the
French army; it is at least some small degree of merit to have
resisted and baffled men of so great reputation in arms. Tho' I think
their attacks were injudicious … one would think that they had
never heard of their great oracle Vauban; the construction of the
batteries in general was too low. Yet their chief engineer has a great

reputation, was esteemed the best before Bergen-op-Zoom, but I can pay him no compliments.

The behaviour of many here, both officers and private men would do honour to the most boasted time of antiquity. If I might presume to mention any particular person when all have done so well, Brereton must stand foremost, he is a most glorious fellow. Monson has put my battalion into such good order and discipline that they were enabled to march out of the garrison the second day after their landing. He makes an excellent Major. Our want of beasts of burden and the scarcity of provisions will I fear prevent us from making the most of the enemy's retreat. Their desertion and dissatisfaction is prodigious, about 250 of them have enlisted in our service; half of them French. They say that M. Lally has given them no pay for above a year; all their hopes depended upon the booty of Madras in which I suppose there was a million in specie, but they were kind enough to let us keep it.

What a glorious conclusion this is for Colonel Lawrence; the third time he has saved this country yet he is not worth a groot while Clive, for one or two most trifling affairs, has got a million. What an unexpected distribution. As they gave Lord Blakeney a red ribband for giving up Minorca, Col. Lawrence is surely entitled to it for saving this coast of more value than twenty such islands.[2]

Pox take the poverty of these Frenchmen. I shall not be able to scrape up a winter's play at Arthur's; I have spent two years of my battalion already. I hope my wife's house is within the verge of Court for as I take it for granted that my regiment is to be reduced and my stipend one hundred and fifty pounds a year my figure and means will be very small; but no matter, I began with less; as long as my behaviour does not shock my friends my poverty will never affect me. Can I but once meet you and Burton, a fig for the treasures of the East. Love to all friends. I particularise none for fear of saluting the dead. Pray, is poor Jenison of that number, it was so reported. If he is alive, tell him I embrace him and his bottle[3] ... Your affectionate servant ... PS. Little More has behaved very well ...[4]

A list of the principal officers of Lally's army was then appended, including some of the most illustrious military names in France; D'Estaing, Montmorency, De la Tour du Pin, and De Crillon.

This private letter, not bound by any rules of official discretion, illustrates the assumption that all military action carried with it the prospect of booty. It also sheds light on the great respect which Stringer Lawrence commanded among his professional colleagues as well as the recurring and widespread irritation that Clive's victories had not only gained him easy glory but vast riches in comparison with Lawrence's pittance.

The letter conveys an understandable sense of relief and yearning for home. The strain of enduring the siege fell equally on the whole garrison which had suffered losses of thirty-three officers, 580 European troops and 300 Sepoys, but the daily danger from bombardment, scarcity of fresh food and water, and cramped conditions in Madras' humid heat, must have stretched resilience to breaking point.

Draper reported more formally to Lord Barrington all the details of the siege, endorsing the tributes paid by others to the behaviour of the defending troops.[5] He concluded by saying that the regiment had lost about 160 men since leaving England and ended with another plea for reinforcements:

> Even after this success all we can pretend to the enemy is yet 2000 European foot ... if we do not muster a force sufficient to recover the province the East India Company will be obliged to make peace upon any terms they can get ... 2000 more men would make us sovereigns of the East.

The call of the commander for just a few more troops to tip the balance resonates through centuries of military endeavour.

In the aftermath of the siege, new dispositions had to be made. Stringer Lawrence, suffering a breakdown in health, made known to the Council his intention of returning to England as soon as possible, preferably by the next available ship. Facing the need to replace him in command, the Council then offered overall command of troops, both royal and Company forces, to Draper. He faced two dilemmas; his own health had suffered during the siege, and the command being offered to him by the local Council of the Company could have compromised his commission as an officer commanding a force of royal troops.

The prospect of possible riches, and greater honour, must have been tempting. Pursuit of Lally's tattered army with the fresh troops arrived from England holding out the possibility of a major victory would have appealed to his professional ambition. The state of his health was the deciding factor. On 28 March 1759, he replied to the Council:

> ... their polite and unmerited compliment might well infuse vanity into any man, but as neither the ill state of my health, but much more of my mind, makes me worthy of the honour or equal to the burden, I beg leave to decline ... I am a stranger to rest, and have no object or attention but that of home and making my escape from this country, the heat of which is grown insupportable to me. This is really my disease, tho' more will call it madness; for so it will

be certainly thought when I quit a regiment, lose two-thirds of my income, impair my private fortune.

With this assertion that it can do the service little good to drag thither a miserable distempered carcass loaded with afflictions and attentions quite foreign to the business of the field, and some domestic circumstances too delicate for any public explanation, all I can say is that I will go to die for, but cannot live in, your service ...

Your service is in such good hands that you will be in no pain for its success. Major Brereton's modesty makes him diffident of himself but he will do well. He will be aided by the counsels and assistance of the persons in whom, had I acted any longer, I should have placed my own chief dependence, I mean Majors Caillaud and Monson, as I think I can hurt no man by declaring the former by far the fittest person for the command of the war in this country of any one now in it. His knowledge of the people, country, experience, generosity and happy turn of mind, which I also so much feel the want of, gives him superiority over any man whatsoever ... All the favour I have to beg is an order to be admitted on board Mr. Howe's ship.[6]

The letter, which was accepted by the Council with regret, was a surprisingly frank admission from Draper that his ill health was made worse by a streak of melancholy in his character which he was honest enough to recognise and unable to ignore. The 'domestic circumstances much too delicate for any public explanation' remain elusive but presumably referred to some news received recently from Caroline. Belated news of a miscarriage, or some other strain on their marriage, would have reminded him that he had already been absent for more than a year, and acceptance of a new command would prolong the absence indefinitely. It is also possible that he had received news, whether or not via Caroline, of the birth of a 'natural' daughter who was referred to, after his death many years later, as 'the offspring of an illegitimate passion'. Although prolonging his stay in India might have seemed a preferable option, his letter to the Council gives insight into a man courageous enough to admit that he was at the end of his tether.

With the impending departure of both Lawrence and Draper, the Council accepted the inevitable, and in their place appointed Major Cholmondeley Brereton to command the 79th Regiment, and Major John Caillaud the Company's forces based on Madras. They were both to see much further action against the French in the coming months, carrying forward the pattern of co-operation established during the siege.

This spirit of unity was referred to by Draper in his parting message to the Company officers:

> Permit me to return my sincere thanks for the great harmony,
> unanimity, and many courtesies you have all shown to me and
> my battalion ever since we have had the honour of serving with,
> and being among, you. I am extremely sorry that some untoward
> circumstances have deprived me of the continuance of that happiness
> by obliging me to return to Europe where I shall go with the
> satisfaction that I left the public service carrying on as it ought to be,
> with credit and glory to the nation and unencumbered with the dirty
> partial differences which do sometimes distract and interrupt the
> general good ... As for the events of the war it is almost needless to
> wish it a fortunate conclusion for you have assured it so thoroughly
> by such a cordiality between yourselves that I think I can answer
> for its success and shall with great truth inform His Majesty that I
> left no kind of confusion among you but that of doing the King and
> Company most service.[7]

Beneath the flowery phrases of the message runs a sense of relief that the tensions of Adlercron's relations with the Company had not been repeated.

Stringer Lawrence was equally generous in his commendations. Reporting to William Pitt from his camp outside Madras, to which he had moved his troops to follow the retreating French, he ended his despatch by writing:

> I cannot conclude this address to Your Excellency without begging
> leave in a most particular manner to express how much we are
> indebted on this occasion to the great service of Colonel Draper and
> Major Brereton whose unwearied attention, discipline, conduct and
> bravery cannot sufficiently be praised and can only be rewarded by
> Your Excellency's approbation of their merit. Their good example
> could not but have a happy influence over their troops. Those of His
> Majesty's officers and soldiers distinguished themselves in a most
> particular manner, those of the Company's and all in general did
> honour by their behaviour to the name of Englishmen.[8]

Lawrence's despatch would not have reached Pitt in England until late in 1759, long after he and Draper had left Madras in separate directions, both of them believing inaccurately that they were leaving Madras for the last time. The news of the repulse of Lally's siege would have been added to all the other dispatches of that astonishing year in which Pitt's plans as a war leader came to fruition and 'bells were worn threadbare with ringing for victories'. Louisberg, Minden, Quebec, Quiberon Bay; all of them victories simplified and magnified in the retrospect of history but at the time regarded by their author Pitt principally as factors to bring an advantageous conclusion to the war.

As Draper prepared to depart, his regiment, now fully up to strength, moved towards Pondicherry. Brereton, in a despatch to the Earl of Holdernesse in

London summarising the events immediately after the siege, identified the core problem of the division of command and control between the royal and Company forces as well as the clash of priorities between the three major Company Presidencies of Madras, Calcutta, and Bombay:

> On 7th April we made a show of besieging Wandiwash which drew out the French, and on 12th April we went into Conjeveram. Major Monson received a wound which went in through his ear, passed through his cheek and came out near his nose, but happily he never found any inconvenience from it and is now quite well. Myself and Caillaud were also wounded. Numbers of the enemy are deserting, but our own force being in rough shape we decided to retire to Madras ... Lally's force have mutinied for want of pay.[9]

He grumbled that he wished to take the field again but that the Governor and Council had forbidden any further immediate action, adding that the French forces 'are coordinated, but the British troops are always having to fit in with East India Company priorities'.

Brereton's wound, to which he had referred so laconically, had been serious enough to delay Draper's departure on the East Indiaman *Winchelsea*. The Diary of Fort St George had noted:

> [T]he reason for the delay of the *Winchelsea* was that Colonel Draper had proposed taking his passage, but the Board having received the advice of the taking of Conjeveram and that all the principal officers had been wounded, Colonel Draper had offered to stay and take command of the army if Major Brereton's wounds were such as rendered him incapable of acting; but it appeared by subsequent advices that Major Brereton's wound is but slight ... Colonel Draper now proceeds on the *Winchelsea*.[10]

The proof that Draper was prepared to continue in command if Brereton had been incapacitated suggests that his sense of duty would have overridden his malaise if there had been no alternative. He must have been relieved with the news that both his friends Brereton and Monson had been no more than 'inconvenienced' by their wounds. The *Winchelsea*, under the mastership of Lord Howe's brother, Thomas, sailed from Madras on 22 April 1759. Its voyage provided the sounding board for the idea of an expedition against Manila.

II

CHIMERA:
THE LURE AND THE REALITY

7. *Admiral Lord Anson (1697–1762), First Lord of the Admiralty during the Seven Years War, whose personal support for the Manila expedition in 1762 sprang from his own successful capture of the Manila galleon twenty years earlier.*

6

IDEAS FROM
A VOYAGE TO CHINA

The *Winchelsea*[1] left Madras not heading directly for England but on the final leg of her planned voyage to China on the normal business of the Company, the profitable tea trade. The great extra distance to be covered on the round voyage to China not only added months to any voyage, but also dictated that the ships sail to the seasonal time-windows of the South China Sea. The *Winchelsea* was thus leaving Madras in the early months of the year to move through the Malacca Straits into the China Sea to be borne to Canton on the south-westerly trade winds, to await the contrary north-easterly winds a few months later for the return voyage.

Travelling on the *Winchelsea* as one of the few passengers along with the recuperating Colonel Draper was the remarkable young Company servant, Alexander Dalrymple, then aged only twenty-one. Dalrymple remains one of the most unjustly ignored figures of British maritime history. If his obstinacy had not prevented him from being given command of the *Endeavour* only a decade later, he, rather than James Cook, might have earned the immortality of discovering the coast of Australia. His other achievements as navigator, cartographer, chronicler and entrepreneur would have been given the credit they deserved. Instead, apart from recognition as founder of the Admiralty Hydrographic Office, he remains a forgotten figure.

Dalrymple's presence at the siege of Madras, and his subsequent voyage in the *Winchelsea*, were fortuitous. Despite relative lack of seniority he had earlier persuaded George Pigot, Governor of Madras, to sponsor him on an unofficial 'voyage of observation among the Eastern Islands'. The intention was to explore the possibility of setting up a new trading station somewhere south of the Philippine Islands. Both Pigot and Dalrymple knew that the directors in London would have refused to approve such a venture, and that the voyage would have to be unofficial. Its departure had been postponed because of the siege of Madras.[2]

Dalrymple had gained Pigot's support for his voyage by his study of the navigational records then available in Madras. While cooped up in Fort St George during the siege, he had time to discuss his ideas with his fellow-traders. One of these was a William Roberts whose career with the Company had included being a 'supercargo' on ships sailing to Manila. Trade between India and the Philippines was conducted on a 'nod and wink' basis since the British were officially excluded by the Spanish from trading there and usually conducted their voyages thinly disguised by sailing under 'Moorish' colours. The links, though unsanctioned, produced both trade and intelligence; and Roberts was particularly knowledgeable about Manila, the state of its commerce, and its inadequate defences. Roberts was killed during the siege of Madras, and the Company, trying to keep business as usual, auctioned his effects, with most of his books on the Philippines being bought by Dalrymple.[3]

The young man's presence on the *Winchelsea*, as far as Malacca, would have given him the opportunity of discussing the merits of a possible attack on Manila with the one man who was eventually given the command to mount such an attack. The log of the *Winchelsea* noted that the voyage from Madras to Malacca lasted a month. On 27 May, Dalrymple disembarked from the *Winchelsea* to join the schooner *Cuddalore* for his three-year odyssey around the Pacific islands and the South China Sea. Although he coincided briefly with the *Winchelsea* in Canton later in the same year it seems that the four weeks at sea shared by the thirty-nine-year-old Colonel Draper and the youthful Dalrymple was the catalyst for the future expedition.

The *Winchelsea*, arriving on the China coast in July 1759, did not sail on her return voyage to England until January 1760. This six-month period was spent on the normal business of negotiating for tea, refitting the ship and moving between the two ports accessible to the European trading community, Canton and Whampoa. During that time William Draper would have had plenty of time to brief himself on the concerns of the Company's traders if Spain were to enter the war. He would also have become acquainted with the coastline off Canton where his elder brother, Ingleby, had drowned more than twenty-five years earlier.

The British community on the China coast was then tiny, accustomed to trading under the arbitrary regime of the Chinese bureaucracy, or through the nearby Portuguese enclave at Macao. Until the previous year there had been no resident 'supercargoes'; and the season of 1758 was the first in which a Company Council had been appointed, though the Council consisted of no more than four traders. Representation of other nations trading into Canton was equally restricted by the Chinese authorities determined to keep all trade at arm's length. The Chinese Viceroy at Canton was wary of overstepping the limited powers allowed to him by the Imperial powers in Peking, and embodied the concept that trade should only be permitted at all if it produced clear commercial advantage to China, and even then not openly encouraged.[4]

The other European nations trading through Canton were the French, Dutch, Danes and Swedes, with Portuguese trade channelled almost entirely through Macao. The season's ships tended to arrive on the monsoon winds and their simultaneous presence in Whampoa, though numerically small, made market conditions fiercely competitive.

The one notable absentee from this pattern of raw-nerved commerce was the Spanish. Their absence was historically and strategically explained by the fact that their ships had no need to trade onto the China coast. Spanish control over the Philippine Islands, only 700 miles from Canton, gave them a trading base to which Chinese junks were only too willing to travel, away from their own overbearing bureaucracy. The Spanish were also uninterested in the tea trade and were content to allow the Chinese to come to them in time for the only trading season of importance to Manila; that which matched the arrival and departure of the legendary Manila galleon.

The Manila galleon, as distinct from the galleon fleets which plied between Mexico, the Caribbean and Spain had acquired its legendary quality because of its inaccessibility, its rarity, and its value. Its inaccessibility was the result of the historic direction of Spanish maritime conquest, westward via the Caribbean, across Mexico and thence across the Pacific to the Philippines. In the Caribbean the Spanish were dominant despite constant friction with the mariners of other powers. Across the enormous stretch of the Pacific between Mexico and the Philippines, they were simply unchallenged.

The galleon between Mexico and the Philippines made its lonely passage of three thousand miles on a year-long round schedule. There were rarely more than two galleons on the route at any one time, their tracks crossing in mid-Pacific. The largest of the ships employed on this solitary run were the size of a man-of-war, carrying fifty guns and a complement of marines. They travelled without escort, capable of repelling almost any attacker, usually safe in their protective isolation. No other European nation had any base around the Pacific which might be used for an attack.

The Manila galleon was recognised to be the single most valuable prize in the world. The memory of Anson's extraordinary achievement in intercepting the galleon and its immense treasure in 1743 was still fresh in the British consciousness; and the prospect of commanding a repetition of this triumph would have excited the most diffident man of action.

The galleon followed an absolutely predictable seasonal routine. For the eastbound voyage across the Pacific from Manila in the Philippines to Acapulco in Mexico she was loaded with silk and lacquer goods from Japan and China, and spices from the nearby Spice Islands, to the value of around three million dollars. She left Manila in early summer before the typhoon season became a threat, arriving in Acapulco by the end of the year. Her merchandise was then sold at the annual Acapulco Fair which had itself become a legend embellished by travellers' tales. Quite often the galleon brought no less than 50,000 pairs of silk stockings for onward transmission to Spain and the rest of Europe.[5]

On its return journey to Manila, usually sailing in March to arrive in Manila in June, the galleon carried the treasure which had produced its mythical reputation. The treasure, in silver specie from the mines of Mexico, represented not only the profits from the Acapulco Fair but, more substantially, the annual subsidy for the Government of the Philippines from the Royal Treasury in Madrid. This subsidy stemmed from the fact that the Government of the Philippines had been established by the Spanish as much for religious as for trading reasons. The Jesuits, intent on expanding the Catholic faith into the Pacific region, had leveraged the Royal Government in Madrid into providing for the colony from the outset. Trade had inevitably followed in the wake of the original proselytising but the religious influence remained strong, and the Jesuits still supplied senior figures in the local government. The needs of the other islands of the Philippines archipelago took precedence over other options for the extension of Spanish power, and there was no pressure from Madrid to pursue an expansionist policy. Indeed there was a strong body of opinion in Madrid that the colony represented a major drain on Spain's finances, and that the burden of an annual subsidy should not be increased by any warlike initiatives. Hence the run-down state of Manila's defences, and concentration on maintaining the existing pattern of profitable trade.

These links included a network of unofficial trade and contact points with the East India Company. To the extent that the Company was not a direct trade rival, both sides were prepared to accept the advantages of discreet commerce, disregarding formal directives from London or Madrid. The availability of Spanish silver, the most widely used currency in the Pacific region, was important to British traders especially when the supply from London was patchy. Trade between Manila and India was looked upon as a useful lubricant for the whole commercial system of the region. Recognition of this by the Company, overtly in the region, tacitly in England, explained the reluctance to engage in hostile actions when the two countries went to war. Disruption of trade would always outweigh any short-term gains.

The small community of the Company traders in Canton, in particular, had no cause to argue the case that protection from Spanish naval power was essential for commerce to flourish. In the event of war breaking out there was no likelihood of a Spanish fleet suddenly materialising over the horizon from Mexico. Distance alone made this an impossibility. So although the traders would have discussed the likelihood of any threat from the Spanish should war break out, there was a strong element of special pleading apparent in the William Draper's subsequent plan when he submitted it to the Government at the end of 1761.[6] This postulated a threat which was never likely to arise. By raising the bogey of a Spanish blockade, and making the call to arms likely to appeal to those almost ignorant of the thinness of Spanish naval power in the Pacific, he was arguably being imaginative with the truth.

He was certainly beginning to allow his enthusiasm as a soldier and potential commander of any expedition to the Philippines to be affected by personal considerations. This he would have justified to himself by the knowledge that when he arrived back in England he would be at least forty, unlikely to receive any worthwhile command in Europe (even assuming the war was still continuing), short of money and bypassed by his juniors. An expedition against Manila could well be his last chance to distinguish himself as a senior commander, repair his financial situation, and fulfil his potential. The concept of an expedition, and his confidence that his experience in India could well qualify him for such a command, must have grown within him during the months of the return voyage.

The *Winchelsea* set sail from Whampoa in January 1760, and by April was near the coast of Natal. On 12 May, she encountered a Portuguese ship which passed on all the news of the British victories which had made 1759 Pitt's 'annus mirabilis'.

The long time-lag between events and the arrival of news about them was a chronic source of concern in the eighteenth century; and in this instance doubly frustrating for a soldier conscious that he still had not received news of action in India following his departure from Madras, now more than a year ago. One of the oddities caused by these lapses of time is that there remain on files in England copies of letters sent to recipients who may never have received them. This is certainly the case with letters sent to Draper in Madras by John Calcraft, his regimental agent in London, which would have arrived there months after Draper had left on the *Winchelsea*. Calcraft's letters have the liveliness of correspondence between friends, as well as the immediacy of current London gossip. The first letter, dated January 1759 when the siege of Madras was at its most exacting stage, reports on despatch of clothing and subsistence pay:

> I have applied to Lord Barrington for six months further advance which if obtained I shall get invested in foreign gold and sent by the last of the Company's ships sailing this season which will be in about three weeks time …

> I will now relate as many occurrences as I can recollect which have happened since you left us … Col Burton has run away with Lydius's daughter, the Helen of Albany, has settled £200 a year upon her, and has a fine son six months old … Col Gage has the command of a regiment of Light Infantry and is since married to a Miss Kemble of good character but no fortune … Lord Granby has got the Blues and is now in Germany with them …

An expedition commanded by the Duke of Marlborough, who is since dead in Germany, was sent against St Malo. They found the town impracticable but destroyed two King's ships, 25 privateers, and about 100 merchantmen in the harbour without any loss on our part ...

Gen Amherst and Admiral Boscawen have taken Louisberg where Wolfe gained great reputation, and Wolfe is to have command of an expedition now sending up the river St Lawrence ...

A battalion on the same plan as yours is formed this year for the East Indies and given to Coote, late a Captain in Adlercron's, at the recommendation of the East India Company to the very great heartburning of his seniors here and the great prejudice, nay injustice, of your two Majors. How it came to pass that Major Monson's friends have let him remain a Major when so many promotions have been stirring is to me amazing ...

We long much to hear of you I heartily hope that you will have some successful operation in the part of the world you are employed where I have no doubt of you gaining credit, tho' I much question if your great soul will let you stoop to riches. Remember they will enable you to serve your friends, to cut a figure at Arthurs', and what may be as well, get you a seat in St Stephen's Chapel ...

There has been smart work at the Round Table; Lord Robert Bertie and George Selwyn are both broke down and silenced for the winter ... Lord Edgecumbe is dead; Dick is left in good circumstances and pretends he will be prudent, tho' his friends won't believe him.[7]

The news of the death of the Duke of Marlborough, struck down by dysentery while serving in Germany, would have brought not only a feeling of personal loss to Draper, but an equally strong awareness that he had also lost another powerful patron who might have been instrumental in helping him towards further command on his return to England. Two months later Calcraft again wrote on pay matters, but bringing his gossip up to date with the news that:

Col. Campbell is married to the Duchess of Hamilton, and Lord Weymouth has concluded a treaty of the like with the Duke of Portland's eldest daughter to whom, ugly as she is or the £40,000 she brings, he at present sacrifices his whole time. Adair the surgeon has carried off Lady Caroline Keppel, and Dr Duncan is to do the same by Lady Mary Tufton ...

We are in a great state of alarm about an invasion, the French having 26,000 men about Dunkirk ... We also have reports of very bad news from India, but as they come from France will I hope prove groundless. What is now said is that the French have taken Fort St David and were proceeding to Madras ...

I saw Mrs Draper a few days ago and she seemed very well. She has been forced to call for more than her allowance on moving house, which on seeing the necessity I let her have, thinking that you would have done so had you been here, and I hope you will approve but she will write particularly on the subject ...

Brudenell is an old married man, he seems in much better spirits than when single. Adieu, keep your health, make 100,000 among the Nabobs, and come home as soon as you can.[8]

Draper would have been ignorant of his own promotion to Colonel which had been gazetted while he was somewhere in the South Atlantic heading towards St Helena. The Court of the East India Company, writing to Fort William in Calcutta in April 1760, conveyed the message that:

His Majesty has been graciously pleased in consequence of our application to grant commissions for the promotion of Lt-Col. Stringer Lawrence and Lt-Col. Robert Clive to the ranks of Colonel in the east Indies only ... at the same time His Majesty has been pleased to promote the officers of the battalion at Fort St George, viz Lt-Col Draper to be a Colonel, and Majors Brereton and Monson to be Lt-Cols.[9]

By the time the *Winchelsea* reached St Helena in June, events in India had moved towards the final defeat of the French. Since the siege of Madras a succession of hard-fought encounters on land and sea had swung the balance in favour of the British. A major naval battle off Pondicherry in September 1759 resulted a month later in Admiral D'Aché's final withdrawal from Indian waters. The British blockade of Pondicherry, where Lally still held out, became a stranglehold.

At the end of the same month, Colonel Eyre Coote had arrived back in India with his newly raised regiment, the 84th Foot. Coote, who holds a place in the pantheon of the Indian Army alongside Stringer Lawrence, had arrived first in India in 1754 with Adlercron and had played a notable role in Clive's victory at Plassey. It was on Clive's recommendation that Coote was sent back to England to raise a regiment for service in the Indies, thus giving him the seniority which aroused the jealousy of his military peers.

Coote assumed command of all the Madras Presidency forces on his return to India, including the 79th now commanded by Brereton. He moved swiftly against Lally, diverted him by seizing the fortified town of Wandiwash, and induced him to besiege the town. Despite being outnumbered, Coote awaited his moment and, bursting out of the town on 22 January 1760, completely routed the French. The victory of Wandiwash finally sealed the fate of the French in India, though a further year was to pass before the reduction of Pondicherry.

The 79th played a major role at Wandiwash, though much dismayed by the loss of Brereton who was killed during the action. His death meant that command of the regiment devolved onto George Monson, who was to retain command of the regiment for the remainder of the campaign.

The slow process of mounting the siege of Pondicherry was beginning at about the time that William Draper finally arrived back in England, in September 1760, after an absence of almost two and a half years. News of his contribution to the successful defence of Madras had long preceded him, and in recognition of this he was appointed within a month to be Deputy Quarter Master General to a secret project being organised under the command of Major-General Kingsley.

His appointment could well have been influenced by the need to spread disinformation about the project which was planned to be a major amphibious raid on Belleisle, the island commanding the northern sector of the Bay of Biscay. The raid was to be another in the series initiated by Pitt between 1756 and 1761. The results of these raids had been patchy, disliked both by army and navy as invitations to disaster.

The decision to mount the expedition against Belleisle was made in September 1760 though Pitt, discounting all the likely difficulties, also kept open the option that the expedition might suddenly be switched to an attack on Mauritius. The fact that an expedition to Mauritius in the Indian Ocean would involve a minimum voyage of four months, in contrast to a week's voyage down the Channel to Belleisle, was an obstacle which would simply have to be overcome if the need arose. The readiness of political and military commanders of those times to undertake such seemingly impossible ventures still commands respect.

There was not a great deal of secrecy about the project, perhaps intentionally. Horace Walpole, writing to George Montagu from Strawberry Hill on 14 October, noted:

> Mr Conway has pressed to command the new Quixoticism on foot, and has been refused. I sing a very comfortable Te Deum for it. Kingsley, Craufurd, and Keppel are the generals, and Commodore Keppel the Admiral. The mob are sure of being pleased; they will get a conquest or a court martial … Draper has handsomely offered to go on the expedition and goes.[10]

By the time the troops had trundled their way to Portsmouth, a reconnaissance report from Admiral Hawke had cast doubt on the outcome of an expedition so late in the season. The whole project was suddenly put on hold by the unexpected death of King George II at the age of seventy-two. The accession of his grandson George III and the arrival on the scene of the new King's adviser and favourite, the Earl of Bute, inevitably produced political and strategic permutations. Though Pitt and Newcastle remained the guiding figures in the ministry, the political landscape had shifted.

During the first weeks of the new King's reign, plans for the Belleisle venture were reactivated, but it was not until mid-December that sense prevailed. The expedition was postponed. The unfortunate troops came ashore, after three weeks enduring channel gales, no doubt grumbling fiercely about the incompetence of their military and political masters.

The aborted Belleisle expedition had nonetheless, almost accidentally, achieved one major strategic success; that of ensuring the final downfall of Lally's forces in faraway Pondicherry. Skilful disinformation about the objective of the expedition had resulted in the French believing that the fleet was to be sent against Mauritius rather than Belleisle. The disinformation would have been strategically valid: an expedition leaving England in the late autumn to reach Mauritius at the end of the dry season in March of the following year was a great deal more plausible than an attack on a well-defended fortress in the Bay of Biscay during the winter gales.

The resulting orders sent from France to D'Aché in Mauritius to prepare for a major British attack meant that he in turn passed on the news to Lally that he could no longer rely on any further naval support or ground reinforcements. The immobility of the French fleet in Mauritius, awaiting an attack which never happened, sealed the fate of the French forces in India.

Meanwhile, as the expedition was stood down, its Quarter Master General, Draper, was faced with the immediate problem of finding some steady income. As a colonel separated from his regiment, he was, as so often happened to officers at the time, supernumerary within a system which made no real provision for supernumeraries. It was a problem which could only be solved through patronage. Ligonier, as Commander-in-Chief, was still overseeing the availability of sinecure posts for deserving officers. He would have been involved with agreeing to Draper being appointed Governor of the Forts and Batteries of North Yarmouth in February 1761, at an annual salary of £181 and 10s.[11] The Governorship involved no executive duties whatever, even in wartime.

The small salary attached to the post was no more than a cushion against his immediate financial problems. It would certainly not have allowed for 'a winter's play at Arthur's' with much to spare, let alone keep himself and Caroline in any great state. However, it tided him over the intervening months until his great opportunity came at the end of that momentous year.

In April he received a letter from Major John Call, who had been Chief Engineer for the defences of Madras during the siege. The letter had been sent from Madras in July 1760, letting him know of the victory at Wandiwash, Brereton's death, and Lally's behaviour while still at bay in Pondicherry.

The amiable tone of the letter must have reassured him that his period of command had not been forgotten, and that he had created lasting goodwill on both a personal and professional level. After describing at length the arrival of Coote's regiment and the Battle of Wandiwash he goes on:

> I wish I could omit the death of that brave soldier Major Brereton to whom our success and Mr Lally's defeat were largely owing. The enemy bestowed great praise on the behaviour of your regiment under his command and acknowledge that they laid the foundation of that day's glory. Every soldier of sense and impartial reflection laments Brereton's loss and I must claim a place amongst those who sorrow most.[12]

He ends with yet another of those sideswipes at Clive which seemed to run through the thoughts of almost all those who were close enough to the reality of events at the time:

> Everybody in Madras wishes they may have the opportunity of expressing their esteem for your services. Many who wish the laurels lately gathered on this coast had fallen to Lawrence's or your share.

Draper was soon to be in a position to make a claim for his own laurels.

7

PEACE DELAYED:
WAR WIDENED

Weariness at a war which had now been in progress for five years was shared by all the combatants as their treasuries were drained. Yet the outcome of the continuing search for peace was the prolonging and enlargement of the war until the end of the following year.

Pitt, as Britain's effective war leader, was not hostile to the idea of peace. His basic insistence was that it should justify all the sacrifices made and embody all the victories gained. He was determined that the French should be driven into peace from a position of weakness. During any period of negotiations the pressure must be maintained on as many fronts as possible to ensure that Britain negotiated from strength.

In pursuance of this policy Pitt reactivated the Mauritius project in January 1761, but the need for it was already being overtaken by events in India. Pondicherry, besieged by Coote's forces for more than a month, surrendered in the middle of January. Eyre Coote, reporting this victory to the Council at Fort St George, was laconic in his description of an event of such profound long-term importance – the virtual elimination of France's power in India.

The brevity of Coote's message might have been tinged with sarcasm, as he was already embroiled with Pigot, Governor of Madras, who had arrived shortly before the conclusion of the siege to ensure that the Company's interests would be given first priority. Coote claimed Pondicherry for the Crown by virtue of the fact that the conquest had been principally the work of royal troops. Pigot, in turn, insisted on the Company's right of possession and threatened to stop further supplies unless the city was delivered to him as the Company's representative. The heat was taken out of the row not only by the appointment of six commissaries to oversee the division of booty but more effectively by the fact that there was very little booty to be had from the conquest. However, yet another precedent for future disagreements had been set.

Lally, as the principal prisoner of war, was transferred to Madras with other senior members of the French community to await repatriation. They seem to have behaved with remarkable arrogance towards their reluctant hosts, and Pigot, writing to the directors in London, vented his irritation at French extravagance:

> Immediately after the capture of Pondicherry, Mr Lally came to
> this place, as did shortly after M. De Leyrit, and many others of the
> late Council ... We thought we could do no more than entertain
> them at the Company's expense. Mr Lally was lodged in those
> apartments of the Garden House which had escaped his fury at
> the siege of Madras, and after his departure M. De Leyrit had the
> same accommodation, and, that they might not complain of their
> treatment a table was ordered to be kept for them at their discretion
> without limitation of expense. Had these gentlemen possessed
> any degree of sensibility they would have been the more sparing
> for being unrestrained. We have, however, experienced in them
> sentiments very different from these. They repaid our politeness with
> reproaches, and seem to have intended revenge by profusion.[1]

Lally was sent back to Europe by the East Indiaman *Onslow*, which sailed in March 1761. The Council wrote to the directors pointing out that he was likely to be an expensive passenger, and Lally apparently made the most of the hospitality available on board.

His departure brought respite for his hosts, but more importantly the realisation that the war in India had been brought to a successful conclusion, despite the continuing presence of residual French forces in Bengal. The idea of an expedition against Mauritius was still, however, being given consideration by both the Company and the Royal Navy, seemingly intent on following up the fall of Pondicherry with a final blow against French power in the Indian Ocean.

George Monson, writing to Draper both as a friend and now as commanding officer of Draper's Regiment, brought him up to date following the French defeat, as well as expressing his chronic irritation that the royal forces were being deployed at the Company's behest:

> Mr Stevens [Admiral Pocock's successor] is gone with his squadron
> to Bombay to refit. His recommendation is to attack the islands
> [Mauritius and Reunion] by which the French would be totally

destroyed in India and the Company left to enjoy their trade without molestation ... Private Interest in this Eastern world has got so much the advantage of the public good that I fear our force, which is very considerable, will be employed making nabobs and moguls which will be set forth with all the flowery oratory; and a very few made rich at the expense of the public ...

Lt-Gen Lally goes in this ship, and declares that if it had not been for you and poor Brereton, Fort St George would have been his own. All the French prisoners are to be sent to Europe as soon as possible ... Pondicherry is destroying as fast as they can ... I have sent six of your men to be recommended to Chelsea, all being disabled. We have thirty more without legs or arms ... it is with greatest difficulty that I can get Mr Pigot to permit them to pass on board the ships. I am as well as can be expected and walk tolerably well on my crutches ... If the expedition against Mauritius should not take place I think of taking my passage on board the next ship for Europe as the national war is now over here.[2]

A PS suggests that Pigot, as Governor of Madras, assumed the right to initiate an assault on Mauritius entirely on his own authority and with the power to co-opt the Royal Navy squadrons. In the end no expedition was undertaken against Mauritius, either from India or the more improbable direction of England. The planned expedition against Belleisle was reactivated and successfully carried through in May 1761. It coincided with the first stage of peace negotiations. Horace Walpole commented that:

Pitt prosecuted with unusual warmth an expedition he had meditated against Belleisle; a conquest of so little value and so inadequate to the expense with which it was attended that the plan was by many believed calculated solely to provoke the court of France to break off negotiations.[3]

The seizing of Belleisle was only a small issue within the complexity of the peace discussions which stalled in July 1761. The point of rupture was over access to the fishing grounds of Newfoundland. Britain's conquest of Canada, made possible by Wolfe's success at Quebec and completed by the greater successes of Jeffrey Amherst, had totally disrupted France's access to these traditional sources of the immense cod trade. It was a matter of profound importance to France that any peace settlement should result in her maintaining some access to the Newfoundland Banks.

The difficulty of resolving this issue had also, over the last year, become entangled with Spain's claims to share the same access. Although Spain had so far stayed neutral since the outbreak of war the sources of friction between her and Britain remained constant, and the accession of Charles III to the throne of Spain in 1759 had brought a new dynamic to the scene. Charles was not only a Bourbon and cousin to Louis XV of France but had good reason to feel personal rancour towards Britain for submitting him to the indignity, as the young King of Naples in 1742, of having to decide whether to withdraw his troops from Northern Italy or face the bombardment of Naples by ships of the Royal Navy under Commodore Martin. His humiliation had not been forgotten; and following his accession he had sent a message to Pitt that 'His Catholic Majesty could not see with indifference the English successes in America.'

Pitt managed to defer any crisis but was keenly aware that the possibility of Spanish intervention on the side of France was likely to grow rather than diminish. Charles was alert to the opportunity of Spain benefiting from the give and take in the moves towards peace. He instructed the Spanish Ambassador to keep alive the list of vexed questions, which in turn had convinced Pitt that the Spanish were prepared to consider some direct alliance with France in return for French help in obtaining redress for Spanish grievances against England.

When the French envoy to London submitted a memorandum in July 1761 relating to Spanish grievances he succeeded only in uniting the hawks and doves in the Cabinet behind Pitt's reply that:

> His Majesty will not suffer the disputes to be blended in any way whatever in the negotiation of peace between the two crowns ...
> Moreover it is expected that France will not at any time presume a right of intermeddling in such disputes between Great Britain and Spain.[4]

On top of this rebuff, the London government then hardened its prospective terms for peace, buoyed by the news of the French collapse in India. The French reply in August made no attempt to break the impasse. Within two weeks the French and Spanish signed the second Family Compact between the Bourbon monarchs. The Compact included secret provisions whereby Spain was to enter the war by May 1762, and to take over the garrison of Minorca from France, the original *casus belli* of 1756.

The reason for the long lead-time between the signing of the Compact and a formal declaration of war by Spain against England was to allow the Spanish treasure fleet, the Flota, to make its annual autumn voyage from Spanish America to Spain without fear of being intercepted by the Royal Navy. The movement of the Flota was still an event of crucial importance to the Spanish economy. The galleons carried goods and bullion worth around three million pounds, consisting not only of silver produced in Mexico, but also the Asian goods brought to Acapulco on the Manila galleon earlier in the year. The loss of such a treasure would heavily outweigh any possible advantage which might come to Spain from an early declaration of war.

Conversely, the possibility of capturing such a prize fascinated the London government, and Pitt, sensing that war was not far away, favoured a pre-emptive strike. At a Cabinet meeting in September 1761 he expressed the opinion that 'an immediate action gives us the best opportunity to extricate ourselves ... Every Spanish flag on the high seas ought to be taken ... If the means to do this are doubtful will it not be more so next spring? ... I am for it now.'

His vigour merely served to isolate him further from the Cabinet majority which had viewed with dismay the stalling of the peace talks and blamed Pitt's intransigence for the fact that the long war seemed suddenly more likely to expand than end. Political tension in London developed within weeks into a crisis, as it became increasingly obvious that Pitt, whose claim in 1756 that he alone could save the country had been so richly fulfilled, was intent on resignation.

On 2 October, he met the Cabinet for the last time during the Seven Years War. He reaffirmed his belief that Britain was still prepared for open war, while Spain was not; ending his long speech to his patient colleagues with his declaration:

> Without having asked any one single employment in my life, I was called by my Sovereign and the Voice of the People to assist the state when others had abdicated the service of it ... That being so, no one can be surprised that I will go on no longer since my advice is not taken ... Being responsible I will direct, and will be responsible for nothing I do not direct.[5]

In the dismayed aftermath of Pitt's departure, the Earl of Bute assumed the management of foreign affairs, though aware of being forced to accept responsibilities for which he was inadequate both in personality and experience. While he attempted almost immediately to resuscitate the stalled peace negotiations, he was conscious that Pitt's certainty of imminent war would not disappear with Pitt's resignation. The momentum towards war was stronger than the pull towards peace.

Relations with Spain had deteriorated progressively during the year Pitt had weighed the military options open to him. Once again the plans for a major strike against Spain's overseas possessions had been discussed, with the veterans Anson, as First Lord of the Admiralty, and Ligonier, still Commander-in-Chief, contributing their opinions. Cumberland, now a portly figure in the wings, was ready as ever to press the merits of commanders whom he still considered to be 'members of his family'.

Pitt's original strategy was to strike at Panama with a naval force carrying troops from North America. Once this had been captured the force would be split, part to attack Havana in Cuba, while a large detachment would be sent from Panama across the Pacific to Manila. The hazards implicit in carrying out such a plan over such vast distances had not changed since the disasters of 1741 in the Caribbean, yet the broad concept was still being optimistically regarded as feasible.

Pitt's resignation did not stop further discussion during the autumn of 1761, and the overall responsibility for the plan fell onto the desk of the Earl of Egremont who had succeeded Pitt as Secretary of State for the South.

Charles Egremont, a political lightweight and nominee of Bute, had no delusions about his stature and authority in comparison with the giant he had replaced, but was conscientious about the burden thrust upon him. He did not wish to be seen abandoning any of Pitt's projects before a formal declaration of war with Spain. Indeed, he, Bute and the other new ministers were only too anxious to be judged worthy of wearing the mantles which had descended on them, resolute in war should the need arise. This made them less inclined to challenge the military enthusiasms of Anson and Ligonier than might otherwise have been the case.

Anson in particular never wavered in his belief in the merits of an expedition against Manila. The veteran admiral spoke with the personal authority of his triumph in seizing the Manila galleon twenty years earlier. No other member of the Cabinet was qualified to challenge him on the likely hazards of a major amphibious expedition.

Thus, when the memorandum from William Draper entitled 'Reasons and Considerations upon the enterprise against the Philippine Islands' was submitted to Egremont in the autumn of 1761 and eventually came before the Cabinet, it was Anson's authority which ensured not only that it would be given due consideration but that it was given more weight than it would otherwise have received, or possibly even deserved.

8

THE MANILA PLAN
IS LAUNCHED

Draper submitted his plan to Egremont in the autumn of 1761. At the time, there was no protocol which deterred serving officers from putting forward ideas on their own initiative and his memorandum carried the authority of direct experience.

The memo was a clear and practical assessment of what might be achieved, and an accurate forecast of what was achieved. Yet its opening two sentences were undeniably a piece of special pleading:

> The Spaniards, from their possession of Manila, are enabled to fit
> out large galleons to cruise upon our China trade and may by taking
> positions at the Mouth of Canton totally interrupt our commerce
> unless our India ships go there under convoy of men of war which
> has never yet been done. The capture of this settlement will disable
> them from such attempts and entirely remove the seat of war from
> the East Indies.[1]

The existing reality was that the Spaniards had neither the resources for nor the intention of doing anything of the sort, as Draper would have known. Having raised a non-existent threat to justify all that followed in the plan, he moved immediately to an arguably valid objective:

> Our possession of Manila will give our India Company a most
> convenient magazine and port to carry on not only their trade to

China but enable them to extend their commerce all over that part
of the world.

This was certainly a point which had been discussed within the Company
over the years but had never attracted much support. There was little to be
gained from confrontation with the Spanish and much to be risked. Hence
Pigot's earlier insistence that Dalrymple's 'voyage of exploration' around the
islands close to the Philippines was no more than that and could be denied
if necessary.

The sentence which followed then revealed the finally compelling reason
for the expedition – the prospect of booty:

> Manila is a proper object of war from its known wealth and
> opulency, and if the expedition is properly timed the Acapulco
> ships will have brought their treasure there such as will add to the
> importance of the conquest and the further detriment of the enemy.

Draper then crisply got down to the military business, with asides to show
that he was well aware of the current state of affairs in India:

> In the proposed attacks the following considerations naturally take
> place: First to weigh the difficulties of the enterprise, the strength of
> the place and the proper force to act against it. The rainy seasons
> are to be guarded against and the shifting of the monsoons ... The
> place itself has never been reputed strong or well garrisoned, and if
> the expedition is carried on briskly can hardly be reinforced from
> America from whence alone it can receive succour.
>
> I should conceive that 2000 troops would do the business, exclusive
> of the marines and a company of artillery. As I presume no forces
> can be spared at present from Britain all the necessary arrangements
> must be made at our settlements on the coast of Coromandel ... We
> must then consider what we shall have left for the defence of the
> coast and trade and settlements, and whether the French have at
> present any fleet at Mauritius capable of attacking any of our places
> during the absence of our troops and squadron.

His next point illustrated the difficulty of planning any operation when news
from distant scenes of action was always months behind events:

> [T]he enterprise against Manila must be conditional only ... His
> Majesty's Regiments which may be expected to join in the enterprise
> are Lt-Col Draper's, Lt-Col Monson's (the Highlands Lt-Col
> Morris), and the Company troops. If we compute these corps one

with another, to have 500 men fit for duty would be a fair estimation ... The Company's troops may be reckoned at 1200 exclusive of some thousands of sepoys who when mix't with our troops are not to be despised ...

The town of Manila is built part of stone, the upper part of wood for fear of earthquakes, so that a bombardment will infallibly destroy it. In 1757 the garrison was about 700, ill-armed and worse disciplined, the cannon old with rotten carriages. The wall is irregular and much out of repair, as well as other works eight or nine small towers flank the place, two sides are almost washed by the sea. The chief entrance towards the land is strongest and has a ravelin, ditch and covered way, but Virtus Britannica quid non donat?

The memorandum, though unsigned, was in Draper's light controlled handwriting and ended with the slight vanity of a Latin tag befitting a Fellow of King's – 'What can British courage not bestow?' – to finish on an optimistic note.

Its great merit for Egremont and the Cabinet was that it envisaged a fast stand-alone operation. The forces needed were already in Madras, available for action. Draper's Regiment, the 79th, would form the reliable main body of the expedition. Above all the cost of such a project would be shared with the East India Company and would therefore not represent a major new burden on the Treasury. The final recommendation would be that its author would be its most appropriate commander.

The memorandum formed the basis for all subsequent discussions, which included a further paper from the East India Company embodying the thoughts of Alexander Dalrymple on the possibility that the capture of Manila would open the way to establishing one or more trading settlements for the Company on the island of Mindanao, south of the main Philippine island, Luzon.[2]

Plans for the twin attacks both on Manila, and Havana in Cuba, began to take shape even before the declaration of war between Britain and Spain on 4 January 1762. Spain's refusal to clarify her relationship with France was deemed to be justification for a state of war, and the British government took the initiative in formalising the breakdown. By then, as Pitt had forecast, the Spanish treasure fleet, the Flota, had safely reached Cadiz and replenished Spain's Treasury.

One week before the declaration of war, Lord Anson had a meeting with Laurence Sulivan, Chairman of the East India Company, letting him know of the Government's decision to attack Manila and sounding him out on the likely extent of help which would be available from the Company. The Secret Committee immediately responded that it would be proper to give all possible assistance towards the attempt against Manila, consistent with the interests of the Company. It then stipulated that the Secret Committee should pay attention to the following points:

- that a sufficient sea and land force be left at the Company's settlements for their protection.

- that none of the Company's ships should be employed on the expedition without their consent.

- that in case Manila or other settlements be taken, they shall be delivered to the Company.

- and that proper measures be taken for the division of booty to prevent differences between the King's and Company's officers.[3]

The Court of Directors was thus, from the first approach by Anson, laying down firm markers for the limits of its support. It would have been negligent to have done less. The experience of more than a century of trading and surviving in Asia had taught the value of caution. The more recent experience of commands split between the Company's and royal forces had made them even more cautious. They were nothing if not realistic in pinpointing four issues which were likely to, and eventually did, cause trouble.

Yet these concerns of the directors were a product of the unresolved problems of demarcation between the powers and authority of the King's government and those of a private chartered trading monopoly. The debate on these lines of demarcation went on throughout the eighteenth century, and was scarcely nearer solution at the end of the century than at the beginning. Problems were inevitable when the interests of the nation and those of a giant trading company were inextricably linked. Within the entangling web of legal, financial, political and military relationships the overriding objective of the directors was to protect the monopoly trading status of the Company, granted and renewed by royal charter. At the same time the Company, while pursuing its priority of profitable trade for its shareholders, could never afford to challenge too obviously the wishes of the King's ministers on whom it depended ultimately for its charter and greatly for naval and military support on the sea routes and in India.

The directors were also then just beginning to grasp the enormous implications of Clive's victories in Bengal, when entirely new responsibilities for administration and sovereignty had suddenly been acquired. The more immediate problems implicit in an expedition to Manila were a burden they could well have preferred to reject.

The Cabinet too showed evidence of accepting the idea of the Manila expedition without much understanding of all that might be involved. The Duke of Newcastle reporting to Lord Hardwicke on Cabinet approval for the major naval venture against Havana, added almost as an afterthought:

After this was over Lord Egremont acquainted us that Colonel

Draper had a scheme for taking Manila with some troops which are already in the East Indies; that was also in a manner agreed to.[4]

It was possible that the Company nursed secret hopes that the Cabinet might be persuaded to take the matter no further than 'agreeing in a manner', but Anson's authority was sufficient to maintain the momentum which he had established.

The Company's defensive reluctance was apparent in all the discussions following Anson's initiative, with the directors amplifying their misgivings at every opportunity. On 14 January, the Secret Committee offered their sentiments to Egremont that:

> the Company will cheerfully assist in carrying this important scheme
> into execution so far as their abilities and the safety of their trade
> and settlements may allow. But, My Lord, the Committee are under
> the necessity of acquainting Your Lordship that their affairs in
> Bengal and Madras are in a very critical situation, the security of
> these important acquisitions gained at an immense expense to the
> Company will require their utmost care and attention.[5]

The Committee went on to seek assurances that it would be for their officers in India to decide what practical help should be given to the expedition, and that there should be no doubt that the Company's agents would embark with the squadron destined against Manila to take charge of that settlement if conquered. The Committee also asked that 'His Majesty's express will be signified respecting the division of booty and plunder, as unhappy disputes have arisen and are still subsisting,' and ended with the observation that Manila would almost certainly have to be returned to Spain at the end of the war and 'these considerations, of such moment to a trading company, oblige the Committee most earnestly to entreat they may be secured in an equivalent for all disbursements should they be ordered to restore Manila to the Spaniards.'

Having expressed its position the Company was allowed no respite. The Secret Committee reported that on Saturday 16 January:

> Colonel Draper came to East India House to confer with the
> Chairman and Deputy Chairman who happened to be there, upon
> the subject of the Manila expedition. After some general discourse
> upon it he said that Mr Wood from Lord Egremont would attend
> them whenever they would be pleased to appoint and the next
> morning being Sunday was agreed upon.'[6]

At the meeting on the following day:

The several gentlemen mentioned in yesterday's minute being met, Mr Wood answered the Deputy Chairman that His Majesty had greatly at heart the carrying the project for attacking Manila into execution ... There was discussion over the eventual authority over Manila ... Colonel Draper then withdrew and the East India Company outlined the hazards and gave Mr Wood a secret briefing ... and Mr Wood said he would report their misgivings to Lord Egremont and the Cabinet.[7]

This last hope that the whole plan might be aborted came to nothing, and the Company gave its formal approval to the project on 19 January. Two days later the King signed his Instructions for 'Our Trusty and Well-Beloved William Draper, esq, Brigadier-General of Our Forces in the East Indies only', whereas:

We judging that a successful attack made by Our Forces now in the East Indies on the Spanish settlement in the Philippine Islands would be greatly for the advantage of our trading subjects in those parts and at the same time would give a very sensible blow to the commerce of Spain, and We relying on your loyalty, courage and military abilities have thought fit to entrust the conduct of such an enterprise to your care and to give you the following Instructions.[8]

There followed ten specific Instructions, including consultation with Pigot, Lawrence and Admiral Stevens to establish whether the attempt 'shall be judged advisable'. Assuming that it would be, a vigorous attack was to be made and 'in case by the blessing of God upon your arms, you shall succeed in the reduction of Manila, possession is to be kept of the same.'

One of the Instructions, relating to the possible establishment of a settlement on the island of Mindanao, was unusual in that it was subsequently totally ignored after the capture of Manila. This particular Instruction had resulted directly from the successes of Alexander Dalrymple during his voyage after he had left the *Winchelsea* back in 1759. Dalrymple, pursuing his belief that there could be advantage to the Company in setting up a new settlement astride the main route between China and the Spice Islands, had not only concluded a commercial treaty with the Sultan of Jolo who commanded the seas between the Philippines and Borneo, but also continued to press the merits of the nearby island of Mindanao. The fact that Mindanao was indisputably Spanish territory was judged by the entrepreneurial Dalrymple as no absolute barrier to establishing a settlement, and war between Britain and Spain would present an opportunity which could be realised through the instrument of the royal forces.

Instructions on the division of booty were much shorter. Their brevity was itself to become a source of friction from the outset of the expedition and for years afterwards:

> [W]ith regard to any booty which may be taken at land during
> this expedition we are pleased to leave it you and the Commander
> in Chief of Our ships to make such agreement with the East India
> Company or their Officers for the distribution thereof, as you shall
> judge equitable and reasonable.

The authors of the Instructions, familiar with the incessant quarrels which always accompanied the division of booty, probably opted for deliberate vagueness in the hope that those directly involved in the action would decide among themselves what could be judged equitable and reasonable. They possibly never foresaw the significance of omitting any mention of booty taken at sea.

As Draper was receiving his Instructions, Egremont was also despatching a letter to Stringer Lawrence in Madras, timed to arrive ahead of the expedition commander. The veteran Lawrence, now a Major-General, had returned to Madras for further service after recovering his health in England following the Madras siege. By now he was sixty-five, and more inclined to exaggerate his problems than search for new challenges. The tone of Egremont's letter suggests an awareness of the need to massage Lawrence into co-operating, rather than give him direct orders:

> Colonel Draper having represented to His Majesty that during
> his stay in China he had had the opportunities of collecting such
> satisfactory information with regard to the state of Manila as
> to make him of the opinion that the conquest of so important a
> settlement might be attempted with well grounded probability of
> success, employing only such a force as may be spared from India,
> consistent with the security of the Company's settlements and
> conquests there; His Majesty, reposing his entire confidence in your
> experienced abilities and known zeal for His Service, has judged
> proper to dispatch Colonel Draper to confer with you as well upon
> the practicability of this scheme as with regard to the number of
> troops which may with prudence be spared from Bengal and the
> coast of Coromandel ...

> I shall only add that the King is greatly encouraged to hope that this
> important undertaking will take place from a thorough dependence
> on your perfect knowledge of the Company's settlements where
> your presence, your vigilance and abilities are absolutely and
> indispensably necessary during the absence of so considerable a
> force as the attack will require ... I hope it is needless to recommend
> all possible despatch and celerity on this occasion, fully trusting
> that every facility and assistance in your power will be cheerfully
> and zealously given towards the success of an enterprise which His

Majesty has so much at heart, and which is so important to the success of the war in general, and to the interest of the East India Company in particular.[9]

Another letter on similar lines was simultaneously being sent to the Secret Committee stressing the King's hope for the fullest support. In his last sentence Egremont gave the Committee an elegant reminder of just how much the Company owed to royal support:

> [A]ll the facilities which the East India Company shall give in expediting ... will be highly agreeable to His Majesty; nor can the Company give a more acceptable testimony of their due sense of the King's most gracious attention to their interests during the course of this war in those ample and effectual aids which have not only been sufficient to protect but to enlarge and extend their settlements.[10]

This quid pro quo would not have been lost on the Committee though it probably did little to diminish the Company's devotion to its own interests.

The most remarkable detail of all these preparatory exchanges was the acknowledgement that the expedition was dependent entirely on the presence and personal leadership of William Draper. Confirmation of this military oddity was conveyed in the Company's letter to Fort St George, dated 19 February:

> We are now to observe that His Majesty's instructions and orders for carrying this project into execution are delivered to and entrusted with Colonel Draper only, appointed a Brigadier General on this occasion ... so that although you may be preparing for the said expedition, as far as may be consistent with the situation of the Company's affairs and the safety of their several settlements, yet nothing further can be undertaken until the Brigadier arrives with His Majesty's orders and instructions beforementioned, being assured from the Government that sending duplicates thereof was supposed needless as the undertaking depends upon Brigadier Draper's arrival, and should he not get to India, duplicates could be of no use.[11]

In short, no William Draper, no expedition. Yet it was a realistic acknowledgement that there was no one else with comparable experience in the Indies available to organise and lead such a venture. Stringer Lawrence in Madras, and Clive in Bengal, owed their first allegiance to the Company and were in any case fully committed. Eyre Coote, the senior royal officer, was about to return to England following his victory at Pondicherry. It was thus reasonable for the Company to assume that if Draper never reached India, either through shipwreck or illness, there would be no expedition.

It was equally true that the whole idea of the expedition had required the backing of men with the authority of Anson and Ligonier to have reached even the preparatory stage. Anson, though a sick man now in the last year of his life, brought all his remaining energies to bear on planning the major attack on Havana while also ensuring that his enthusiasm for the Manila expedition was translated into effective support. It was characteristic that he personally should have conducted the discussions with the directors. They were given little time to prevaricate, and no real opportunity to exercise a veto.

To Anson the possibility of seizing Manila would have had a personal appeal as the fulfilment of an ambition worthy of his own stature. He had also certainly discussed the idea with William Draper during the previous year on any of the occasions when they would have met as fellow members of White's.

Anson ordered a fast frigate, the *Argo,* to get Draper to India speedily. Anson's orders to Captain King of the *Argo* told him to proceed with Draper, 'his attendants, servants and baggage without a moment's loss of time ... and then make the best of your way to Madras.[12]

Plans for both the expeditions to Havana and Manila were meant to be surrounded by secrecy. Yet, as early as 16 January, even before the Company had given its formal consent to helping the Manila venture, the London newspapers were beginning to circulate rumours about the objectives. The *St James's Chronicle*, muddling the two ventures, wrote: 'this great naval armament is supposed to be destined against Manila, the principal of the Philippine Islands ... it was near this spot that Lord Anson took the rich Acapulco ship.' On 30 January, it spelt out that 'Our squadron in the East Indies reinforced might make an attempt on Manila.' By 12 February, there was 'open talk that the great expedition implied Havana ... and another expedition is already approved of'.[13]

As if to leave no doubt as to the public feeling about these proposed expeditions the *Chronicle* on the same day ran a long jingoistic song to be sung to the tune of 'The Roast Beef of Old England', some of the appalling doggerel in the verses including:

> Let's away to Manila, the pride of Old Spain
> Where with gold silk and diamonds great plenty doth reign
> The noblest of all the rich isles near the Main
> O the brave fleet of Old England
> And O the bold British fleet ...[14]

Further verses, full of equally breezy inaccuracies, took no account of the fact that these early warnings about the expeditions would soon be circulating in Paris and Madrid and could add an extra dimension of hazard to all the plans.

Draper meanwhile had left London for Plymouth where he had to curb his impatience because the *Argo* was delayed in fitting out. The extra days in the city brought one of those bizarre coincidences of military life when he was asked to go to the Common Prison and identify as the Comte D'Estaing a prisoner who had been brought there off a French ship captured in the Channel a few weeks earlier.

The prisoner was indeed the Comte D'Estaing, who had been captured by Draper's troops during the sally from Fort St George at the siege of Madras and who had been a reluctant guest at the Fort throughout the siege. His presence in the jail at Plymouth had been explained to readers of the *London Chronicle* of 21 January:

> They write from Plymouth that the Count D'Estaing, a French
> officer of distinction who was taken prisoner by our forces in the
> East Indies and discharged upon his parole not to engage in any
> expedition against the English and who afterwards did considerable
> damage to the East India Company was taken ... in his return to
> France ... by the Venus, Captain Harrison, who used him with great
> respect and allowed him to carry off all his plate and valuables too
> with leave to reside at Tavistock; but since it was proved he acted the
> dishonourable part above he has been commanded from thence and
> committed to the common prison to his great mortification, even to
> the shedding of tears ...[15]

A week after this news, a reader of the *Public Advertiser* responded with the thought that:

> On 22 Jan I saw a paragraph wherein mention was made of the
> Comte D'Estaing being sent to the Common Prison at Plymouth.
> In my heart I think it is no more than he justly deserves, for in the
> manner he has acted, had our admirals met with him in India I
> believe his fate would have been to hung at one of their yards for an
> hour by the neck.[16]

The anonymous writer went on to detail D'Estaing's various actions in commanding two French frigates against Company settlements in Sumatra, after he had been released from Madras en parole for his return to France as a prisoner of war, and ended by declaring that 'in the eyes of the world he is looked upon as no better than a pirate.'

Draper correctly identified D'Estaing as the prisoner and writing to the directors in London said:

> For my part I wish him gone most heartily as he is a dangerous
> person and capable of great enterprises and understands English too
> well ... Perhaps as an old acquaintance I pity him more than any
> one else does ... He should be treated either better or worse; if he is

guilty he should suffer more, at present he suffers too much for an innocent man.[17]

D'Estaing was eventually released and made his way back to France to prove his 'capability for great enterprises' by becoming an admiral in the French navy. During the War of American Independence, his fleet came to be a constant source of concern for the Royal Navy. Had the British government been able to foresee his later career they might well have found reasons to keep him in Tavistock, tears or not.

The *Argo* was finally in Plymouth Sound almost ready for her voyage by 13 February. On board, Draper wrote to William Pitt, expressing his appreciation of Pitt's evident recommendation that the expedition should be entrusted to himself:

> His Majesty has been pleased to honour me once more with
> His Commands to the East Indies and I am most sensible that
> His favourable ideas of me are greatly owing to your kind
> representations when Minister of State. Permit me, Sir, to assure you
> of the deep sense I shall ever retain of your great goodness to me
> upon all occasions. To prove myself worthy of your recommendation
> is my utmost wish, and I know no way to secure your esteem as
> doing my duty to the public in a proper manner and shall do my
> utmost to deserve it.[18]

The *Argo* sailed on 25 February, reaching Madeira in early March. From there, Draper wrote to the War Office expressing the hope that he would be in India 'in time enough to put His Majesty's commands in execution – it is so much the interest of the Dutch to give the enemy there all possible intelligence that I am under no small uneasiness that we sailed from England so late.'[19]

He was acutely conscious that Dutch ships might pick up news of the outbreak of war between Spain and Britain in time to bring it to Manila before the arrival of his expedition. There was no way by which the news could be conveyed directly from Madrid to Manila more rapidly than by the Manila galleon which had probably already sailed from Acapulco. French ships would be intercepted by the Royal Navy should the opportunity occur. Only the Dutch, as neutrals, were likely to break the news. The hope that 'a good passage may retrieve all, so blow good winds' was foremost in Draper's thoughts. The *Argo* reached Madras on 26 June after a remarkably fast passage of four months.

A few weeks earlier Lord Anson had died in England, destined not to hear of either of the great successes at Havana and Manila, the final testimony to his abilities as First Lord of the Admiralty throughout the Seven Years War. Pitt, by then the Earl of Chatham, paid tribute to Anson a few years later in saying, 'To his wisdom, to his experience and care the nation owes the glorious successes of the late war.' Anson would have particularly enjoyed the capture of Manila as a natural sequel to his own adventures as well as vindication of his strategic vision. Had he lived he would surely have lent his authority to ensuring that the gains from the conquest were not allowed to leach away into a diplomatic quagmire.

9

HUSTLE AND ARGUMENTS

Timing was absolutely critical for assembling the expeditionary forces at Madras. Each passing day made it more likely that news of the outbreak of war would reach Manila ahead of the expedition. It was just possible that the Spanish in Mexico might not have heard the news before the departure of the galleon from Acapulco, but this could not be taken for granted. Surprise could only be assured by speed of action. The need for surprise was increased by the hope that the expedition might intercept the Acapulco galleon as it arrived at Manila, or capture the city before the galleon's treasure had been dispersed. The success of this part of the project alone would justify the whole venture.

Madras awaited with impatience for the appearance of the naval squadron. When the ships finally arrived on 7 July, they were commanded not by the expected Admiral Stevens but by Rear-Admiral Samuel Cornish who had taken command following Stevens' sudden death almost a year earlier.

Cornish was fitted by character and experience to joint command of an expedition setting out for unknown territory. Describing himself as 'a sailor who had come up through the hawser hole', he had started his naval career as a seaman, rising to be Commodore by 1759, attached to Pocock's squadron off the Coromandel coast. When Admiral Stevens succeeded Pocock, he detached Cornish to help in the siege of the port of Carical, whose capture opened the way to the fall of Pondicherry. Cornish was also present at that action, and knew both Eyre Coote and George Monson from that time of success. He had also been party to all the subsequent quarrels with the Company about the division of the spoils of victory.

When he reached Madras, Cornish was preoccupied with the problems of deteriorating ships, inadequate supplies, and makeshift crews. Just after he reached Madras, writing to John Clevland, Secretary to the Admiralty, Cornish reported major concerns with two of his ships and went on to express his apprehensions that:

> [T]he *Lenox, Grafton, Elizabeth,* and *Weymouth* will not long continue fit for service. The *Lenox* is become very weak and leaky and is much broke; the others by age are constantly complaining their timbers, many of them are quite rotten and in general so bad that I am afraid to inspect into their complaints.[1]

Yet all these ships were to play a crucial part in the Manila success.

In the same letter, Cornish, reporting on the first planning meeting held in Madras on 10 July, noted that 'General Lawrence indeed objected against the expedition but his reasons appeared to us imaginary rather than real.' Lawrence had proved negative, if not actively obstructive, from that first meeting of the small group assembled to direct the expedition. The members were George Pigot as Governor of Madras, Lawrence, Draper, Cornish and Commodore Richard Tiddeman, naval second-in-command. Lawrence declined to put his name to the group's initial assessment that the expedition was feasible with the limited forces available as long as their absence from India was kept short. On the same day the full Council wrote back to the planning group noting:

> It is a matter of very great concern to us to find General Lawrence's name not subscribed thereto, as we have from his long experience and abilities ever entertained a great opinion of his judgement.[2]

It appears that it was only the personal enthusiasm of George Pigot as Governor which tilted the balance in favour of the expedition. Lawrence had valid concerns about the security of the coast and the hinterland. Although Pondicherry's fall had sealed the fate of the French in India, this was more apparent in the retrospect of history than in the year immediately following that victory. Lawrence regarded the Manila venture as a drain on his limited resources which, if unsuccessful, would be a disaster and, if successful, a burden demanding further military commitments. His colleagues on the Madras Council looked upon the project even more sceptically as likely to upset normal patterns of trade for questionable advantage. They gave no more than minimum assent.

Cornish, writing later to Anson to report the success of the expedition (not knowing that Anson was then long dead), retrospectively vented his frustrations:

I am very sorry to mention that the Company servants at Madras took every method in their power to obstruct the expedition, except Mr Pigot who proved himself very hearty in it and wished it success. Their behaviour on this occasion was shameful; they would admit only two companies of their troops to go, and those comprised of French deserters and prisoners they released on this occasion; of 2000 Sepoys they were to furnish only 500 embarked; they even refused a small vessel which would have been of great use, the master being a good pilot in the Straits of Malacca, well acquainted with the Bay of Manila.[3]

Despite all the minor squabbles preparations went ahead swiftly and, by 23 July, only two weeks after his arrival in Madras, Cornish was able to report:

The artillery and stores being embarked and everything in great forwardness on the part of General Draper, I hope to leave this place the 31st Inst with the following ships; viz, *Norfolk, Lenox, Grafton, Elizabeth, America, Panther, Falmouth, Argo, Sea Horse, Seaford and Southsea Castle, storeship.*[4]

Draper, four days later, was ready to report the salient details of his plan to the Secretary at War. The new holder of the post, who had replaced Lord Barrington, was the brilliant but volatile Charles Townshend, brother of Draper's friend George Townshend. The letter noticeably refrained from commenting on disagreements with the Company officers:

I have the honour to transmit to you the returns of His Majesty's forces allotted to me for the enterprise against Manila. Their very small number will sufficiently show the impossibility of my acting against the place with the formalities of a siege. My hopes depend upon the effects of a bombardment or a Coup de Main, for both of which we are prepared ... This service alone will not be inconsiderable and tho' perhaps we cannot do all we wish, we are determined to do all we can, and try we will ...

My further expectations of success are founded chiefly on the goodness of my own regiment (my tenth and indeed my only legion) and some very good officers who are so obliging to follow and assist me on this occasion. Colonel Monson goes with me as Second-in-Command, and acts as Quarter-Master-General ... Your friend Major Scot of the Highlanders acts as my Adjutant-General ... Major Barker of the Company's troops, who commands our artillery ... Captain Stevenson and Captain-Lieutenant Cotisford of the Company's troops act as engineers ... Captain Fletcher of the

Company's troops is my Major of Brigade ... These officers form
my little staff, tho' I fear the handful of men under my command
will scarce justify such pomp, for, exclusive of my battalion and
the artillery, the rest are a composition of deserters of all nations
who I take with me more to ease the fears and apprehensions of the
people at Madras than from any service I can expect from them; as
perhaps I shall only carry recruits to the enemy, but I have no choice.
Those or none; such banditti were never assembled since the time of
Spartacus.[5]

He went on to list the difficulties endured by the royal troops in their contacts
with the Company, including the fact that sick or wounded officers had to pay
masters of East Indiamen £100 to ensure a passage home:

As these things cry aloud for redress, the troops most humbly hope
for your protection and application to His Majesty on their behalf
... Mr Pigot's private generosity has been the sole resource which has
saved many of His Majesty's officers from ruin. What he could not
do for them in his public capacity as Governor he has done from his
own purse and great benevolence ...

The prize money due to the troops and navy from the capture of
Pondicherry is not yet paid, from a pretence of not knowing His
Majesty's intentions on that subject. All these circumstances added
to the heat of the country have put them somewhat out of temper.
Yet they have ever gone upon every service recommended to them
with the greatest spirit and cheerfully, and have embarked upon the
present occasion with such joy that I cannot but look upon it as an
omen of my good success ...

We propose sailing by the first of August as we have no time to
spare or trifle away ... If we take the place I shall be at a loss how
to garrison it, as most of the Regulars are to return to the coast
after the affair is over. The Company has stipulated to me to furnish
me with 2000 Sepoys, but their averseness to a sea voyage, the
difference of religion, and particular methods of diet make me fear I
shall not carry a fourth part of their number, so that I have little to
say in my justification for venturing on such a slight foundation but
that the zeal and ardour of all the gentlemen of the navy and the few
under my command bid me hope for success.

We shall make an effort all the same with the land forces; carry it we
will or perish in the attempt.

The unanimity of military effort on which Draper pinned his hopes was in sharp contrast to the inevitable clash of opinion on the division of the likely spoils of victory. While all the logistical problems were being solved during the final three weeks before departure, arguments about booty remained unresolved even as the expedition was about to depart.

The preliminary airing of views soon hardened into formal exchanges of correspondence. On 23 July, Draper wrote to Pigot that the King's Instructions limited his powers to any booty taken on land, and that he felt a one-third share for the Company would be reasonable and equitable. He went on:

> I will likewise, agreeable to His Majesty's commands deliver up
> the place and fortifications ... to the officer or officers who shall be
> duly authorised on the part of the Company to receive the same.
> But I will not deliver them up for the use and benefit of the same
> Company, as by His Majesty's Instructions they must be in deposit
> and kept possession of until His Majesty's further pleasure shall be
> signified ... As to all bonds and engagements of that sort, I shall
> enter into none, as it is a thing unheard of in His Majesty's service.
> The word or promise of the Admiral or General has ever been
> thought a sufficient security for all affairs where men of honour are
> concerned.[6]

The rebuke contained in the last sentence, charged with the contempt of a Guards officer and a Fellow of King's Cambridge addressing traders, could hardly have helped the tone of the exchanges; and five days later Cornish and Draper wrote jointly to the Council:

> His Majesty having been pleased to leave to us the powers of making
> such an agreement with the India Company or their agents with
> regard to booty taken at land during the expedition ... we have
> therefore determined a third part of the booty so taken to be a fair,
> equitable and reasonable distribution. We had an intention to give
> a moiety (half) of the whole had the situation of the forces under
> our respective commands admitted of such a great cession in their
> favour, but the present ill humour and heart burning of our people
> arising from the affair of Pondicherry, and the small advantage
> derived from its capture, have obliged us to take all the means in our
> power to secure the hearts and affections of the forces to the service
> they are shortly to embark upon, and we look upon the distribution
> we have now mentioned to be the effectual means of so doing, as the
> hopes of future advantages may serve in some degree to compensate
> for the former disappointments of His Majesty's squadron and
> army.[7]

This reminder to the Company that its sharp practice over the division of booty at Pondicherry was still a lively issue had been made even more pointed by an additional letter from Cornish to Pigot stressing that 'as to prizes at sea by the squadron under my command, His Majesty's naval laws can be my only guide on that head, nor can I deviate therefrom; the Company cannot share therein nor have I the power to consent to any such agreement.'[8]

The thought that the great prize, the Manila galleon, might result in no share for the Company if it were to be captured at sea only served to sharpen the disagreement. On 31 July, the day before the expedition sailed, Cornish and Draper must have spent most of their hours in the humid heat of the Madras summer drafting their responses, as no less than four long letters were exchanged between the parties.

The first from Cornish and Draper sidestepped the issue of booty taken at sea, while underlining the firmness of their argument:

> We look upon the Navy, the Army, and India Company to be
> three distinct parties concerned in the division of any booty or
> plunder taken at land during this expedition … and of course that
> the majority of these parties can *determine* the point in question,
> especially as the Instruction given by His Majesty to his general at
> land expressly declare that He is pleased to leave it to him and the
> commander-in-chief of his ships to make such agreement with the
> Company for the distribution of any booty taken at land, as they
> shall *judge* equitable. His Majesty does therefore make us the *judges*,
> and as such we have clearly given our determination and reasons
> for it … We have no objections to your appointing an agent to take
> the share allotted to you and what we have *determined* to be fair
> equitable and reasonable you shall certainly have.[9]

Hardly surprisingly this dismissive take-it-or-leave-it attitude evoked an immediate response from the Council:

> … declining to accept your authority to *determine*; and that we
> may avoid altercations, to refer the decision on that point to His
> Majesty. It is however our indispensable duty to take notice that as
> His Majesty has been pleased to declare to the Company His Royal
> intentions to apply to his Parliament to reimburse the Company the
> charges they may be put to in this expedition should the conquered
> places be restored at a peace, the less they receive from the plunder,
> the greater the sum will be to be reimbursed, so that in the end the
> Nation and not the Company may suffer.[10]

This sudden invoking of the national interest was followed immediately by the rather more self-interested suggestion that:

As you are pleased to reject the first part of our proposal that half the plunder be deposited, we cannot do otherwise than adhere to the alternative proposed, that we, the Deputy Governor and Council appointed to receive possession of your conquests will receive whatever you think proper to tender on account of the plunder and booty, not as the Company's share, but merely as such tendered by you.

Cornish and Draper countered with:

Our intentions are most upright. Your agent may certainly join with ours in taking an inventory and account of the whole Booty and plunder. We want to secrete nothing from you, but we adhere to our first determination to allow you only a third of the said booty and plunder as a fixed and positive share, as such offers and tenders as you are pleased to mention afford only room for the chicanes and tricks of attorneys.[11]

Pigot and the Council, determined to have the last word and conscious that time was running out, made sure that they had given themselves a negotiating position which they could use in the months to come:

It is certainly right to be so plain in all dealings as to leave no room for the chicanes and trick of attorneys ... There is a passage in your letter ... on which we think it necessary to explain ourselves, that future understandings may be prevented. Speaking of the garrison to be left in the conquered places by General Draper, you add that the military instructions will be given by him according to circumstances. We hope that these instructions will be such as not in any degree to derogate from the power and authority of the Company's representative to govern, manage, and direct all affairs ... These and these alone are the terms on which we have empowered the representatives of the Company to receive the charge of any conquests; should it so happen (which we hope will not) that any military instructions should be given tending to abridge them of that power and authority they have our directions to return thither.[12]

Within this letter, the Council nominated a group of five Company servants, drawn from the Madras Council, to proceed with the expedition to fulfil the role of an interim administrative body for Manila. The position of Deputy-Governor of Manila, reporting back to Pigot in Madras, was allocated to a senior trader, Dawsonne Drake, with no apparent qualifications for the complex task facing him.

After these acrimonious exchanges the military commanders must have left Madras with nothing but relief. They would have felt some sympathy for George Pigot, who found himself having to discount the scepticism of his Council colleagues, who in turn could not have enjoyed haggling with a general who had been one of their saviours during the siege of three years earlier and an admiral whose squadron guaranteed their continuing safety. All the parties were trying to reconcile conflicting tensions within an experiment, and given all the possible complications it was remarkable not that disputes should arise but that so much was resolved.

The total of the forces assembled and embarked came to around 6,600, with ground forces of around 2,300 and naval forces including marines of around 4,300. These numbers were deceptively large as the ground forces effectively only constituted the 79th Regiment, the small contingent of Company artillery under Major Barker, and a motley collection of French and German deserters, Sepoy soldiers, and various volunteers prepared to fight on the chance of sharing any eventual booty.

8. *Rear-Admiral Samuel Cornish (1710–1770), Captain Richard Kempenfeldt, and Thomas Parry, Cornish's secretary, depicted on board the Norfolk off Manila. Cornish commanded the squadron which played the vital naval role in ensuring success for the Manila expedition.*

Cornish's squadron consisted of eleven men-of-war. His flagship, the *Norfolk*, captained by Richard Kempenfeldt, himself a distinguished sailor, carried seventy-four guns and a crew of 600. The *Elizabeth*, a sixty-four-gun ship with a crew of 480, carried Commodore Tiddeman. The remaining nine ships together represented a competent striking force, but all showing signs of dilapidation from continuous service around the Indian Ocean.

The *Seahorse*, a twenty-one-gun ship, was despatched ahead of the fleet through the Straits of Malacca to patrol the entrance to the China Sea to intercept any ships heading for Manila. The squadron's voyage was to last almost six weeks, itself a considerable test of patience for both mariners and soldiers, as well as a navigational challenge into new waters. A few days before departure, Draper, in an Order to his officers, had stressed the need to regard the expedition as combined operation between the naval and ground forces, spelling out the need for soldiers to help man the ships when necessary and for mariners to man the batteries after any landing.

The main force set sail from Madras on 1 August 1762, arriving at Malacca on 19 August and sailing again eight days later, as the fleet headed north-east parallel to the coast of Borneo. The Company nominees were following the fleet in the fifty-gun *Falmouth*, which had been left behind in Madras to act as escort for the *Essex*, an Indiaman en route to China.

The Company, meanwhile, determined to safeguard its interests in any future negotiations about trade around Manila in the aftermath of the expedition, had sent a letter to the absent Alexander Dalrymple, still on his voyage elsewhere in the region, suggesting that:

> In case this enterprise should meet with success we recommend
> you to call at Manila on your return from China as the island is by
> His Majesty's orders to be put in the possession of the Company's
> agents.[13]

Dalrymple's eventual arrival in Manila, albeit a year later, was to be a fitting conclusion to his own involvement in the germination of the whole project.

10

PRESSURES OF
WIDER EVENTS

The fleet under the command of Cornish headed slowly towards the Philippines, still in advance of the news of the outbreak of war but already unknowingly overtaken by events on the wider stage. The success of the much larger expedition to Havana in Cuba, seat of Spanish power in the Caribbean, which capitulated to a British force in August 1762 while Cornish's fleet was still at sea on the other side of the world, led directly to the renewal of the peace talks. Their outcome coincided with the Manila conquest in a way fatal to it ever receiving the credit it deserved.

The expedition to Havana was the major project of Pitt and Anson's strategy against Spain's overseas empire.[1] It was commanded by the formidable Admiral Sir George Pocock, who had achieved so much against the French around the coasts of India. His second-in-command was Commodore the Hon. Augustus Keppel, who had served with Anson on the circumnavigation twenty years earlier. The land forces were commanded by Keppel's brother, the Earl of Albemarle, whose appointment to such an important command was widely and accurately held to have resulted more from the influence of the Duke of Cumberland than from his own merit. The duke was still involved in many senior military appointments so Albemarle, whom Cumberland considered as one of his 'family', was given precedence over more qualified officers. As if to emphasise that royal favouritism had made a comeback since Pitt's resignation, yet another Keppel brother, William, was given command of a division of troops. This guaranteed that no less than three members of the Keppel family were in line for a major share of the expected booty. Even by eighteenth-century standards of probity this was broadly agreed to be outrageous, though nothing could be done about it.

During the months in which the Manila and Havana expeditions were being assembled, peace negotiators were still striving for compromises which could stop the human and financial haemorrhages of war which had become intolerable not only for Britain and France but also for Prussia, Austria, and to a lesser extent Spain and Portugal.

As the first arm of the Havana expedition sailed from England in March 1762, the Earl of Bute sent renewed terms to the Duc de Choiseul, the French Foreign Minister. Choiseul's delayed response was undermined by the news of the fall of the French islands in the Caribbean, and negotiations again went into a state of suspended animation. During the months in which they remained stalled, the ministry in London was preoccupied with arguments over the scale of support for the Portuguese in their struggle against Spain and the level of subsidies for Prince Ferdinand of Brunswick, whose generalship had contributed so much to the Allied successes in Germany.

The outcome of these wrangles was the final resignation of the Duke of Newcastle, bringing to an end four decades of public office. His departure, outflanked by Bute and his younger colleagues, was the culmination of George III's plan to clear the way for Bute to head a ministry more congenial to himself.

Bute's dilemma was to obtain a peace without conceding too much to Choiseul. The tortuous exchanges continued through the summer of 1762. In August, treasure seized by two Royal Navy frigates from the Spanish ship *Hermione*, worth over half a million sterling, was paraded through London to the Tower 'amidst the acclamation of a prodigious concourse of people'. It was known to the public that forces had already landed near Havana. Any further concessions to Spain or France at that moment would have been politically hazardous to Bute.

In September, the Duke of Bedford was sent to Paris with plenipotentiary powers, though his instructions caused further dissent within the Cabinet, and pamphleteers inflamed public opinion with the idea that British conquests were to be surrendered and Frederick of Prussia betrayed. Into this turbulent diplomatic scene came the news on 29 September that Havana had fallen in the early weeks of August.

The Havana expedition had been carried through with a professional expertise which took the Spanish by surprise. The master plan had been Anson's own, based on a daring and novel approach of the fleet of almost sixty ships along the north coast of Cuba through the Bahama Channel. The siege of Havana, involving British ground forces of around 14,000, lasted almost six weeks at the hottest period of the Caribbean summer. Besiegers and besieged suffered more from the climate than from each other's fire; but the lessons of Cartagena from twenty years ago had been remembered and the British pressed for a quick victory. A major breach led to capitulation, Havana's reputation for impregnability lost for ever.

It is probably impossible to recapture the sense of triumph or shock produced by the fall of Havana. From the days of Drake onwards, Spanish power in the Caribbean, Mexico and America had depended on Havana. Oliver Cromwell had described it as 'the gateway to all the riches of the Indies'. The idea of the British flag flying over the Queen City of the Indies after two centuries of uninterrupted Spanish domination was an event of global significance.

More immediately, the loss was a decisive blow to Spain playing any further effective role in the war. Fourteen ships of the line, almost one-fifth of the entire Spanish navy, were destroyed. One hundred merchant ships were seized, together with booty of goods, specie, and other valuables worth an estimated £750,000.

Admiral Pocock and General Lord Albemarle each eventually received the gigantic sum of £122,697 as their personal share of the conquest, and the rest of the forces were proportionately rewarded according to the usual unjust arrangements; sums ranging from £6,816 for a major-general, £1,600 for a naval captain, and downwards to £3 or £4 for seamen and private soldiers.

When Albemarle reported the victory to Cumberland the Duke responded with the pleasure of one whose choice had been vindicated.[2] His joy was entirely at one with the nation's which sensed that the loss of Havana would paralyse the whole Spanish empire. The annual movement of the treasure on which Spain's economy depended was now to be denied. Spain, having entered the war to help France and receive Minorca as her reward, had now catastrophically lost the most prized of her overseas possessions.

Bedford in Paris was immediately instructed to include in his negotiating the possibility that the return of Havana to Spain might be swapped against the cession of Puerto Rico or Florida to Britain. Choiseul, coordinating his tactics with Grimaldi the Spanish Foreign Minister, recognised that Spain's defeat at Havana, and a possible further defeat at Manila, had hardened the demands of the British to the point where the best peace obtainable must be immediate.

Accordingly, on 3 November 1762, the Preliminaries of Peace were signed at Fontainebleau. The passions aroused by the terms of the treaty could not obscure the fact that Britain had achieved the principal objective for which she had gone to war seven years earlier – the protection and enhancement of her territories in North America.

The one absolutely indisputable outcome was that Britain had gained Canada, while restoring to France some limited access to the Newfoundland fisheries. In the strategic area of the West Indies, France ceded Grenada, Dominica, St Vincent and Tobago, while Britain restored Martinique and Guadaloupe to France. In India, the *status quo ante* of 1749 was agreed by both parties, which allowed Pondicherry to be reactivated as a trading post; though neither party had any illusions about the disappearance of French military power.

In Europe, France evacuated and restored Minorca to Britain, while Belleisle was restored to France. Spain, with little bargaining power, conceded Florida in return for Havana, and also withdrew her forces from Portugal.

Despite France's recognition of Canada as British, Choiseul had won terms far better than he could have expected at the outset. His success was immediately the subject of controversy in England and it became imperative for Bute, and the King, to obtain parliamentary approval for the preliminary terms before opposition could be fully marshalled.

The shadow of Pitt still dominated the political scene. Since his resignation a year earlier, his stature as a national figure had grown. His attitude to the peace terms may no longer have been crucial to their acceptance by Parliament but was nonetheless regarded as the expression of the national sentiment. He felt he could speak as the war leader who had been so largely responsible for the victories which Britain had gained.

Pitt's speech on the terms of the peace in the Commons debate early in December 1762 was thus more of an act of Parliamentary theatre than pivotal to the arguments, but was heard throughout its three hours in the silence which he could still command.[3] Declaring himself 'determined … to raise up his voice … against the preliminary articles of a treaty that obscured all the glories of the war, surrendered all the interests of the nation, and sacrificed the public faith by the abandonment of our allies', he went on to range across all the areas of conflict expressing anguish at the outcome of the negotiations. The restoration of the French trading posts in India was dismissed in the phrase which has come to represent the whole of his speech: 'We retain nothing, although we have conquered everything.'

Pitt's conviction that the continuation of the war would have been preferable to an ignominious peace might have had historical validity but was never likely to carry the day with a war-weary Parliament. The House divided 319 to 65 in favour of peace. Bute had thus opened the way for the final completion of the negotiations and, in turn, for the public odium which within a few months was to contribute to his own departure from office.

In the cause of moving rapidly towards a definitive treaty, the question of Manila became a victim of the pressure of time. No news could be expected for months. Whatever the outcome of the expedition it could not be allowed to delay the ending of the war. It had inadvertently slipped into a diplomatic, political and historical limbo.

11

COUP
DE MAIN

In the same week in September 1762 as the Duke of Bedford was negotiating in Paris and news was arriving in London of the fall of Havana, Spanish lookouts on the citadel of Manila were startled to observe a squadron of ships heading towards the city across the great sweep of the Bay of Manila. They assumed at first that the ships might simply have been driven into the bay to seek shelter, but within hours realised that the British fleet had not arrived there by accident and that its intentions were hostile. The expedition had reached Manila before the news of the outbreak of war, gaining the crucial advantage of surprise.

Manila was then a small city, less than three miles in circumference, sheltered within ramparts and bastions, and dominated by the Santiago fortress controlling the point at which the Pasig River ran into the bay. It had no harbour, and all port traffic and trade was channelled through the small port of Cavite, a few miles around the bay. The city walls had twelve bastions and six gates and should have presented an almost impenetrable challenge had they been manned by a well-equipped defending force; but the loneliness and inaccessibility of Manila had over the years lulled the Spanish into a false sense of security. They had discounted any possibility that a rival European power would be rash enough to dispatch an invading force over such enormous distances in strength sufficient to overcome their permanent garrison.

The defences were in a lamentable state of disrepair and presented, if not an easy, at least an attainable target. The artillery dispersed around the walls was, even by the Spaniards' own assessment, in no condition to repel a siege, almost a third of the 130 pieces being defective in some degree. The garrison available to defend Manila and Cavite was in an equal state of unreadiness. In theory, a full regiment of royal infantry was based on Manila; but it was dispersed around the main island of Luzon, elsewhere in the archipelago, or even at sea on the galleons between Manila and Mexico. Its fighting strength around the city was in the low hundreds, of whom a considerable number were local Filipinos never tested in battle.

The commander of the Spanish forces, the Marques de Villamediana, was suddenly faced with a situation in which he could only play for time as the British fleet anchored offshore and the first reconnaissance boats were lowered to sound the entrance to Cavite harbour on the evening of 23 September.

At this moment of crisis, Villamediana was at one with the Governor of the Philippines, Archbishop Manuel Rojo, a priest whose long Jesuitical training was to be a valuable weapon in the Spanish armoury. He had become Governor only the previous year in succession to another bishop, and the thought that he might one day be called upon to command a city under siege would have seemed improbable at the time of his appointment. Yet he was to prove equal to the surprising challenge.

While the Spaniards debated their opening response, the British commanders considered whether their first attack should be upon the port of Cavite. If this were seized it could be a firm base for further action around the bay against Manila; if not it might become a rallying point for Spaniards in their rear. The need to get this immediate decision right was crucial, and when William Nichelson, the master of the *Elizabeth*, reported to Admiral Cornish and Brigadier Draper that his night reconnaissance proved it would be possible to take the men-of-war close inshore to seize Cavite, 'the General was so much elated that he clasped me in his arms and said many pleasant things to me for the good news I had brought him.'[1] Draper's unconcealed joy showed immense relief that this first part of the operation was feasible.

The following morning, a Spanish officer boarded Cornish's flagship with a letter from Rojo, written in his capacity as both Governor and Captain-General. The letter was in Spanish, asking by what authority the squadron had entered the bay and what was their purpose if not to seek shelter. It concluded by saying that if the British had come with hostile intent, 'which he could not think possible not having heard of any declaration of war', he was determined to defend the honour of the Spanish Crown to the utmost extremity.[2]

Cornish and Draper replied with a letter in Spanish so dotted with grammatical errors that it seems they could not have included a Spanish interpreter in their team. Their clumsy phrases did not blunt the message that the King of England had sent them to conquer Manila and 'to convince the Spaniards that the most distant dominions of their sovereign are not proof against the force and power of our King, or beyond his just displeasure'. They called upon the Spanish authorities to avoid the sad extremities which would inevitably follow fruitless resistance by surrendering Manila. Their claim to be moved 'by the principles of moderation and humanity so peculiar to the British nation' sat slightly uneasily alongside the simultaneous advice that the Spaniards should 'think seriously of the means we have to enforce our demand'. The letter closed with the splendidly courteous and inaccurate 'Vouestras mui obedientes serbidores'.[3]

More importantly, Rojo's letter had confirmed to the British commanders that they had arrived ahead of the news of war, and that the Spaniards had therefore made no advance preparation for defending their territory. They decided immediately to move against Manila rather than waste time on the reduction of Cavite. That same evening the first troops were landed on the beach about a mile and a half from the walls of the city. The landing was unopposed, the troops relieved to have disembarked so easily after almost two months at sea. The Spaniards meanwhile set fire to houses outside the city walls, and received into the city 500 Filipino soldiers summoned urgently from nearby towns.

The next day was spent in moving towards positions where artillery batteries could be constructed, with a company of the 79th under the reliable George Monson taking post at a deserted church which Draper used thereafter as his headquarters. The seamen and marines remained by the beach covering the slow landing of stores from cumbersome rowing boats.

During the day came a moment which must have electrified the whole expeditionary force. A small sailing vessel, a galliot, had been seized as it approached Manila across the bay. Its crew turned out to be from the galleon the *Philipina*, which had just arrived from its cross-Pacific voyage and was waiting off the coast of the island of Samar. The galliot had been sent to Manila to pick up a pilot to guide the great ship through the tricky waters and islands around the south of Luzon.

The closeness of the timing was almost incredible. The *Philipina* had brought news of the outbreak of war on its voyage. If the small galliot had arrived in Manila only two days earlier, the Spaniards would have been alerted against the British force and disaster could have resulted. Equally important, and more exciting, was the realisation that there was now a possibility of seizing the galleon itself with its immense treasure, and justifying the whole expedition even if Manila was able to defy an attack.

Simultaneously it was obvious that the galleon could be alerted to the presence of the invaders, and that her treasure might be dispersed before it could be seized. Cornish immediately despatched two of his fastest frigates, the *Panther* and the *Argo*, to seek out the waiting galleon, though their search would take at least ten days through hazardous and unknown waters.

Archbishop Rojo, equally aware of the vital need to protect the treasure, had learnt of, and probably witnessed, the capture of the galliot. He urgently sent a letter, overland through the primitive roads across Luzon, to the captain of the *Philipina* ordering him to unload the silver bullion and carry it inland.

If necessary the galleon could be scuttled. He assured him that the Jesuit missionaries in the inland town of Palapag would help to guard the treasure.[4] So the race for the treasure was on, with all parties knowing that there could be no news of success or failure for at least two weeks.

Meanwhile, as the British slowly deployed closer to the city, Rojo and Draper continued to exchange letters. On 26 September, Draper, writing from his headquarters in the little church of Malate, reminded Rojo, in English:

> how unequal your people are to support this affair. I beg you therefore to consider your position before it is too late. I have a multitude of most fierce people who are unacquainted with the more humane parts of war; it will not be in my power to restrain them if you give us more trouble.[5]

Rojo responded by complaining that, although he had briefly suspended all operations against the British under flag of truce, they were bringing their battery closer, and asked the general to order his soldiers to return to their former lines. Draper ignored the specific request in thanking the Governor for his polite message:

> Be assured that this war will be carried on as becometh polite and humane nations. I have the pleasure to inform you that your nephew is safe aboard the Admiral's ship, and that he will be sent ashore as soon as possible, till which time I shall give the strictest orders not to fire upon your city and suspend all hostilities, and do not doubt that Your Excellency will observe the same punctilio.[6]

Rojo's nephew, Antonio de Serra, had been captured on the galliot as it came towards the city. It seems that he was reluctant to leave the safety of Admiral Cornish's ship for the dubious pleasure of being escorted into the city, as in another letter to Rojo on the same day Draper noted:

> I have the honour to enclose Your Excellency this letter from your nephew. It seems he declines entering Manila. As the reason therefore for which only I suspended operations against your palace no longer subsist, hostilities will recommence this night. God have you in His holy protection. If you place a particular flag upon your palace my bombs shall avoid it if possible.[7]

Rojo, in turn, introduced an unexpected gambit. He wrote in Latin, addressing Draper as Dux Excellentissime, and asking not only for the release of his nephew but also for the British commander to consider what a hopeless undertaking it was to try to take Manila by storm and causing so much useless suffering.[8]

It is intriguing to speculate how Rojo could possibly have known that Draper would be able to understand his ornate Latin, and be tempted into replying in his own rusty Etonian Latin. Perhaps the couriers relaying the letters, or the interpreters, had suggested that Latin was acceptable currency among educated people. The Archbishop touched the vanity of the soldier, who thereafter corresponded with him in Latin, except at times when he needed to trust himself absolutely in English.

The need occurred as early as the next day. The Governor's nephew was being escorted into the city under flag of truce by Lieutenant Samuel Fryer, Draper's secretary, when a large body of undisciplined Filipinos and other auxiliaries fell upon them. In the violent skirmish which followed, Lieutenant Fryer was killed and beheaded, while the Archbishop's nephew was also mortally wounded. Rojo himself had shown much bravery on hearing the news of this outrage by riding out and personally restoring order.

Draper wrote immediately in English:

> It is impossible for me to express to Your Excellency the indignation
> I feel at the barbarous treatment of my secretary, murdered under
> the solemn sanction of an embassy; a guilt only known among these
> savages for believe me, Sir, I cannot think or suspect Your Excellency
> or any Castilian to be concerned in so horrid an affair ... I must
> tell you, Sir, that if the authors of this most barbarous murder are
> not immediately given up to our justice, these gentlemen now our
> prisoners will meet with a proper retaliation for this affair. I likewise
> demand the head of my secretary or shall send in all the heads of all
> the prisoners in exchange.[9]

The Journal kept by William Stevenson, the chief Engineer of the expedition, noted immediately afterwards:

> In the evening a flag of truce was hung over the walls, no one daring
> to venture out after such an act of treachery. On our answering
> the flag they sent out the headless body of Mr Fryar maimed in the
> most inhuman manner, with a letter from the Governor expressing
> the utmost horror of such an inhuman act, imputing the fault to the
> ignorance and barbarity of their natives who are unacquainted with
> the customs of war.[10]

Preparations for an onslaught gathered momentum the following day when the store-ship, the *Southsea Castle*, finally arrived with her supplies of heavy mortars and entrenching tools. The building of the batteries was supported by two men-of-war, the *Elizabeth* and the *Falmouth*, which stood in close enough to the citadel walls to effect a damaging cannonade. On the following evening, potential disaster blew up in the shape of a tropical storm which lasted for almost two days. From the account in the Journal it could not have been a typhoon which so often cross the Philippines during the late summer; a full typhoon would have lasted longer and been disastrous to the squadron in its unprotected anchorage.

The storm reminded the commanders that time was not on their side, and the attack would have to be pressed home as quickly as possible. During the storm, the ships lost all contact for a few hours with the land forces, while the unfortunate troops took the full discomfort of a tropical downpour. The official Journal noted that:

> Notwithstanding the deluge of rain which accompanied the wind, by the perseverance of our troops and seamen we completed two heavy batteries, made a communication from the church to the gun battery and established a spacious Place of Arms on the left of it near the sea. The waves prevented the enemy from hearing the noise of our workmen during the night. They gave us no interruption but seemed to trust entirely to the elements ... while the Archbishop gave out that an angel from the Lord was gone forth to destroy us like the host of Sennacherib. On the afternoon of the 2nd the seamen with wonderful activity brought up and mounted all the guns in the battery which we masked.[11]

As the rain continued, a force of around 1,000 Spanish auxiliaries made a night attack, believing that the dampness would have made the muskets of the British ineffective. Throughout the hours of darkness fierce skirmishing went on which resulted in the loss of 300 men by the auxiliaries, mostly Filipinos and Malays. The Journal went on:

> We had scarce finished this affair when another body of them, with part of the Spanish garrison, again attacked the church ... forced the Sepoys from their post in it nearest the town, took possession of the top, from whence they killed or wounded several of our people, who were entirely exposed to all their weapons. Notwithstanding this disadvantageous situation the European soldiers maintained their post behind the church with great firmness and patience and at last dislodged the enemy with the assistance of the field pieces ... The Spaniards left behind them 79 dead, in and about the church ... on our side Captain Strahan of the 79th was mortally wounded and 40 men killed or wounded.[12]

The losses suffered by the auxiliaries convinced them of the futility of risking their lives any further for their Spanish masters, and they started deserting in growing numbers. By the time the assault was made on the city a few days later most of them had slipped away to the safety of their home villages.

The British artillery, now free from direct attack in improving weather, concentrated on making a breach in the citadel walls. Major Barker's limited resources were so well deployed that by the evening of 5 October it was decided that the final assault could be made on the following day.

The Journal, factual as ever, summarised the final action:

> At four in the morning we filed from our quarters, in small bodies to give the less suspicion, and by degrees assembled at St Iago's church observing the utmost silence, and concealing ourselves in the Place of Arms, and the parallel between the church and the battery. Major Barker kept up a brisk fire upon the works and the places where the enemy may be lodged or entrenched. Our mortars were applied for the same purpose ...

> At daybreak we discerned a large body of the Spaniards formed on the bastion of St Andrew which gave us reason to imagine they had got some information of our design and intended to annoy us with their musketry and grape from the retired flank of that bastion where they still had two cannon placed; but upon the explosion of some shells among them they went off. We took immediate advantage of this, and by the signal of a general discharge of our artillery and mortars, rushed on to the assault, under cover of a thick smoke which blew directly upon the town ...

> Sixty volunteers of different corps under Lieutenant Russell of the 79th led the way, supported by grenadiers of that regiment. The Engineers and the Pioneers, and other workmen to clear and enlarge the breach and make lodgements in case the enemy should have been too strongly entrenched in the gorge of the bastion followed; Colonel Monson and Major More were at the head of two grand divisions of the 79th. The Company's troops closed the rear. They all mounted the breach with amazing spirit and rapidity. The few Spaniards on the bastion dispersed so suddenly that it was thought they depended on their mines ...

> We met with little resistance, except at the Royal Gate and from the galleries of the lofty houses which surrounded the Grand Square. In the Guard-House over the Royal Gate, 100 of the Spaniards' Indians who would not surrender were put to the sword. Three hundred more, according to the enemy's account, were drowned in attempting to escape over the river which was very deep and rapid.

> The Governor and Principal Officer retired to the Citadel, and were glad to surrender as Prisoners at Discretion. As the place was in no

good posture of defence Captain Dupont of the 79th, with 100 men, took possession of it. The Marquis of Villamediana, with the rest of the Spanish officers, were admitted as prisoners of war on their paroles of honour; and to conciliate the affections of the natives, all the Indians were dismissed with safety ...

Our joy upon this fortunate event was greatly clouded by the loss of Major More who was transfixed with an arrow near the Royal Gate and died immediately, universally lamented for his good qualities. Captain Sleigh of the grenadiers, and some other good officers were wounded. We had but 30 private men killed or wounded.[13]

Major More's death at the moment of victory would have been a great personal sorrow to William Draper, for More had been with the 79th since its formation in November 1757 and was the senior officer of the regiment after Brereton and Monson.

Draper had ordered the final assault at the earliest possible moment, knowing that there was no alternative to a bold strike. The storming of the city was completed within the early part of the morning, the assault having been concentrated on the weakest bastion. From the time the troops assembled before dawn to the surrender of the Archbishop in the Citadel around 8 a.m. only about four hours had passed.

Losses had been gratifyingly light over the whole expedition, with only twenty-one Europeans killed and sixty-nine wounded, including naval casualties, while Sepoy casualties were even lighter at five killed and twenty-three wounded. The oddest loss was that of Commodore Tiddeman, Cornish's second-in-command, who drowned with five seamen after the capitulation as one of the ships' boats overturned close to ramparts on the river side of the fortress.

As a coup de main, dependent on close cooperation between the naval and military forces, it had thus been a swift and successful amphibious operation. The two commanders, however, had no time to indulge in any self-congratulation. The speed and completeness of the final assault brought them the immediate problem of how to maintain discipline in the hours after the fighting and prevent the inevitable looting and pillage. Their own force was a volatile mixture difficult enough on its own to keep in check; but among the vanquished also were disparate groups ready to take advantage of any breakdown of law and order. The Spaniards had released from the city gaols all the prisoners who were now roaming free. The numerous Chinese inhabitants of Manila, treated as virtual slaves by the Spanish for years, were suddenly given an opportunity to vent their suppressed rage. The undisciplined Filipino auxiliaries, and the large numbers of Mexicans among the Spanish forces, were left without any chain of command.

Added to this combustible mixture were the regular British soldiers, mostly of the 79th Regiment, who had fought unrewarded, except for sporadic pay, since 1758; the Company troops including their Sepoys, the collection of French deserters and others who had joined the expedition in the hope of booty; and some of the seamen and marines who had played a crucial role on land as well as at sea. It was hardly surprising that, as the Archbishop and the Brigadier sought to exchange terms of capitulation in a civilised manner, mayhem got under way around the streets of the prostrate city. In the light of all the subsequent arguments and conflicting evidence about the length and severity of the disorder, nobody ever denied that there was a chaotic day of pillaging, looting and raping in the hours following the capitulation. With so many parties seizing what could be taken in the hours of disorder it was impossible to attribute blame in any measured way.

The British commanders, presented by Rojo with terms of capitulation which he had finished drafting even as the Citadel was being stormed, knew that their greatest chance of gaining the maximum prize lay in restoring order as quickly as possible in concert with the existing Spanish administration. Both Draper, and Cornish who had come ashore to the Citadel, immediately entered into discussions with Rojo, both on his proposed terms of surrender and on their own additional conditions to preserve the city from plunder, irrespective of what was actually happening on the streets at that moment.

Rojo's terms of surrender proposed by himself as Captain-General on behalf of the Audiencia, the ruling council of Manila, and the 'City and Commerce' consisted of twelve articles broadly safeguarding existing rights in relation to commerce, religion, and administration. Most of these terms were granted without debate, although residual animosities surfaced in, for example, the British commanders' comments on the clause seeking liberty to 'instruct the faithful', to which they added 'The ecclesiastical government must not attempt to convert any of our Protestant subjects to the Popish faith'.[14]

The Brigadier and the Admiral then put forward their own conditions offered to the city of Manila, embodied in which was the ransom demand that was to become the bone of contention between the British and Spanish governments over the next decade.

Nowhere in the great bulk of correspondence still surviving between the parties is there any clue as to how Draper and Cornish arrived at the idea of demanding a ransom for the city. There were almost no naval or military precedents for the concept in the immediate past of the British royal forces, and no specific guidelines embodied in military or naval law. Yet they must jointly have discussed the idea on their voyage from India as an option to be used in case of need.

The most likely explanation might oddly enough have come from Madras itself. Back in 1746, Madras had been seized for the first and only time by a French naval force. The city, unprotected at the time, accepted a ransom offer of about double the monetary value of the entire French squadron that extracted it. Having concluded the deal the French returned to Pondicherry, after pledging the honour of France that Madras should remain free from further molestation. This sequence of events would have been recalled in Madras during the months of the siege twelve years later, and possibly gave William Draper the idea towards the initiative he eventually took in Manila.

The British conditions, including the ransom demand, were much shorter than Rojo's proposed terms; five crisp paragraphs covering the disarming of Spanish forces, surrender of all military stores, capitulation of other forts and ports including Cavite, and ending with the straightforward quid pro quo:

> The propositions contained in the paper delivered on the part of the Governor and his Council [i. e. Rojo's terms] will be listened to and confirmed to them upon payment of four million dollars, the half to be paid immediately, the other half to be paid in a time to be agreed upon, and hostages and security given for that purpose.[15]

The response of the Governor and the Audiencia acknowledged the inevitable, but attempted to make the British understand that the ransom demand was easier to make than to fulfil:

> To satisfy the four million of dollars which are immediately demanded by the Commanders in Chief, all the capital of the public funds, such as the Misericordia, the Ordentercera, and the religious communities, as also what belongs to the Archbishop, which shall be found in being, [will be surrendered] … and what shall be wanting of the complement of the said four millions shall be made up by the capitals which the ship Philipina shall bring in, with condition that if the said ship should be taken by His Britannic Majesty's ships before the time that the advice despatched by His Excellency the Governor shall arrive to her, ordering her to come into this Bay, or if the capital therein should not be sufficient to complete the said four millions, they will give a bill on His Catholic Majesty.[16]

Rojo in defeat had been forced to countermand the earlier letter he had sent to Blanco, the captain of the galleon *Philipina* with orders to disperse the treasure and if necessary scuttle the ship. Acting in good faith he dispatched on the day of defeat a letter instructing Blanco to bring the *Philipina* into Manila with or without a British naval escort. He would nonetheless have been well aware that his first letter, sent a fortnight previously, would in all probability reach Blanco before the second; and that the chances of the galleon arriving safely in Manila with her full cargo of treasure were already remote.

It was quickly becoming apparent to the victors that there was very little chance that the ransom sum could be found in Manila alone, especially after the pillage in the hours following the heat of action. Manila was a rich city, with a population of around 100,000, enhanced by its wide range of residences, churches, libraries, convents and colleges. But, as it was not a port, there were none of the great warehouses which would have made it comparable to Havana as a haven of treasure. Nor were there any great merchant ships at Cavite similar to those which had been seized by the victors at Havana. It must have dawned rapidly on the British commanders that if the treasure of the *Philipina* was to slip from their grasp the rewards of victory might turn out to be meagre indeed.

They both gave their authority to bringing the civil situation under control as rapidly as possible. Order was restored, first in the 79th Regiment; then martial law was imposed upon the city. Many of the criminals freed from the Spanish gaols were apprehended and executed without trial by the British with the acquiescence of the Spanish authorities and hanged, as a witness described, 'from window gratings like bananas'. This rough but visible justice enabled the city to be calmed within a further day.

Evidence of the extent of the looting began to flow in to the civil and military powers, as injured parties made their claims as soon as they could move around safely. The Dominican friars asserted that the British had taken vestments and silver to the value of 8,000 pesos; the Jesuit college of San Ignacio lost 3,800 pesos worth of chalices, coins and church ornaments; and the convent of San Nicholas, claiming to have endured three days of pillage, had been ransacked of silver and gold ornaments to the value of 70,000 pesos. Testimony from the Franciscans, submitted later, claimed that the bells from several churches had been taken by British troops and then sold back to them. British redcoats, sweating under the tropical sun and the weight of stolen bells, must have presented a bizarre spectacle to the harassed citizens. Other witnesses claimed that some Sepoys, having stolen all the vestments from one church, had disported themselves on the ramparts clad in full raiment as they danced in celebration of victory.

The general and his staff, while busy negotiating with the Archbishop and the Audiencia, did their personal best to ensure that their commands were obeyed in restoring law and order. Draper himself, responding to the personal pleas of a lady of Manila whose house had already been ransacked, disturbed a looter in her house and killed him on the spot.

As the city slowly started to return to normal, so did the pace of events. The Spanish authorities contrived to spin out the formal negotiating process for a full three weeks, and only signed the formal surrender of all the Philippine Islands on 30 October. The document, even as it was signed, was already behind events in Europe, and the declaration that 'all the islands must be ceded to His Britannic Majesty who must be acknowledged Sovereign 'til the fate of these islands is decided by a peace between the two Kings' was itself no longer valid.[17]

Draper took upon himself the main burden of prodding Rojo towards this definitive agreement. Cornish had to spend much of his time at Cavite, concerned with the practical need to repair as many of his ships as possible before the return voyage to India. He was forced to depend on Draper for the day-to-day haggling with the Archbishop. Much of this was apparently in Latin, and the exchanges of letters during October conveyed increasing irritation on the subject of collecting the ransom; Rojo pleading for patience, Draper anxious for results. He would have been more anxious had he known what was happening to the vital treasure aboard the *Philipina* and how it was already slipping beyond the reach of the victors.

12

FRUSTRATIONS

The chief agent responsible for this calamity was a member of the Audiencia, Don Simon de Anda y Salazar. He had been appointed Lieutenant-Governor of the Philippines by Archbishop Rojo on the evening before the surrender in anticipation of Rojo's likely capture the following day. Anda fled from Manila overnight, making for the interior of Luzon, where he set up a provisional government in the name of the King of Spain, using the town of Bulacan as a base. By the end of the month, he had managed to establish contact with Captain Blanco of the *Philipina* who had decided to move the ship north on hearing reports that Manila had fallen.

It was crucially important for Anda to gain control of the treasure from the galleon, as his only hope for raising and paying any rebel force large enough to become a threat to the British conquerors. He was sufficiently authoritative to persuade Captain Blanco and his officers to entrust the unloaded cargo of the galleon to his command. They had already beached their large ship and unloaded its treasure, worth around three million pesos. The galleon also provided Anda with experienced troops and marines to form the nucleus of his guerrilla army which was to operate against the British until their departure more than two years later.

So the Spaniards had won the race for the treasure though neither side was to be certain for a few more weeks. In the absence of news, the British commanders in Manila assumed that the navy frigates *Argo* and *Panther* would find and isolate the galleon until its captain could be given the Archbishop's orders for it to be escorted into Manila.

In fact, by a strange sequence of events, the frigates captured an entirely different galleon which should not have been there at all and whose presence was not expected by either the Spanish or the British. For twenty-six days during October, the *Argo* and *Panther* had searched the waters between the islands of Luzon and Samar, certain that the *Philipina* could not elude them, not realising that it had already moved north. On the night of 29 October, the *Argo* sighted a large ship beating in through the straits. Assuming logically that it could only be the *Philipina*, the *Argo* closed for action but was beaten off by the enormous galleon.

At daybreak, when the *Panther* arrived in support, both British frigates engaged the galleon but had to battle for two hours before the Spanish ship struck her colours. 'She was a large vessel,' reported the *Annual Register* much later. 'She lay like a mountain in the water, and the Spaniards trusted entirely to the excessive thickness of her sides, not without reason; for the shot made no impression upon any part, except her upper works.'[1]

Had the galleon been ready for action with all her guns mounted she would probably have sunk the frigates, already suffering seventy-eight killed in the action. The British captains were elated when she struck her colours, and understandably confused when she turned out to be not the expected *Philipina* but another galleon, the *Santissima Trinidad*.

The *Trinidad* had actually left Manila almost three months earlier, in August, bound for Acapulco with the customary seasonal cargo. Contrary winds had kept her in Manila Bay for almost a month and she had taken until the middle of September to clear the archipelago and head north-east for her Pacific voyage. She had then run into a storm which carried away her mainmast. As she struggled to make way under temporary rig, a further storm struck her, sweeping her masts overboard. This would have been the same storm which was simultaneously causing such trouble for the British squadron in Manila Bay.

Its unforeseen result was to drive the *Santissima Trinidad* back towards the Philippine Islands. On the third day of the storm, her planking opened so badly that she was in danger of foundering, but she managed to crawl back towards the safety of the straits. Her officers wanted to take her into Palapag, having no idea that the *Philipina* had meanwhile beached herself there, but the pilot refused to take her in at night. It was then resolved to head for the coast of Luzon, and as she was beating in there she was intercepted by the British frigates, and taken as a prize.

The demoralised crew of the *Santissima Trinidad* nursed the stricken galleon back to Manila under escort of *Argo* and *Panther* and their delighted captains, King and Hyde Parker. The galleon had a total crew, including soldiers, of no less that 800. She finally limped into the port of Cavite on 12 November, to become yet another subject of dispute rather than celebration.

The aftermath of conquest had already begun to expose the underlying conflicts of interest among the conquerors. Delay in completing the formal terms of the capitulation, linked with the growing realisation that the conquest was not going to lead to a gigantic prize, had sharpened tempers all round. On 28 October, the British commanders sent a memorandum to the Spaniards over their failure to comply with the surrender conditions, reminding them that by the end of the month they should have contributed a million pesos towards the ransom of the city. On the same day Draper wrote in Latin to Rojo asking that the rest of the ransom for the city should be paid and threatening Manila with pillage unless the other islands were formally ceded.

This blustering pressure concentrated Spanish minds, and in the following two days Rojo not only announced to the inhabitants of all the Philippine Islands that surrender had been made and respect and obedience were due to the British, but also issued a decree that the religious orders should contribute their silver towards the ransom. One million of the four million were to be handed over by 31 October, and on the basis of this agreement the formalities were completed the day before.

Formalities were, however, scarcely in line with realities on the ground. It was becoming obvious that the ransom demand was far beyond what might be gathered in Manila; and that even the process of collecting the ransom would devolve onto the new civilian administration. This would be the under the Governorship of Dawsonne Drake, the appointee of the East India Company. He and his fellow councillors were now installed in Manila ready not only to take up their ill-defined duties but to ensure that the interests of the Company should take precedence over all others.

On 2 November Drake's 'Diary and Consultation Book' noted:

> This morning General Draper assured Mr Drake in the presence
> of the gentlemen of the Council in the most satisfactory manner
> that he need entertain no suspicion of military control but on the
> contrary the settlement will be delivered over in every respect with
> the Company's settlements in India. Mr Drake, attended by the
> Council, was conducted by him to the Royal Palace and, the artillery
> saluting with 15 guns, was there declared Governor of Manila
> in the presence of the officers of the garrison, His Excellency the
> Archbishop, the Audiencia, and the principal inhabitants.[2]

On the same day, Draper issued a general order confirming the handover and the decision to deploy his own regiment and all other troops except the marines as 'a proper competent garrison'. Major Robert Fell was appointed Commandant of the military force, and Captain Thomas Backhouse, senior captain of the 79th, took command of the regiment ahead of the departure of George Monson.

The courtesies completed, tensions once again began to surface. Cornish, reporting to Clevland at the Admiralty on the present parlous state of his ships and their crews, could not resist complaining about the meanness of the

Company in making difficulties about wounded sailors being sent back either from Manila or Madras on Company ships to Europe. He went on to express the customary plea on behalf of his own men shown by the more humane naval commanders of the time:

> I am induced from the principles of humanity to acquaint their
> Lordships that the few men remaining who came out in the ships
> under Vice-Admiral Watson from their long service in this country
> are worn out and become quite infirm. I must further presume to
> recommend to their Lordships consideration of the distresses of the
> inferior officers and seamen serving in India, who by the late Act of
> Parliament are deprived of any means to procure their pay for the
> several ships they have served in this country and from the want of
> which they labour under the greatest difficulty and distress.[3]

Draper, too, in his first Report to the Secretary at War covering the whole action, felt obliged to mention the problems of providing for an equitable distribution of the spoils of victory. After giving the main details of the action, and complimenting his force for their conduct and bravery, he went on:

> But although I have so much reason to be pleased with their
> behaviour, mine, I fear has not been equally pleasing to them. My
> method of dividing the prize money has given much offence and
> made me very unpopular with the captains and subalterns. I must
> therefore beg leave, sir, to state the case to you and to desire you lay
> it before His Majesty ...
>
> The sea and land officers had so near a connection and co-operated
> so fully and cordially upon this service that I thought the best way
> of dividing any prize money that might be taken by us would be
> to adhere to those rules which His Majesty had thought proper
> to fix for the sea service and that the officers should share in their
> respective ranks according to those proportions.

He went on to confirm a crucial point:

> The case of prize money is so rare in the land service that I
> believe no particular laws have been hitherto ascertained for that
> purpose amongst us ... but the captains of foot have thought the
> disproportion of prize money between them and the field officers to
> be too great, a field officer receiving nine times as much as a captain.
> Yet this is the case in the Navy and as the King has not judged or
> ordered otherwise I cannot think I could have acted better. However,
> sir, as this is a grievance complained of I beg you will receive His

Majesty's commands thereon; I am in hopes it will not be thought that I have acted from any interested motives, as I am myself a great loser by this method, sharing only as a subordinate flag officer to Mr Cornish instead of dividing as the Commander-in-Chief at Land.[4]

Draper's scrupulous adherence to the comparability of ranks between the two services meant that he, as Brigadier-General, ranked himself as comparable to a naval Commodore rather than Cornish's rank as Rear-Admiral. Such adherence to the ideas of fairness was not particularly common to senior officers, and rare on the occasions where considerable sums of money might be put at risk. His concern also for the future of his regiment, and its likely disbandment as soon as peace was established, came through in his plea to the Secretary at War as his letter diverted from immediate details:

> As I know that it is impossible for the regiment to be kept up at the peace, I most humbly beg leave to recommend the half-pay officers to your protection that they may be provided for when occasion shall offer. All the favour I can presume to ask at present is some little distinguishing mark for their past services. If His Majesty would do them the honour to name them the Royal Asians, a mere feather in their caps, they would esteem it more highly than any pecuniary reward whatsoever. I can venture to assure you, sir, that no corps has endeavoured to merit His Majesty's approbation more than the 79th. Twenty three officers and upwards of eight hundred men have lost their lives in this severe service since 1758, of which they have constantly borne the chief and foremost service. Most of the old officers now remaining have been wounded.

He then returned to the more pressing problems of the aftermath of the conquest and the chronic irritations of having to maintain workable relationships with the East India Company:

> The great extent of Manila and its suburbs with one hundred thousand inhabitants, and the importance of Cavite, will prevent me sending back any part of my regiment to Madras, as we have no troops besides we can depend on. The Sepoys are ill-disciplined, the rest of the Company's people scarce 300, of which two-thirds are French deserters, so that it is impossible to entrust a place of such consequence in their hands. The Admiral will, I hope, leave the marines. The contingent of Sepoys which the Governor and Council at Madras promised to assist me with was 2,000; they gave me only 600, the half raw and new raised.

> It was not difficult to discern their motives for this shameful

behaviour. They had sent a ship to Manila to trade clandestinely under Moorish colours, most of it the property of the chief people at Madras and Bengal. They were afraid their ventures would suffer at the loss of Manila, and took every method in their power to discourage the attempt. I must except Mr Pigot, as a man of better and more generous principles. They prevailed upon Mr Lawrence to give a negative to the expedition under the pretence of an invasion expected from the French who have neither troops nor a fleet of any consequence in India ... these mercenary people consider nothing but their immediate profit.

He completed his Report by again recommending his senior officers for consideration as 'their merit in their several departments has much facilitated my good fortune, to which the kind protection of you and your family gave the first rise.' As the Secretary at War to whom he was reporting was Charles Townshend, this last cryptic phrase proves an additional and definitive allusion to the patronage which linked Draper to the Townshend family.

The report ended with a crisp, elated PS which simply said, 'We have taken a galleon worth four hundred thousand pounds called the Santissima Trinidad, and are in quest of the Philipina.' His elation would have been tempered had he known that the value of the captured galleon was worth far less than this optimistic estimate, and the resolution of any final figure was to become entangled in all the subsequent haggling between the Navy, the Treasury, the Spanish government and the East India Company.

This process was given immediate impetus by Drake's appointment as Deputy Governor of Manila. It was typical of this experiment in instant government that Drake could make no claim whatever to be qualified for the responsibilities now being thrust on him. He was a trader like all his fellow members of the Council at Madras, and had risen only by virtue of seniority of service. His nomination to his post in Manila was partly explained by the desire of some of his colleagues to put him out of circulation. They realised that the post was likely to be a bed of nails and were agreeable to the idea of Drake being impaled on it. In view of the odium Drake was to attract over the next two years, his selection was a tribute to their foresight.

Cornish at Cavite was furious when he received the news of the handover of the civil government to Drake and wrote immediately to Draper:

I have just seen a letter from Captain Pemble to my secretary wherein you desire him to acquaint me that you have delivered up the city of Manila to Dawsonne Drake, esq, agreeable as you say to His Majesty's instructions ...

I find myself necessitated to acquaint you that I think you have been rather premature in this act as the conditions of capitulation are not yet complied with, nor are the military stores as yet taken account of by which His Majesty's instructions should be delivered up with the Government. Neither do I think the conquest sufficiently complete as yet to resign the power from the military to the civil. I must further observe that from my rank here in His Majesty's service I ought to have been consulted before this cession was made. This step of yours is so very extraordinary that I must represent it home to the Lords of Admiralty ...

I propose dispatching the *Seahorse* in a few days for England and in case you continue your resolution of taking passage in her will send her over to take on board your baggage and retinue with that of the other gentlemen who are to proceed in her.[5]

Draper responded with equanimity to Cornish's complaint, pointing as his justification to the King's Instructions and adding:

The inventory of the artillery and warlike stores were taken a week ago and signed by the Major of Artillery and myself, nor indeed had I strictly a right to keep the Government a moment after that signature unless by Mr Drake's desire. In the second place my instructions nowhere order me to consult with you about the delivery of this place. His Majesty had given me sole command at land in as full a manner as you enjoy at sea. I think the conquest sufficiently complete to justify the cession.[6]

He went on with some mollifying remarks about deferring to Cornish's rank and experience but left him in no doubt that he did not intend changing his mind about his return voyage to England. Between this exchange on 2 November, and Draper's departure just over a week later he probably took the opportunity to clarify his decision to Cornish and to his own subordinates, though all of them would probably have concurred with Cornish's observation that 'the conquest was not sufficiently complete'. An uneasy tension still hung over the city, the Spanish military were still present even if disarmed, and the countryside beyond Manila and the narrow swathe of land to Cavite was virtually untouched. There was every likelihood that Anda's guerrilla army might soon materialise in sufficient strength to become a real threat to the British occupation. There seemed some strong arguments for the continuing presence of the commander of the land forces.

The tone of the letters between the two commanders suggests that there had been some tension between them since the capitulation. Cornish in particular, worried about the condition of the ships at Cavite before their return voyage to India, would reasonably have felt aggrieved that he had not been consulted personally by Draper ahead of the brigadier's decision. The formal politeness of their letters does not disguise the fact that the admiral had reason to feel that he was being let down.

Yet Draper had long proved that he was not inclined to choose the easy option. He probably reasoned that as a soldier he had completed his mission, the reduction of Manila, and that there was no further need for him to remain when he could arguably be more useful to the whole venture by returning to London. He probably suspected that the treasure of the *Philipina* had been lost to the expedition, that by the time he reached London the war might already be over, and that there was a consequent danger that the whole conquest would no longer be able to exert any influence on events.

More importantly, pressure would need to be exerted by London on the Spanish government to honour the bills on Madrid presented by the Archbishop. Of equal importance, his presence in London would enable him to present a pre-emptive case in favour of the royal forces in their arguments with the East India Company over the disposal of the ransom. The original assumption on the Company's part in London was that Draper had agreed that any booty would be divided equally between the Company and the royal forces. The subsequent decision made unilaterally by Cornish and Draper in Madras that the Company would receive only one-third was certain to cause a long and irritable debate in London. His presence in London would at least guarantee that his and Cornish's arguments would not go by default. The admiral was unlikely to be able to get back to London for at least another year. In comparison with the importance of these motives the need to remain in Manila bickering over details of civil government must have seemed less crucially demanding.

In the few days remaining before his embarkation, and while Dawsonne Drake was trying to establish his own authority, Draper continued to press the Archbishop for signs of progress on the collection of the ransom. Rojo was pleading for the release of the *oidores*, the town magistrates, on the sensible grounds that they would be more useful outside gaol than inside. He also made the valid point that much of the city's wealth was actually tied up in the two galleons: the *Philipina* with her inward cargo of bullion and profits from last year's trade, and the *Santissima Trinidad* with her outward cargo of goods for the Acapulco Fair. The *Santissima Trinidad* meanwhile rode at anchor in Cavite under the watchful eye of Cornish's ships. Her cargo had been unloaded and the question of its disposal was about to add another dimension of disagreement.

Before his departure Draper also wrote to Lawrence in Madras, apprising him of events in Manila, but taking the opportunity to express his aggravation about the Company's contribution to the whole venture:

> I am afraid that the situation here makes it impossible for me to send you back any part of the troops. The Frenchmen you were so obliging to provide me with desert every day. Had the gentlemen

at Madras and the number of Sepoys they promised fulfilled their
engagements some Europeans might have been returned. I am
also sorry to be obliged to add that the ungrateful treatment my
people have experienced makes them very averse to have any
further connection with those at Madras ... For my part I have long
determined to have no sort of commerce with them, either as a body
or as individuals.[7]

Lawrence would have received this letter with the resigned irritation of
knowing that his concerns about the continuing drain on his military resources
had been fully justified. He contented himself in due course with grumbling to
the Court of the Company in London, pointing out that Lt-Col Scott of the
89th Regiment, whom he had released from duty in India to serve as Adjutant-
General to the expedition, had returned to England on the *Seahorse* with
Draper without bothering to seek Lawrence's permission or giving him the
courtesy of a letter.

The scene was set for future acrimony when, on the eve of his departure,
Draper reminded Drake of the decision that the booty should be divided in
three, and stressed that the artillery, fortifications and stores were not being
handed over for the use and benefit of the East India Company but to be held
by them only, to await further instructions from the Government in London.
As a long-standing officer of the Company, Drake would have known from
experience that advantage usually lay with the man on the spot and that his
own handling of affairs would now be unencumbered by the presence of a
commanding but irritable general.

Drake nonetheless complied with Draper's request for a bill on the Company
to the value of £5,000, a request which was probably made by the general in
the knowledge that it might be all he would ever receive as his share of the
prize money. Drake noted in his Diary:

> [I]t is agreed to grant his request, tho' our necessities do not
> authorise such a step it being a favour he seems entitled to especially
> as he returns to England by this ship.[8]

The bill was signed by Drake and the Council and delivered to Captain Robert
Fletcher, Draper's Brigade-Major.

The *Seahorse*, a ship of twenty guns and a crew of 160, under Captain
Robert Jocelyn, left Manila on 11 November crowded with as many wounded
and sick men as she could accommodate, to sail directly for England.[9] She
reached England safely in mid-April 1763, but Draper's absence at sea for
those five months left him out of touch with the major points of issue still
awaiting resolution in Manila, Madrid and London.

III

ILLUSIONS IN SLOW DISSOLVE

13

QUARRELS
IN MANILA

The six-month lapse between the fall of Manila and the news reaching
Europe was to be decisive on the outcome of the venture; but even in
Manila the growing discord progressively undermined the chances that the
great prize, full payment of the ransom, would ever be realised.

Within the broad triangle of conflicting interests of the royal forces, the
East India Company, and the Spanish community, there was endless room
for all the parties to argue and dispute. Each of the main characters, Admiral
Cornish, Governor Drake, Archbishop Rojo, and Robert Fell as Commandant,
were ready to make their own contributions to the discord; but each was
himself in an unprecedented situation of being answerable to distant superiors
from whom they had received only the most general guidance and who might
repudiate, months later, decisions taken in good faith to meet the needs of the
moment.

The crucial fault-line lay in the divergent priorities of Cornish and Drake.
The admiral, anxious to get his fleet back safely to India as soon as possible,
was equally aware that this departure would immediately reduce the likelihood
of ransom or prize money ever getting paid. In his impatience he was in no
mood to defer to the authority of Drake as civil Governor.

Drake in turn realised that the departure of the squadron would not
only make impossible the subsidiary objective of setting up a settlement on
Mindanao, but leave him vulnerable in Manila, unprotected except by a small
garrison and surrounded by the guerrilla forces under Señor Anda.

This clash of priorities would have been difficult enough to resolve even with goodwill on both sides. There was precious little to spare between Cornish and Drake. By December, only two months after the conquest, relations between the two men had deteriorated to the point where Cornish, spending most of his time at Cavite, refused to deal officially with Drake in Manila. Cornish was infuriated by Drake's assumption that his power as Governor included the authority to decide on the disposition of the squadron's ships. He rebuked the Governor with all the irritation of an admiral still nursing a justified grudge about the Navy's exclusion from the spoils of victory at Pondicherry. Drake responded that:

> We find ourselves disappointed in the hopes of your leaving a Naval force here. We shall only remark to you that it was His Majesty's order that a sufficient force should be left for the security of the conquest ... and it being not only our opinion but that of General Draper, communicated to us in writing, that the presence of a line of battle ship and two galleys at least is absolutely essential.[1]

Drake citing the departed general's opinion on naval matters would only have added to Cornish's irritation about Draper's early departure from Manila. This irritation became focused on the improbable figure of a Swiss commander in the Spanish service, Chevalier Cesar Faillet, who had been active in the defence of Manila and thereafter played an important role in the negotiations leading up to the capitulation.

Drake, in a deposition to Egremont some months later (not knowing that Egremont was already dead) wrote that when Draper had handed over the conquest to him he had introduced Faillet, whom 'he strongly recommended for having procured from the Spaniards the cession of these islands'. He went on to write that Cornish disliked Faillet because the Swiss 'expatiated in all circumstances and all companies on Mr Draper's many laudable, noble qualities without reflecting that the other (Cornish) considered it as intended to point out the contraries in himself.'[2] Faillet, even if he had been playing the role of neutral broker between the British and the Spaniards, would have had to have been a diplomatic genius to avoid incurring the suspicion of both sides. Cornish at one point accused him of persuading some French soldiers in the Company's garrison forces to desert to Anda's guerrilla army, although it was far more likely that they deserted at the prospect of actually being paid by anyone.

Faillet acted as a go-between in the tortuous haggling of most concern to the Spanish merchant community; the fate of the captured galleon, the *Santissima Trinidad*. Estimates of the worth of the prize seemed to have diminished by the day, proving the first assessment of around £400,000 as wildly optimistic. However, she undoubtedly represented a severe loss to the traders of Manila as her cargo bound for Mexico constituted much of their capital investment for the year. They pressed their claim that since the galleon had been seized after the capitulation which guaranteed them their possessions its seizure was illegal and all its contents should be returned. Cornish sidestepped the claim while negotiating with Rojo on points of detail such as the recovery of official papers, and the release of officers and officials travelling on the galleon.

These details were subsumed into the grumbles over the gathering of the ransom money. In January 1763, Drake and his Council, trying to speed the whole dilatory process, summoned a conference to be held in the Archbishop's presence. As expected, the participants, particularly the religious orders, came up with convincing reasons to show that they had no more funds available. By February, the position was at least becoming clearer, if no more comforting to the occupying powers. On 18 February, Rojo wrote to King Charles in Madrid informing him that since the silver bullion on the galleon *Philipina* was not available he was drawing bills for two million pesos on the Royal Treasury to pay Cornish the amount agreed upon to keep the city from being plundered. Two days later he reported to Cornish and Drake that half the ransom money was to be granted immediately, the other half to come from the funds of the local Treasury, from the treasure on the *Philipina*, and from bills drawn on Madrid.

Even this report was shrouded in ambiguities. The only definitive list which purported to show the actual amounts collected was made the following month. It came to around $520,000, only just over a quarter of the sum originally agreed, roughly divided between $405,000 in specie, and $121,000 in plate and effects. Of the money contributed, the largest sum of $194,000 came from the aptly named local treasury the Misericordia, followed by $58,000 from the allegedly impoverished Franciscans. One particular item of only $26,000 was 'from plunder recovered from the soldiers and sailors after the conquest', which puts into perspective the later Spanish arguments that the city had been devastated by the hours of pillage after the capitulation.

In broad terms, those $520,000 were all that was ever received. Translated into sterling, it came to much less than £150,000. The chimera that the capture of Manila would unlock riches similar to those seized at Havana had been exposed as a huge disappointment. Cornish, exasperated beyond measure and aware that time was running out before his necessary departure, then threatened to use royal and Company forces to pillage the city again, apparently inveigling Major Robert Fell, the commandant, to fall in with his plan. Although he was eventually dissuaded from this wild idea it was used as an accusation later by Drake and others as an example of a commander who had no hesitation about overstepping the bounds of his authority.

While Cornish and Drake aired their disputes, this disunity played into the hands of the Spanish. Of all the correspondence which flowed between the parties, perhaps the most important was the letter sent to King Charles in Madrid by nine magistrates of Manila which alone would have been sufficient to persuade the proud Spanish monarch never to honour Rojo's promise of the ransom.

The magistrates set out their version of events in 'strongly complaining of the proceedings of Admiral Cornish after the surrender ... accusing him of burning the town house of Cavite ... insulting the Jesuits ... taking the *Santissima Trinidad* as a prize ... plundering the house of a married woman four months after the capitulation ... and now pressing for a second contribution from Manila'. They praised Drake as affording them protection from the Admiral and went on to ask:

> If the capitulation were made in the King's name by the two generals
> Draper and Cornish with what right did the latter, in General
> Draper's absence, make himself sole legislator for altering and
> making new laws, and what is more pretend to an amphibious
> jurisdiction both by sea and land?[3]

The letter listed further evidence of Cornish's high-handed attitude and ended by making the most telling point:

> What hurt us most in so strange a behaviour was the Admiral's
> continual contempt of the whole Spanish nation, making a jest of
> us whenever we visited him in public or private, treating us with
> scorn and showing us an angry aspect saying even before us that we
> were bad Spaniards, faithless, comparing us to beasts, with other
> shameful scoffs only because we did not get the money of the ship
> *Philipina* ... thus failing in that common respect due to our nation
> and our sovereign which he ought to have kept up for the honour
> and the advantage of the conquerors themselves, since by good
> treatment great affection is acquired to the new sovereign power ...
>
> The present Governor of these islands has conducted himself in a
> manner diametrically opposite and being of an affable and prudent
> disposition has distinguished himself by his attention and civility to
> all the Spaniards ... We beseech you to deign to receive these just
> grievances against Admiral Cornish in order that he may meet with
> due punishment.

Whatever the intent of the letter, it would have struck a deep chord with the Spanish King, who still bore such strong resentment against the British for the humiliation which Commodore Martin had inflicted upon him in Naples twenty years earlier. Personal and national pride would have made him immediately determined never to hand over a single dollar of the ransom, whatever the legal or constitutional pressures.

While this vital letter was being despatched to Madrid, Cornish and Drake again clashed on the Admiral's decision that the booty taken from the *Santissima Trinidad* should be divided only between the royal troops and sailors, with no share allocated to the Company's troops. Although this may have seemed no more than rough justice in retaliation for the fact that the Navy and army had received nothing from the Company for the capture of Pondicherry, it ensured that the quarrel between Cornish and Drake stayed fully alive up to and beyond the date of Cornish's departure from Manila.

The squadron sailed on 2 March 1763, six months after its surprise arrival. Its voyage back to Madras gave Cornish time to prepare a long report, and room to air his version of the quarrels which he knew would be interpreted differently in any communication from Dawsonne Drake to the Company. Writing to the Lords of Admiralty, he started with a professional assessment of the ships from which he made it clear that he was so worried by their state, even after work done at Cavite, that he would have no confidence in them being able to support any further action towards Mindanao, or indeed anywhere else.[4]

Cornish had made certain before he left Manila that he personally carried the ransom bills from the Archbishop to be channelled via the Admiralty, rather than leaving them to the more uncertain route of the East India Company. His animosity towards Drake and the Company shone through his report, linked with acerbic comments on Draper's early departure. He also vented his fury about the activities of Faillet, particularly when the Swiss had let it be known that the Chinese population of Manila would once again be subject to the taxes and forced labour from which Draper and Cornish had exempted them on the day of victory. The recipient of Cornish's dispatch, John Clevland, Secretary of the Admiralty, months later in London, must have been dismayed to make some sense of the double-dealings of Faillet and aware that in time he was likely to be hearing a diametrically opposed version of the same events from the Company.

Cornish ended the recital of his difficulties with a broadside against the Company:

> Their Lordships may depend I shall continue to exert my utmost
> abilities for the honour of my country and the interest of the
> Company, tho' I cannot but consider it my peculiar misfortune that
> by the nature of my instructions I am connected with a set of men
> who, having no other views than to accumulate immense wealth for
> themselves, too frequently bring discredit on His Majesty's arms.

Cornish, having delivered himself of this judgement at sea via the pen of his secretary, Thomas Parry, concentrated on ensuring that the squadron arrived safely back at Madras in June 1763, ten months after its departure. Stringer Lawrence wrote immediately to Charles Townshend, Secretary at War in London, expressing relief that 'Cornish has arrived back with the fleet from Manila, with four companies of Monson's regiment.' Lawrence in February had pleaded to the Madras Council that 'the expedition to Manila has deprived me of so many men that we are in great want here. I beg you will remind the Governor of sending the remainder of Monson's whenever opportunities offer,' so their arrival must have been a great relief. In April, he had written to Townshend bemoaning the calibre of the reinforcements who had arrived in Madras from England:

> I am sorry to tell you the drafts we received are so bad that there are few of them fit to stand under flintlocks, and many of them invalided by the regiments they went into without doing an hour's duty ... I make no doubt you have heard the particulars of General Draper's success laid before you; that expedition depriving us of so many of our forces has given the country powers an opportunity of making disturbances which will be attended by very disagreeable consequences should we not be strong enough to quell them.[5]

Lawrence's letter shows he never shifted from his original disapproval of the whole idea of the Manila venture, and that he felt subsequent events had justified his stance. His grudging admission that the expedition had been a military success still kept him at one with his Company colleagues in expressing their dismay about the overall value of the expedition.

As the fulcrum of the issues moved slowly back towards Europe, Dawsonne Drake was left in a political and military limbo in Manila, his shaky civil administration propped up only by the presence of the 79th Regiment and remaining Company troops. He was acutely aware that his authority as Governor hardly extended beyond the walls of Manila and Cavite. Archbishop Rojo continued to insist that Anda had exceeded the temporary powers granted to him just before the capitulation but was unable any longer to command his adherence. Anda, primed with the treasure of the *Philipina*, remained effectively in command of the whole island of Luzon outside the capital. The lure of his funds led to a steady trickle of deserters from both the British and Spanish garrison.

Drake and Rojo had to share equal frustrations in their attempts to extend the capitulation agreement to other islands in the archipelago. The slow-motion impasse stayed unresolved, with the outer islands remaining semi-autonomous and the British understandably reluctant to risk sending emissaries who might be taken as hostages by those from whom they were demanding submission.

All the parties were forced into this demoralising state of indecision while they awaited news from Europe as to whether Britain and Spain were still at war, and, if not, how they had decided to resolve the future of the Philippines.

14

A MUTED WELCOME
IN ENGLAND

Coinciding with Cornish's return voyage to Madras, though thousands of miles apart, Draper reached England in the *Seahorse* early in April 1763, after a rapid passage of five months. He was accompanied by Captain Richard Kempenfeldt of the Navy, Captain Robert Fletcher his Brigade-Major from the Company's forces, and Lieutenant-Colonel George Scott, his Adjutant-General; all of them chosen in accordance with the custom that officers who had distinguished themselves in battle should be allowed the privilege of personally conveying the news of victory to higher authority.

On 14 April, Draper sent a note on his arrival in London to the Secretary at War. By then, Charles Townshend had relinquished the post in yet another government reshuffle, his successor being Welbore Ellis. Draper confirmed:

> Lt. Col Scott set out from Crook Haven in Ireland on 5 April with my despatches to Lord Egremont to inform him of the success of His Majesty's arms in the conquest of Manila ... I ransomed Manila for a million sterling, the squadron has taken an Acapulco ship worth two millions of dollars ... In short it is a lucky business. Can I have the pleasure of seeing you for five minutes ... I am quite tired or would come to you.[1]

By the time the three men reached London, they would have been briefed on the two major political developments of the last months which, separately and jointly, were to make their achievement more a cause of embarrassment than celebration; the signing of the Treaty of Paris which brought the Seven Years War to an end; and the departure of the Earl of Bute as the King's chief minister. The first was already old news, but Bute's resignation and its political fallout were even then claiming the full attention of Court and Parliament. The belated arrival of victors from distant lands must have seemed a minor distraction.

The signing of the Treaty had taken place on 10 February, following a ceasefire the preceding November. The final terms of the Treaty were almost exactly in line with those which had aroused Pitt's dismissive epithet, 'We retain nothing although we have conquered everything.' There was no mention of Manila in the Treaty. Havana's capture had been traded against the cession of Florida, but Manila was simply alluded to in a catch-all Clause XXI which briefly stated:

> All the countries and territories, which may have been conquered in any part of the world whatsoever ... which are not included in the present articles either under the title of cessions or under the title of restitutions, shall be restored without difficulty and without requiring any compensations.[2]

In short, there was now no chance that the conquest of Manila could be used as any sort of bargaining counter. It was wariness on the part of the chief British negotiator, the Duke of Bedford, which resulted in Manila being consigned to the margins of the final terms. Bedford had achieved a Treaty in accordance with his own underlying belief that Britain might be in danger of over-colonising if all the conquests outside Europe were retained. The capture of Havana at a late stage in the negotiations had been an embarrassment to Bedford and Bute, making a conciliatory treaty harder to conclude. The possible fall of Manila had to be, and was, neutralised in advance of any news reaching Europe.

In determining this, Bedford was in tacit agreement with his fellow negotiators, the Duc de Choiseul for France and the Marquis of Grimaldi for Spain. Though Choiseul and Grimaldi in theory represented equal allies under the Bourbon Family compact, each had his own nation's interests to protect. Choiseul had become quickly sceptical about the value of the Spanish alliance, and was advising Spain to seek peace within months of joining the war. The fall of Havana confirmed Choiseul's disenchantment, and shocked Charles III and Grimaldi into negotiating seriously on the basis of Britain's demands for the cession of Florida.

The marginalising of Manila was thus agreeable to Spain and France, and acceptable to Britain. The British public was anxious for peace, though reserving its right to criticise the terms. Bute's sense of relief on achieving peace, and the strain of enduring the unpopularity which accompanied his efforts, made him determined to find a successor as soon as possible after the signing. By March 1763, the process of political jockeying was under way and within a month George Grenville, Pitt's brother-in-law, had been made First Lord of the Treasury.

Grenville's reluctant but dutiful advent to power was accompanied by the usual musical chairs among office holders, where most of them moved but very little changed. Some, including the Earl of Egremont, stayed on in their old posts. Egremont, on his way to an early death from overeating, was thus still Secretary of State for the South in the new government and it was his duty to present William Draper to his young Sovereign.

The ceremony took place at St James's on 15 April, the day after Draper's return to London. The *London Gazette* reported 'that he was most graciously received, and presented to His Majesty the colours which were taken at Manila'.

Draper also presented to the new ministry the less welcome gift of how to handle the aftermath of the conquest of Manila, particularly the ransom issue. Under the terms of the Treaty, Manila was to be 'restored without difficulty', which implied that the raising of additional problems at this stage would be unwelcome to both sides. The need to pursue the question of the ransom so soon after the peace agreement must have made the King's ministers feel that the victorious commander had not only brought back the Spanish colours but also a ticking time bomb.

While the Government considered the options, Draper was allowed to enjoy the uncertain fruits of his triumph. His most immediate gesture was to offer the Spanish colours, with Royal permission, to his old college King's, of which he was still a Fellow. Only three days after his presentation at Court he responded to congratulations from William Barford of King's, writing:

> I have got some Spanish colours taken at Manila for the chapel and His Majesty has been pleased to consent that they shall be sent to your College and hung up there. So if you have no objection to see your old friend's trophies over your head, I shall send them down.[3]

His offer was accepted with pride by the Provost on behalf of the College, his exchange of letters with Draper expressing the pleasure of the academics that one of their Fellows should have distinguished himself so notably. The *Cambridge Chronicle* subsequently reported:

> On May 4th 1763 nine colours taken at Manila by Brigadier Draper were carried in procession to King's College Chapel by the scholars of the Chapel accompanied by the Fellows, the organ playing, and the colours preceding them, singing the Te Deum. The colours were erected on each side of the altar rails when the Revd. William Barford, Public Orator of the University and one of the Fellows of the College, made a Latin Oration.[4]

Draper did not attend the ceremony, although he visited the College later in the year. Provost Sumner's hope that the Spanish colours would survive as long as the chapel was hardly practical. They were eventually moved to a side chapel and thereafter disintegrated in the library

The brief pleasures of thus being acknowledged as a hero must have been counterbalanced by awareness that the future was once again uncertain. Draper's Regiment was certain to be disbanded when it eventually returned from Manila and India, along with many other regiments raised during the war. He could lay no particular claim to preference among the host of senior officers faced with the same dilemma. Though his three main patrons, Ligonier, Cumberland, and Pitt were still close to the centre of events none of them could be expected to make a personal intervention on his behalf. His income as colonel of his regiment would disappear. From there on his only certain source would be from his continuing Governorship of Yarmouth, with its princely salary of £181 10s per annum.

The resolution of the ransom issue therefore loomed large in his priorities, despite the fact that the immediate financial pressure seems to have been relieved by his wife, Caroline, who had retained her minor post at Court during her husband's absence. Her health appears to have been fragile, as within a month of his return Draper was reported by the *Bath Journal* to have arrived at Hotwells, the small spa near Bristol, 'with his family'.

The visit to Hotwells would not only have provided Draper and Caroline with the benefits of somewhere to recuperate and enjoy the prospect of renewing their married life, but would also have given him the opportunity of meeting again the rest of his family in Bristol. His mother, Mary Draper, who was still living in Bristol, had survived long enough to enjoy the triumphs of her only remaining son. Caroline seems to have taken longer to gain any benefit from the spa waters than might have been expected, as a month later, in June, Draper writing from Clifton to a distant relation mentioned being 'extremely obliged to you for your kind and friendly offices to me and Captain Fletcher … my own health is quite re-established … and I am now here only on Mrs Draper's account.'[5] Caroline, who remained childless, was probably no more or less robust than any of her contemporaries in an age when even to survive was to defy the usual hazards of quack doctors and lethal potions.

Captain Robert Fletcher stayed close to his old commander during the summer of 1763, depending upon him to press his claims for advancement from the Company's forces. Draper approached Charles Jenkinson at the Treasury pointing out that Fletcher had not received the £500 usually given to officers returning home with captured colours, and possibly justifying his transfer from the Company's into the King's service. Fletcher, who was then only twenty-five, not only received the money in due course, but was also honoured with a knighthood in the same year for his bravery at Manila.

For Draper himself, the high point of the months following his return was the crediting of £5,000 to his account at Drummond's in July, the bill drawn

9. Manila Hall was built on Clifton Down for William Draper after his return from the successful expedition. It survived until early in the twentieth century.

by Dawsonne Drake on the East India Company which had been given to him before he left Manila.[6] This sum might have been deemed to be only the first instalment of what he would eventually receive as his share of the victory. In fact, as events unrolled, it was all he ever received. There were no further payments, either from the Company, or from any other source.

The sum of £5,000, handsome though it was in contemporary terms, puts into perspective the current rumours of prodigious riches being shared among the victors of Manila, and compares with the £122,000 which Keppel gained from the comparable triumph at Havana. Though it might have been a great deal better than nothing, it was also a great deal less than expected.

The money nonetheless enabled Draper to undertake the building of a house on Clifton Down, above Bristol, on land belonging to the Merchant Venturers. Clifton was then still a tiny village on either side of the road which straggled up Clifton Hill. The elegant terraces and squares which would transform Clifton still lay in the future. The house, which was named Manila Hall, occupied a site of about four acres, including its garden. It was built in neo-classical style with four massive columns supporting its portico. Nathaniel Wraxall the diplomat-politician-adventurer who was a contemporary of Draper and a fellow-Bristolian commented in his *Memoirs of My Time*:

> Sir William's vanity which led him to call his house at Clifton near Bristol 'Manila Hall' and there to erect a cenotaph to his fellow soldiers who fell before that city during the siege, exposed him to invidious comments. But Lord Amherst, in whom vanity was not a

predominant passion, gave in like manner the name of 'Montreal' to his seat in Kent.[7]

Wraxall seems to have ignored the much more notable fact that nobody held it against the great Duke of Marlborough that he should have named his own seat after his greatest triumph at Blenheim. To name a house, or even a palace, in commemoration of a victory which had made it possible seems to rank fairly low on the scale of personal vanity.

Manila Hall enabled Draper at last to provide Caroline with a home appropriate to her own family background. It was also large enough for him to allow his mother, Mary Draper, to enjoy the last year of her life in considerable comfort. She died in Clifton aged seventy-four in September 1764 and was buried in the churchyard of St Augustine the Less in Bristol alongside her husband, Ingleby Draper, who had predeceased her by more than forty years.

Draper was also able to renew contacts with his two surviving sisters, particularly Anne Moore, whose husband had been a surgeon with the Company in Bombay where Anne had married him in 1732. He had now been in Bristol for a number of years as a prosperous apothecary, and in time became the family doctor. From the constant payments to him noted during the 1760s it would seem that his services were frequently needed, most probably for Caroline who could already have been suffering from the early stages of the illness which cut short her life at the end of the decade.

While thus having the chance to give priority to his personal life, Draper would also have been enjoying the sudden fame thrust upon him. As Admiral Cornish was still absent in the Indies, Draper was the sole available recipient for the public enthusiasm which followed the news of an unexpected triumph against the traditional enemy in a quarter of the world so distant that few knew accurately even where it was. To the excitement of a military victory, regardless of whether the war was over, was added the spice of it being achieved in a region inaccurately labelled 'the South Seas'. Manila seemed to have the magic of a place on the outer edges of the known world.

Draper and Cornish received the formal thanks of the House of Commons in April, only a few days after Draper's return,[8] a tribute which alone would have been sufficient to further their careers in wartime but in peacetime amounted to little more than a warm valediction. There was no suggestion of a parliamentary gift being voted, as it was assumed that when the ransom issue was resolved and the other spoils divided, both Cornish and Draper would be sufficiently recompensed not to need further thanks from the public purse. The bleak reality took years to become apparent.

The slow grinding of the diplomatic wheels between London and Madrid began as the year progressed. Lord Rochford was appointed ambassador to Spain in June 1763, the first since the end of the war. He set out on his leisurely journey to Spain later in the year, to take forward all the issues outstanding from the peace treaty, of which the Manila ransom was only a minor item.

Rochford on departure may have shared the optimism of the Earl of Halifax, who had succeeded Egremont as Secretary of State for the South during the year, that the Manila issue would soon be resolved. In October 1763, Halifax wrote to John Weyland, Deputy Governor of the Bank of England:

> According to the request of the Governor and Court of the Bank of England, His Majesty has commanded me to forward to the English Ambassador now on his journey to Spain the copy of a bill of exchange for two millions of dollars drawn by the Archbishop of Manila on the King of Spain's First Lord of the Treasury, together with a letter of advice from the Archbishop to His Majesty ... I will not fail to instruct the Earl of Rochford to procure the two millions to be sent on board one or more English ships-of-war as proposed.[9]

The optimism of Halifax that the Spanish Treasury would simply hand over two million dollars to the first available British man-of-war was soon to be shown as wildly unrealistic. The ransom issue was to become a pawn in a succession of gambits played slowly and jointly by Grimaldi as Spain's foreign minister, and Choiseul on behalf of France.

15

INTRUDING
REALITIES

The principal objective of Choiseul's foreign policy in the years after the Treaty of Paris was to avoid conflict while France rebuilt her economic and military power in preparation for a future pre-emptive strike against England. The treaty had given him a useful basis for his diplomatic initiatives, in that it had effectively isolated England. The very completeness of the victory, gained largely through the exercise of global maritime strength, had alarmed all the European nations. They saw in the power and arrogance of the British a long-term imbalance and threat which could not be ignored.

In the face of this threat, always more apparent than real, Choiseul found no difficulty in maintaining the Family Compact and alliance with Spain. He nonetheless did not allow Spain to forget that if she pursued her policies to the point of renewed war, she would be on her own. France would not be drawn into any premature renewal of conflict. The Spanish, in turn, were still so scarred by the debacles of Havana and Manila that they were prepared to accept France's role as leader of the alliance, whose support was vital in the resolution of continuing quarrels with Britain.

Thus the question of the Manila ransom could not avoid being subsumed into a tripartite process which was eventually and bizarrely complicated by involvement with the first disputes over the colonisation of the Falkland Islands. The Spanish attitude to the payment of the ransom was at least consistent. The first indications came as early as January 1764, shortly after the arrival of Lord Rochford *en poste* in Madrid. Halifax sent to the Governor of the Bank of England a copy of an immediate dispatch from Rochford to the effect:

> that the Marquis of Grimaldi had declared to His Excellency that
> the King of Spain will not consent to pay the draft of the Archbishop
> of Manila upon His Catholic Majesty's Treasury; and that the
> representations made by the Ambassador to show the justice of the
> claim had not prevailed to obtain a change of that resolution.[1]

In diplomatic currency this could be deemed to be the first statement of a negotiating position rather than a definitive refusal. The Spanish government based its case on two propositions: that the levy of a ransom as an exemption from pillage was a violation of international law; and that in any case the Archbishop of Manila had no authority to sign any capitulation or to draw drafts on the Spanish Treasury. Having thus dismissed any legal basis for the ransom demand, Grimaldi also countered with the contention that the British commanders had undermined the de facto basis of their demand by allowing uncontrolled pillage immediately after the capitulation.

The pace of any British rebuttal of the Spanish arguments depended partly on the availability of Admiral Cornish who, as joint commander of the expedition, would be needed to add his personal evidence to any response. He was known to be returning to England with some of his ships but was not expected until midsummer. Until then, not much progress could be made.

In the meantime, Rochford in Madrid was attempting to deal with two additional issues which complicated the picture: an interim claim by the East India Company for reimbursement of funds which had been borrowed by the Spanish authorities in Manila after the capitulation to pay their own troops; and the unresolved status of the galleon *Santissima Trinidad*. These two linked topics gave the Spanish the opportunity to play a slow game. In March 1764, Grimaldi informed Rochford about the Company's claim:

> I have laid the said office before the King and upon sight of it and
> in consequence of some indirect and unsatisfactory informations
> received from Manila; as well as upon account of other irregularities
> which the Archbishop is known to have committed through his
> pusillanimity I am commanded by His Majesty that before a positive
> resolution can be taken it will be requisite to receive very direct
> express and circumstantial information of all that has happened
> relative to this affair.[2]

The implication was that at least another year could be added before any decision could be taken. Simultaneously Halifax was communicating with Draper, about the status of the *Santissima Trinidad*. He forwarded a memorandum from the Spanish Ambassador in London, Prince Masserano, reclaiming the galleon unjustly taken, and complaining of some other proceedings there as contrary to the capitulation. Halifax asked Draper:

> that you will furnish me with every information in your power concerning the matter of complaint therein set forth and particularly that part of it which relates to the pillage that you are charged with permitting.[3]

Draper produced in his own handwriting a long memorandum which was to form the basis of a pamphlet published later in the year stressing:

> I flatter myself I shall afford you the clearest conviction that the people of Manila have most grossly misinformed and imposed upon their court in every particular ... and are most impudent and fallacious as my just exposition of facts will demonstrate ... I have first proved that the capitulation cannot be objected to by the Spaniards under the pretence of force and violence which I am charged with having made use of to extort it from them, secondly that I neither ordered nor permitted the place to be pillaged after the capitulation was signed ... and lastly that we have an indubitable right to the two millions of dollars ... upon which article I had intended to have delivered a memorial in the beginning of winter but was in hope that the punctuality and good faith of the Spanish nation would make it unnecessary, being also very unwilling that factious and designing men should make any use of this subject to the distress of the administration.[4]

The letter reflects the dismay of a man coming to realise that he has been caught in the toils of diplomatic and political wrangling where his experience as a military commander counted for little. More importantly, it expresses awareness that the arguments are beginning to irritate the very people in government on whom he depends for any future advancement.

Masserano replied to Halifax, countering Draper's arguments, casting doubt once again on Archbishop Rojo's authority to handle the whole affair,[5] and commenting on Rojo's inexperience in military affairs. Having moved towards making the unfortunate Archbishop a scapegoat, Masserano then challenged that:

> [W]ith little reason and foundation General Draper pretends to insinuate that it is breaking the capitulation to deny the validity of one of its articles. There never was an example before of a governor of a fortress having granted, or being forced to grant, such a condition ... Even a Minister plenipotentiary has to seek

acknowledgement and ratification by their respective masters.
How could a greater latitude be allowed in the limited terms of the capitulation of a fortress?

He ended with the hope that the *Santissima Trinidad* should be delivered up to Spain as soon as she arrived in England, 'as taken contrary to agreement'.

This rebuff was being delivered coincidentally with Draper's involvement in a furious quarrel between the Duke of Bedford and the Prime Minister, George Grenville, over the timing of the award of Knighthood of the Order of the Bath to him. Membership of the Order was a signal honour which had been promised to Draper for his services at Manila, as soon as a vacancy occurred. Membership was limited to thirty-eight.

The row blew up because the vacancy which had been allotted to Draper had suddenly been given to Lord Clive, who was shortly to return to India as Governor-General of Bengal. Bedford had apparently given his considerable weight to the nomination of Draper, possibly from a sense of embarrassment that the timing of the Treaty of Paris had deprived the general of his just awards, and the difficulties over the ransom could well deprive him of any others. A Knighthood of the Bath, the highest military order, would at least be some tangible consolation.

The Earl of Sandwich, Draper's friend from their cricketing days in the 1750s, who was now First Lord of the Admiralty, alerted Grenville on 23 April to Bedford's wrath:

> From some conversation I had today with the Duke of Bedford I fear he is a little uneasy at the disposal of the Red Ribbon without your having mentioned a word to him on the subject, more especially as he says that the King promised him that Colonel Draper would have the first that was vacant. I told him that I was persuaded your having said nothing to him was owing to your hurry to go to Bath, and to take it for granted that you could persuade Colonel Draper to acquiesce the present occasion, which however as Mr Jenkinson informs me is not the case.[6]

Jenkinson, writing to Grenville on the same day from the Treasury, confirmed that the King had told the Duke that such was the case, but that the King had then decided that Draper should give way to Clive on this occasion. Apparently, Clive felt that the award of a KB to himself would reinforce his authority on his return to India, and in view of his imminent departure the King acceded to his request. Bedford a day or two later vented his wrath on Grenville, writing of his anger on arriving at Court to find that Clive had already received the honour: 'I did remonstrate to the King that I thought that Colonel Draper and myself had met with hard treatment ... Mr Draper being disappointed and myself being disavowed.'[7]

Draper, in thanking the duke from Clifton, took the opportunity to convey his own feelings about Grenville's role in the affair:

> I am truly and highly sensible of the kind part you have been pleased
> to take in my behalf and beg leave to return my sincerest thanks. It is
> not part of your Grace's character to abandon those you have been
> pleased to honour with your profession of friendship and assistance.
> Such an imputation was never charged to the Duke of Bedford;
> but a minister of the House of Commons is seldom so steady in
> his profession. All merit with him is weighed in the Parliamentary
> scales; it is no wonder that I flew and kicked the beams when
> balanced against Lord Clive ...

> But I own to Your Grace it is not a little mortifying that we who
> serve government from principle and affection should be so often
> sacrificed to those new converts to administration who serve it only
> from self-interest and convenience. Whenever I am employed again I
> will be a most dirty dog, rob and pillage whenever I can, deserve to
> be hanged and then carry every point for myself and my associates.
> But God forbid my hand that this idle affair should give Your Grace
> a moment's uneasiness. I am sure it will give Grenville much more ...
> let us be revenged that way.[8]

Horace Walpole, writing from Strawberry Hill to Horace Mann, who also nursed hopes of being admitted to the Order as reward for his years of service in Florence as Ambassador to the Grand Duke of Tuscany, summarised the imbroglio with his usual cynical clarity:

> Your Red Ribband is certainly postponed. There was but one vacant
> which was promised to General Draper who, when he thought he
> felt the sword dubbing his shoulder, was told that My Lord Clive
> could not conquer the Indies a second time without being a Knight
> of the Bath. This however I think will be a short parenthesis for
> I expect that 'heaven-sent' hero to return from whence he came
> instead of bringing all the Moghul's pearls and rubies. Yet before
> that happens there will probably be other vacancies to protect both
> Draper and you.[9]

Walpole's conjecture that Clive might die in India proved inaccurate, and Horace Mann was knighted in the following year at the same time as Draper. With his honour known to be pending, and he in a position where he could easily call upon some powerful patrons, it is surprising that Draper made no attempt to become a Member of Parliament. The wish expressed by his regimental agent, John Calcraft, as far back as 1759 that he should get 'a seat in St Stephen's Chapel' on his return from India could have been helped by Calcraft himself, who had become an experienced political fixer in the intervening years. Calcraft was closely linked with Bedford and could easily have championed any quest for a parliamentary seat. There would have been little difficulty in arranging for a suitable constituency, and no surprise that Draper should have sought one. Among his most immediate military colleagues, Cornish, Fletcher, and Monson all obtained seats within a few years. Possibly he believed that in the aftermath of his triumph his freedom to pursue the ransom issue might have been constrained by being under the obligations of a political placeman. Perhaps more simply he was temporarily soured by the compromises of public life and wished to bide his time in private.

In the close-knit society of London, gossip about the queue-jumping of Clive to his KB had made the rounds within hours. The public also was well in touch with the issue of the Manila ransom, not least because so many troops and sailors stood to gain from the outcome of the arguments.

Draper's urge to keep the issues alive was renewed by the arrival of Admiral Cornish at Spithead on 16 July. Cornish was immediately faced with trying to sort out the outstanding claims of his sailors. The *Scots Magazine* of August 1764 showed that there was no way in which these questions could be shunted into a bureaucratic siding. The magazine reported:

> A large body of sailors waited on Admiral Cornish in London on 23 August to know in what manner they were to receive their prize money for the capture of Carical and Pondicherry; and received for answer that he had made application to the directors of the East India Company ... and no further satisfaction could be given to the captors as 50,000 pagodas had already been distributed to the Navy.[10]

The fact that Cornish was not immediately assaulted by the unfortunate and disappointed sailors, who had now been waiting for more than four years for their deserved share, was proof of how highly he was still regarded by the men who had served with and under him.

Following his return to England, Cornish submitted a further petition, again jointly calling with Coote on behalf of the royal forces serving in India, broadening their complaint to include the Company's behaviour on the whole Coromandel coast. Neither petition made much headway against the obduracy of the Company playing a long game, and armed with the counter-grievance that Cornish had not allowed the Company's troops to share in the prize money and booty from the *Santissima Trinidad*. Now the Manila ransom had added another, and larger, area of controversy. Both Cornish and Draper felt the need to present their case to the public, not simply to justify their actions, but to prove to their troops and sailors that they were not prepared to let the case go by default.

They took advantage of the freedom allowed to serving officers at that period to launch into print on issues of public interest or personal concern. The absence of libel laws, the spread of newspapers, magazines and pamphlets, and the uninhibited pugnacity of the age had all created conditions in which a rich and varied stream of argument, insult, claim and counter-claim, invective, special pleading, sarcasm, wit, and pomposity could be, and was, brought before the public. Throughout the century, naval and army officers produced a constant output of publications, most of them dedicated to justifying the conduct of the author in the face of criticism from fellow officers or the wider public.

Cornish and Draper's *Plain Narrative of the Conquest*, signed jointly by them and published after Cornish's return, was therefore not unusual by the standards of the time.[11] Indeed, it might have been thought unusual if they had not published, suggesting a reluctance to set forth their explanation for the success of the expedition and their conduct during it. Although Cornish signed the document jointly, it was written by Draper who expressed the view with Cornish that 'it is a duty incumbent on me to set the material transactions of the expedition in a proper point of view as much in my justice to my own conduct and character as to the officers and men serving under me.'

The *Plain Narrative* was a factual document, giving a concise version of the naval and military action and containing few elements of special pleading. It included some paragraphs on the difficulties which faced the commanders in establishing where eventual responsibility for allocating the booty should lie:

> As soon as the place was in the possession of the East India
> Company, the Spaniards perceived that the King's officers had
> no further power over them, and therefore stopped any further
> collection towards the payment, and from the excess of lenity shown
> them grew insolent, broke every part of the capitulation by retiring
> into the country and joining Anda ... who had taken up arms and
> proclaimed himself Captain General, while their priests and friars
> publicly exhorted rebellion.[12]

The document included reference to the various galleons, and Rochford in Madrid could have been forgiven for becoming confused about which of the galleons should, or should not, be included in his discussions; the *Philipina*, the real prize which had eluded the British; the *Santissima Trinidad* which had been captured by accident yet was not included in the capitulation; and a small ship the *Santo Nino*, captured at Cavite and sold for a small sum, which the Spaniards were trying to pretend was the *Santissima Trinidad*.

The position was clarified a little when the *Santissima Trinidad* entered Plymouth Roads in June 1764, having been sailed back from Manila by a motley crew including fifty French prisoners, under the command of a Royal Navy lieutenant. The arrival of the prize galleon, then the largest ship ever seen in England, was reported as attracting crowds from all over the south of England.[13] She weighed more than 2,000 tons, in comparison with the average of 500 tons for an East Indiaman, drawing twenty-eight feet of water. After her arrival she moved to anchor at Spithead awaiting a decision as to her eventual fate, a source of amazement to all who came to see her.

While the Spanish Ambassador in London kept pressing Halifax for release of the galleon, he was also forwarding complaints about treatment of the Augustinian friars in Manila following the restoration of civil government. One of these evoked a testy response from Draper to Halifax:

> I have the honour to inform you that the violence complained of in
> the memorial of the Spanish must, if committed, be subsequent to
> my departure from Manila ... I am convinced there is not a single
> man of the Order of St Augustine undeserving of the gallows and
> they are responsible for all the blood shed there since my departure.
> They spirited up the people to disobey the Archbishop's orders
> and have been guilty of so much treason against our government
> there that I am surprised Mr Drake did not long hang these fellows
> instead of sending them off the islands, but all these counter-claims
> of the Spaniards are made purposely to evade the payment of the
> two million dollars we have an undoubted right to.[14]

The Augustinian Friars had been exiled from Manila by Dawsonne Drake for their seditious activities, and eventually arrived, bizarrely, in London where they presented a further minor problem for Masserano, the Spanish Ambassador. He was understandably much more concerned that the British had decided that the case of the *Santissima Trinidad* should be adjudicated by the Admiralty Courts. The predictable judgement, handed down in November 1764, that both the ship and its cargo were free to be sold in England, triggered an angry response from the Spanish which, in turn, resulted in a lengthy report from the Advocate-General to Halifax for onward transmission to Madrid.

The nub of the Advocate-General's conclusions was that the *Santissima Trinidad* could not be considered as coming within the terms of the capitulation. In short, there was no way in which the King of Spain, or his subjects who owned the cargo, could expect any further redress of their grievances on the *Santissima Trinidad*. Nor did they receive any, as the great galleon, too large to be commercially viable or usable as a man-of-war, was eventually sold in England and quietly broken up.

The decision of the Admiralty courts only served to harden Spain's position on the ransom, which had already been set out clearly and widely distributed in England via the Spanish Ambassador's 'Memorial'. This in turn inspired Draper to publish at the end of 1764 a pamphlet entitled *Colonel Draper's Answer to the Spanish Arguments* in the form of a public letter to Halifax as Secretary of State for the Southern Department.[15]

In his *Answer*, Draper showed his keen awareness of how much his own troops, and Cornish's sailors, still depended upon him to plead their case in the absence of any formal channels available to them:

> I was in great hope that the good faith, honour, and punctuality of
> the Spanish nation would have made this publication unnecessary.
> But finding that they have absolutely refused payment of the
> ransom bills, and do now claim the restitution of the galleon, I am
> constrained for the sake of those brave men to whom I am obliged
> and indebted for my success, to assert their rights in the best manner
> I am able ...

> Many of them, My Lord, from the too usual and sanguine hopes of
> their profession have already anticipated their supposed profits and
> may live to repent their fatal success in a jail unless the powerful
> intercession of the Government will rescue them from impending mis-
> ery or destruction. They vainly look to me for their protection, which,
> in their names, I again request from Your Lordship's good offices ...

> I must add that the calumnious and envenomed attack upon my
> character demands the most public justification; being described
> both at home and abroad as a man void of all faith, principle, or
> common honesty; and so indeed I should be most deservedly thought
> were I guilty of what the Spanish Memorial accuses me.

The core of the Spanish argument was that the capitulation ought to be void because it was extracted by force, and that Draper first violated and then broke the capitulation by permitting the city to be pillaged. He answered:

> It is a known and universal rule of war amongst the most civilised
> nations that places taken by storm without any capitulation are
> subject to all the miseries that the conquerors may choose to inflict.
> Manila was in this horrid situation ... but Christianity, humanity,
> the dignity of our nation, and our own feelings as men induced us
> not to exert the utmost rigour against those wretched suppliants.

He then went into detailed comments on the confused sequence of events in the hours following the capture of the Citadel, arguing that the pillage, regrettable as it was and virtually impossible to control, could have been a great deal worse. He countered the Spanish suggestion that the Archbishop had no authority to draw bills on the Spanish Treasury by pointing out that:

> the persons entrusted with such remote commands must be left
> to their own discretion; to the fertility or barrenness of their own

resources and invention. A state may undoubtedly punish the man who is found to have betrayed its dignity or interests, but at all events it must abide by his decisions, however prejudicial soever.

Draper's hope that the pamphlet might influence the Government into taking more positive steps towards resolving the problem had been given added urgency by his concern for the veterans of his regiment, the 79th, which was thought to be on its way back from Manila and India for disbandment. Although many of the troops had probably chosen to transfer from the royal to the Company forces, preferring the hazards of continued service in India to predictable penury following discharge in England, there would still be a sufficient number of survivors dependent on the Government's haphazard charity to be a cause of worry for their old commander. Draper, as colonel of the regiment, had been kept in touch with events in Manila following his departure, and nothing he had learnt from his officers via their infrequent reports would have done anything to lessen his concern for their future.

16

MANILA:
THE LAST STAGES

While post-expedition quarrels in Europe were conducted on a diplomatic level, in Manila itself they deteriorated to somewhere between farce and tragedy. From the time of the departure of Cornish and his squadron for India in March 1763 to the final embarkation of the remnants of the royal and Company forces in April 1764, a fourteen-month purgatory of confusion and bickering among the British victors seriously undermined any chance that the Spanish court in Madrid would feel any obligation to honour the terms of the capitulation.

Lack of news and instructions from Europe and India created wearisome months of uncertainty in which all the parties could, and did, find excuses for provoking or maintaining feuds. The complex situation would only have been manageable with clear, acknowledged lines of responsibility and authority. There were none. In the ensuing hiatus, the senior Company, Navy, army and Spanish leaders manipulated every opportunity to pursue their narrow interests. The systemic friction among the British played straight into the hands of the Spaniards.

The basic decision to hand over the running of Manila to the East India Company might have been valid if the Company's nominee had been a man of the stature of George Pigot, the Governor of Madras. Dawsonne Drake, saddled with a burden which would have taxed the qualities of a first-class administrator, hardly rose above the level of a trader presented with unbounded opportunities for dealing.

Under Drake's inadequate authority it was not surprising that the British garrison began soon to show signs of demoralisation. The excitement of battle had given way to the tedium of garrison life in a tropical setting with plenty of time to brood on real or imagined grievances. A punitive sortie against Anda's forces almost immediately after the conquest, in search of the treasure from the *Philipina*, had proved too hazardous and unrewarding to be worth repeating. Thereafter the royal troops, chiefly the 79th Regiment, now under the command of Captain Thomas Backhouse, shared their discomforts, sickness, sense of isolation and lack of pay with the larger number of Company troops; all aware of being in a restive city surrounded by a guerrilla army, with no hope of reinforcement, and beset by the gloomy thought that all their discomforts and dangers might never even receive recognition or reward.

The two naval guardships were at least occupied in the continuing search for the vanished galleon on the far coast of Luzon. They were still absent when news arrived in Manila in July 1763 of the cessation of hostilities and the preliminaries of peace. This news could not, however, be taken as confirming the end of the war; nor did it give any indication as to the future disposition of Manila and the Philippines. It merely added to the miasma of uncertainty.

Backhouse, writing later to the Secretary at War, focused on one of the immediately malign effects of this unsettling news; the decision by Major Robert Fell, Draper's appointee as Commandant of the land forces, to allow junior officers in the 79th Regiment to recruit or engage troops which they might then command in the service of the Company. This decision made sense in the context of the known likelihood that the 79th would be disbanded if and when it returned to England. Nonetheless as Backhouse reported:

> This at once disunited the corps, and destroyed that attachment, spirit, and pride which had on every occasion distinguished their superiority since their arrival in India; what ensued was disputes, quarrels, drunkenness and desertion; the non-commissioned officers looked upon themselves as dismissed and slighted; the enemy took advantage of this and offered great sums to such as would desert; this and the visible advantages that this island has over all other parts of the Eastern world were motive sufficient to minds agitated to fly from their colours, as they had lost all hope of being carried to their native country. Supposing Major Fell has received His Majesty's liberty for such procedure surely never was anything so ill-timed ... both for the service of our Royal Lord and Master and the East India Company.[1]

Backhouse's dismay at the breakdown of discipline in his command is mixed with understanding of the urge among royal troops for guaranteed pay-in-hand from any paymaster, preferable to unfulfilled promises of continued service in the army. Pay in a warm climate was more attractive than the likelihood of poverty in a cold one.

Major Fell, a few months after his demoralising initiative, suddenly found himself embroiled in a ludicrous sequence of events resulting in his eventual arraignment for mutiny and departure in disgrace from Manila. The events were related in depositions sent by Dawsonne Drake later to the Earl of Egremont, when Drake was attempting to justify his own conduct and diminish the odium into which he himself had fallen.[2]

At the centre of this absurd row was, yet again, the Swiss Chevalier Faillet, who had been such a source of irritation to Cornish earlier in the year. Months after Cornish's departure Faillet, still in Manila, wrote to a friend with an account of his treatment at Cornish's hands, and making disparaging remarks about the Admiral. Cornish, in Madras, somehow intercepted the letter, and sent orders to his naval commander in Manila, Captain William Brereton, to apprehend Faillet. The Swiss, getting wind of this order, sensibly absconded from Manila, but in October was taken into custody by Drake who had received similar orders from the Council in Madras. The dispute flared over whether the Swiss would be a Company or a royal prisoner.

Brereton attempted to deprive Drake of his prisoner and, on 5 October 1763, alongside a parade of Company and royal troops, there was an unseemly scuffle between the Governor's escort for the prisoner and troops detached by Fell to help his naval colleague. Major Fell came off best in this demeaning encounter and promptly fled to the naval base at Cavite with his prisoner; where the next day they were both arrested by a land party sent by Drake under his authority as Governor.

Fell was charged with mutiny and, so that his continued presence in Manila would not add to the tensions, was placed on board an East Indiaman leaving Manila. This ship was heading for Canton before its return journey via Madras, which meant that Fell's arraignment on charges of mutiny was delayed until May of the following year, by which time Faillet the unfortunate Swiss had also been transported to Madras.

Drake meanwhile had also been dealing with discontent among officers of the Company still stationed in Manila. They too shared the emotions of the royal forces that their fate was of no great interest to their masters. In September, a memorandum signed by thirty-four of the Company officers grumbled at length about their distress at hearing that they were not going to receive the usual bonus for their service in Manila and lamenting to the Governor about the maltreatment being meted out to them from Drake's superiors in Madras.

Captain Mathew Horne, one of the Company's officers in Manila who had been promoted after Major Robert Barker went back to Madras, was able to express his dismay to a correspondent in England, giving him a detailed account of all the quarrels, and commenting:

[E]ver since General Draper left us we have had nothing but
disagreements and a villainous enemy to deal with. Anda has daily
increased his strength ... there is a continued scarcity of provisions.
and as now the monsoon is changing and there is no confirmation of
peace or assistance we are in a very disagreeable position ... I think
my situation owing to all these disagreements the most disagreeable
I was ever in.[3]

Whatever sympathy Drake may have had for the plight of the Company's
officers, he was hardly in a position to plead their case with his superiors in
Madras. The Council at Fort St George, becoming increasingly irritated by the
consequences of the expedition, was reluctant to commit any further resources
to Manila. Drake, as their nominee, was an easy target for this irritation, and
his tenure of office was marked by letters from Madras chiding him on his
sloppy accounting and other negligence.

Stringer Lawrence, still in command in Madras, was particularly impatient
to see the return of the troops from Manila. Throughout 1763, despite the fact
that no firm guidance had been received from London on post-war arrangements, Lawrence nagged the authorities in London for the return of the royal
and Company troops, observing in a letter to Egremont in October 1763:

In an address to Your Lordship of 25 April I could not help
observing that I had all reason to fear my disapprobation of the
expedition to Manila would prove to be just. The sending of so great
a part of our strength to so great a distance has been the foundation
of all the troubles we are now involved in.[4]

The troubles referred to were minor confrontations with local rulers along
the Coromandel coast, but gave Lawrence the chance of repeating his original
misgivings. The forces in Manila were in fact playing a useful if necessarily
passive role; as protection against the continuing activity of Anda and his
guerrilla army. Anda had chosen to pay no attention to the news of the
cessation of hostilities, continuously harassing British patrols outside Manila,
and interrupting food supplies to the city.

Captain Backhouse, early the next year, commenting in a letter to the
Secretary at War on the pressures exerted by Anda, took the opportunity to
air his ongoing complaints about dealing with Drake and his minions:

The insolent enemy seem every day more determined to pay no
regard to the suspension of arms agreed to between their Majesties.
All possible means are used by them to prevent our getting supplies
of provision. At present we pay a most extravagant price for every
article. The disadvantages we labour under on this head are owing
to the measures taken by the Company's Governor and Council.

The grain that we found in the garrison and the quantity that we
added to it immediately was sufficient for our support for some
years. The greater part of this they put on board their ships and sent
it to China. What remained they sold out of the garrison to the best
bidder so soon as it bore a high price. In fact when I came to the
command of the troops I found the place swept ... I shall do all in
my power to save the arms of my Royal Lord from stains, but even
in this I am interrupted and made most wretched at times.[5]

Backhouse was even more outspoken about his problems in a letter to his
colonel, William Draper, written on the same day:

You will see by the returns how much our numbers are decreased by
desertion, death, etc. The whole Council who you left here belonging
to the Company are gone to the Coast, except Mr Drake ... From
such another Governor and Council Good Lord deliver all honest
men. Believe me, Sir, the condition of His Majesty's troops exceeds
all description. No hell that human nature ever experienced can
equal it. In this I have a most heavy share. This is principally owing
to the Governor who appears to have but one view and sticks at no
length to obtain it ...

The Archbishop, late Governor of Manila, was interred in the
cathedral a few days ago with great solemnity. I paid him such
honours as were due his rank. He behaved well on all occasions and
was a good man. His death gave much pleasure to Senor Anda and
his party who are in arms against us in the province.[6]

Archbishop Rojo had died on 30 January 1764, his death accelerated by the
strains of the previous eighteen months. Draper received the news of his death
via Backhouse's letter which arrived at Clifton in August 1764 and forwarded
it to the Secretary at War, formally adding his complaints about Drake, and
adding for good measure:

In order to secure a few friends in a country which abounds with
enemies, Mr Cornish and I exempted the Chinese and Indians from
some heavy taxes. I find that Mr Drake has laid them on again with
additions, so that the whole island is now against us; but as long as
these rascals get more money they care not for any consequences
how fatal soever ... The ships that were sent by Admiral Cornish
to bring off the King's troops have most unfortunately lost their
passage; so that my poor regiment has neither clothing nor pay,
which was sent to Madras where the regiment was expected; nor
have they received any authentic account of the peace, nor is it

possible for them to be in England until next year. They are brave fellows and deserve a better fate.[7]

Had he known the final sequence of events as the British prepared to depart from the Philippines he would have been even more dismayed. Confusion and quarrels continued to the bitter end.

The news for which they were all waiting in Manila – definitive terms of the peace – finally arrived on the Company ship, *Revenge*, on 8 March 1764, a full year after the signing of the Treaty of Paris. The news had itself been unnecessarily delayed by the fact that the captain of the *Revenge* had taken his time getting to Manila, preferring to search for possible trading opportunities en route.

The *Revenge* brought orders from Cornish to Brereton to deliver up Manila to the Spanish authorities as soon as possible. Brereton had had a few final frustrating months trying to track the long-lost *Philipina*, which he had eventually found beached near Palapag. To prevent its further use, he put it to the torch. Thereafter he saw little purpose in acting as a watchdog around Manila's waters and was as anxious as his military colleague, Backhouse, to see the last of the city.

Even the handover now became the subject of another furious tripartite quarrel. As Rojo was dead, the first problem to be solved was that of negotiating with Anda, who, bizarrely, by the powers devolved to him by Rojo, was legally the person authorised to receive back the conquest, despite having been officially declared a rebel by Drake and his Council.

This potential impasse was solved when Don Francisco de Torre shortly afterwards arrived from Spain, via Mexico and the Pacific, with full powers as Governor and Captain-General. However, his party immediately complicated the delicate situation by declaring that they would only deal with Brereton and Backhouse, the commanders of the royal forces, to whom they had delivered their King's orders. This early decision had been their reaction to discovering that the Company had virtually stripped Manila of its stores and supply of rice by selling it into China. Drake and his Council were not considered fit persons for negotiations.

Drake naturally took umbrage at being ignored, and challenged the right of Brereton and Backhouse to issue any orders at all. From 18 to 25 March the commanders laboured to forward the embarkation of the troops onto the limited number of ships immediately available, thwarted at every turn by Drake and his Council. According to Backhouse they 'threw every obstacle in their way that rancour could invent'.

Matters came to a head on 25 March when Drake, via instructions to Captain Sleigh of the 79th, ordered the arrest of Backhouse who reported later that:

about two o'clock in the morning of the 26th he was alarmed in his bedroom by Lieut Richbell and a party of grenadiers of the

79th Regiment with fixed bayonets. The latter accosted him in a very mutinous manner ... adding that he had orders to take him prisoner and confine him in the Citadel. He did this, he said, by the Governor's orders. On being ordered by Backhouse to obey him as his commanding officer, and being reminded of the punishment of mutiny, he said he had no time to talk and ordered his party to make the arrest which was done with the utmost violence. The men employed seemed to be in liquor. The colours were also seized and carried away without decency.[8]

In the confusion of the next three days, while Backhouse attempted to restore his authority from his cell, it became clear that Drake was about to be presented with a series of lawsuits 'setting forth his oppressions and vile actions' by Spaniards in Manila emboldened by the arrival of a restored Spanish Governor, and encouraged by Brereton still smarting from the memory of the imbroglio over Faillet.

Drake, sensing that retreat was probably now his best option, embarked in the covering darkness of the night of 29 March on board one of the Company ships, the *Admiral Pocock*, which had put in to Manila on voyage to Madras. Drake, consistent to the last, had purloined some treasure from the dead archbishop's palace and placed it on board in barrels labelled 'Rice for Governor Drake'. Backhouse was then released from the Citadel, and he in turn issued orders divesting Drake of all his powers, 'he having absconded'.

As if these events were not sufficiently confused to baffle the Spaniards, they were further complicated by the totally unexpected arrival from Sulu en route to China of no less a figure than Alexander Dalrymple, who pronounced himself Deputy-Governor. His arrival was fortuitous, but beneficial. He brought authority to the remaining Company officers and their forces, and neutrality between the royal commanders and the Spanish. His presence had an immediate calming effect.

On 1 April 1764, Manila was thus formally handed back to the Spanish authorities, not to the new Governor Francisoco de Torre, who was diplomatically indisposed, but to Anda himself, to whom de Torre allowed the honour of riding in triumph back into the city. The British troops marched out at the Sea Gate and had all the honours of war paid to them by the Spaniards.

For a few days afterwards, there was another inevitable muddle around the port of Cavite as makeshift arrangements were made to transport the royal and Company troops back to India. There were only one or two ships available, and the north-east monsoon which would have given them a fair wind had already died away. Supplies were short, responsibilities ill-defined. Sickness was already taking its toll.

Backhouse and most of the troops of the 79th embarked on the *Falmouth* on 12 April, but did not reach Batavia (the modern Jakarta) until mid-July, 'arriving in a sickly condition having suffered much in a passage of four months which has frequently been made in sixteen days'. The *Falmouth* by then was in such poor condition that she would need six months' repair work before she could proceed any further. Two Company ships had then arrived unexpectedly, one of the captains offering to take some of the troops back to Madras, the other taking the rest to Bengal. Backhouse had no alternative to accepting these offers because 'by the time the Falmouth might be ready to sail again death would have put an end to this battalion.'[9] Dalrymple remained in Manila in nominal charge of the residual British presence until 16 April, when he too departed for his return journey to Sulu.

The voyage of the *Admiral Pocock*, carrying the absconding Drake and no fewer than 300 Company troops as well as other passengers, which should have had a straight run to Madras, then turned into one of those agonising epics of eighteenth-century sailing. After leaving Manila, she was forced by bad weather and contrary winds to put in to Sulu, hundreds of miles south of her intended course. The 300 Company troops, mostly Sepoys, were disembarked and left as a problem to be solved in due course. The ship, having already been at sea for six months, was then despatched back to Canton late in September by Dalrymple who had completed his return to Sulu. Her captain's laconic description of the next stage of her voyage is a masterpiece of understatement:

> I sailed for Canton, but meeting with a severe gale of wind which
> lasted three weeks with little intermission in 21 Degrees North I lost
> all my topmasts and most of the sails, which so disabled the ship
> that I bore away for the island of Hainan, but not having sufficient
> sail to work into the port, and the hull of the ship being so disabled,
> I bore away for the Port of Turan in the Kingdom of Cochin China,
> where I arrived on 21 November in a very shattered condition.[10]

While the ship, her crew, and passengers, were recovering from this ordeal their stay in the port of Turan, on the coast of modern Vietnam, was eventually cut short because of a threat posed after the accidental killing of a Cochinese subject by one of the *Pocock*'s sailors:

> This occasioned a great dispute, and the affair not being settled to
> the satisfaction of the King, he sent down an army of ten thousand
> men and eight elephants with orders to cut off the people on shore,
> and if possible destroy the ship ... Dawsonne Drake, esq, late
> Governor of Manila, narrowly escaped falling into their hands, had
> he not bravely stood his ground until assistance was sent from the
> ship ... Mr Nodes in the Honourable Company's service fell into
> their hands, and Mr Arundine and his daughter, late inhabitants of
> Manila. I intended to have endeavoured to release them, but found
> the natives so determined to cut the ship off by force or destroying

her by fire I judged it most prudent to leave the port; and upon my sailing was attacked by six of her galleys.[11]

There was no further mention of the unfortunate Mr Nodes or the Arundines.

The *Pocock*, having made good her escape, finally arrived at Macao in June 1765, no less than a year and a half after her departure from Manila and still thousands of miles from her intended destination of Madras.

The 300 Sepoys, who had been disembarked from the *Pocock* in Sulu, had meanwhile been involved in their own continuing saga which lasted even longer than that of the *Pocock*. They were provided with a passage from Sulu in 1765 but, owing to contrary winds and other problems, the ship somehow ended up back in Manila. They sailed from Manila finally in March 1766, but the captain was more interested in private trade around the region than in heading straight for Madras. The officer commanding the troops finally forced the captain to put in to the Company's nearest settlement, Fort Marlborough in Sumatra. The troops were disembarked in September 1766 to wait for the next available ship. They only reached Madras in August 1767, having spent three years on the voyage, during which at least one hundred of them had died of sickness.

Dawsonne Drake, a born survivor, had also finally returned to Madras, but finding himself under the residual cloud of disapproval, resigned from the Company, remaining as a free merchant in Madras until his death in 1781. By accepting his nomination before the expedition he was probably hoping for an opportunity similar to that which had come to Clive in Bengal. On his return to Madras, discredited and richer only by his plunder from the Archbishop's palace, he must have rued the optimism which had allowed him to accept the nomination in the first place.

All of them would have shared the opinion expressed by Matthew Horne, the Company officer who endured the whole expedition until his return to Madras, when he wrote to a friend in England:

> With respect to us except the admiral and general, and a few captains of men of war, I don't know a person but what are considerable sufferers; indeed chiefly owing to the misconduct of our chiefs (who if they have their deserts all deserve the gallows) and to the Company not only an enormous expense but the loss of the troops from this coast has almost undone what they have been doing these ten years past ... You will imagine I am very happy in being returned from so disagreeable an expedition.[12]

The remnants of the 79th Regiment would have concurred. They arrived in batches in Madras and Bombay in January 1765, where they were given the opportunity to re-enlist in the Company's forces. Having been at sea for more than six months on their journey via Batavia, only those with a strong urge to return to England were prepared to set out on another long voyage home.

The number of survivors of the 79th who arrived back in England still hoping to gain a share of the Manila ransom was small in comparison with the numbers who had served with the Regiment since its formation in 1757. The London papers reported in mid-June 1766 that 'the colours and remains of His Majesty's 79th Regiment had arrived at Chelsea under the command of Captain Thomas Backhouse ... They left Manila on 1 April 1764 and have buried near one half of the troops on that tedious voyage.'

Eight years of almost continuous action had taken a heavy toll of officers and men. Of the senior officers at the formation in 1757 only William Draper, George Monson, Robert Fell and Thomas Backhouse were still actively involved with the Regiment.

The survivors were to find that the 79th had been formally disbanded at Chatham in the autumn of 1763, almost two years before the last of the companies arrived home from India. Its disbandment, along with that of more than twenty other young regiments, was no more than an item in a process determined by Parliament and encouraged by the public, financially exhausted by war.

To a colonel saying farewell to survivors of such continuous action, it would at least have been an occasion of deep regret. To this particular colonel, the disbandment of his regiment must have been additionally galling from the knowledge that the survivors were unlikely ever to receive what might have been their due. He would also have known that the achievements of the regiment would rapidly fade in the public memory.

As a mark of his wish that so much gallantry and hardship should not be left totally unrecorded, Draper commissioned for the garden of Manila Hall the small cenotaph which now stands on Clifton Down. At its base, a Latin inscription addresses the passing traveller with the hope that 'to thee may fortune kinder be' than it had been to those commemorated, thirty-three officers and 1,000 men who had fallen between 1758 and 1764. Medallions bear the names of the regiment's major battles; Madras and Conjeveram in 1759, Wandiwash, Arcot and Carical in 1760, Pondicherry in 1761, and Manila and the Philippines.

The surviving members of the regiment remained in contact with their colonel in the faint hope that his public pleas to the Government might sometime yield some tangible reward. None could have foreseen that their arguments were about to be absorbed into, and given new impetus by, a confused sequence of events in an area hardly known to any of them – the Falkland Islands.

17

THE FALKLANDS
LINKAGE

The unforeseen and improbable linkage of the Manila ransom issue with that of the Falkland Islands meant that the claims of the disappointed commanders, and also those of the East India Company, became pawns in a game being played for much higher stakes – not just between Britain and Spain, but France as well. Cornish and Draper were forced by the accidental timing of history to be no more than minor onlookers on events over which they no longer had any influence.

Events were set in motion by Choiseul, the French Foreign Minister, in his policy of restoring France's colonial network following the Treaty of Paris. Shortly after the signing, Choiseul had encouraged a private expedition to colonise for France the small group of islands in the South Atlantic, now known as the Falkland Islands. The enterprise was organised by the young Antoine Louis de Bougainville on behalf of the town of St Malo whose long-distance fishermen had for many years used the uncharted islands as a base, naming them after their home port as Les Malouines.

Bougainville landed on the eastern island of the uninhabited and desolate group in March 1764, formally claiming it for France. He returned the following year with further supplies and settlers, whose base was named Port Louis. By then, the Spanish authorities in Montevideo were expressing anxious curiosity about the French moves. By the time of Bougainville's second visit in 1765, the Madrid government was informing Choiseul that a French settlement would be prejudicial to Spanish interests and likely to produce a British response.

Choiseul was understandably reluctant to surrender the new French colony but entered into tortuous negotiations. Meanwhile, creating complications which have endured to the present, the British mounted an expedition, under the command of Commodore the Hon. John Byron, grandfather of the poet, to establish a settlement on the islands. This was not in response to the French initiative; Byron had left on his voyage before news of the French venture reached Europe in August 1764. Byron's expedition was the long-delayed fulfilment of yet another of Lord Anson's visionary projects – to secure bases for the expansion of British interests on the alternative routes to India and the South Seas via Cape Horn. Byron's Instructions were:

> to call at His Majesty's Islands called Falklands and Pepys Islands
> situated in the Atlantic Ocean near the Straits of Magellan in order
> to make a better survey thereof ... and to determine a place or places
> most proper for a new settlement or settlements thereon.[1]

His Instructions are noteworthy in that 'His Majesty' had no sound claim whatever on the islands. They had occasionally been visited by British ships but they had never been settled, there was even confusion about their exact location and names as between Falklands and Pepys Islands, and the British had never before tried to claim possession or sovereignty over them.

Byron arrived on the western island in January 1765, using as his base a spot which he named Port Egmont in honour of the current First Lord of the Admiralty, Lord Egmont. Having laid claim to the islands by virtue of landing unopposed, he then sailed away, having no reason to suspect that, in the recesses of a cove on the eastern island, Bougainville's tiny settlement was already in position and ready to claim prior sovereignty.

News of Byron's landing on apparently uninhabited islands reached England in June of the same year. It prompted the British government to mount a further expedition which, in view of the reported presence of the French somewhere in the same group was instructed:

> If, contrary to expectation, the subjects of any foreign power
> in amity with Great Britain should under any real or pretended
> authority have taken upon them to make any settlement ... the
> commanders of His Majesty's ships are to visit such settlement and
> to remonstrate against their proceedings, acquainting them that the
> said islands having been first discovered by subjects of the Crown
> of England. The subject of no other power can have any title to
> establish themselves without the King's permission.[2]

Egmont at the Admiralty showed himself heir to Anson's thinking in a letter to the Duke of Grafton, then Secretary of the Northern Department, drawing his attention to:

the great importance of this station which is undoubtedly the key to the whole of the Pacific Ocean. This island must command the ports and trade of Chile and Peru, Panama, Acapulco, and in one word all the Spanish territory upon that sea. It will render all our expeditions to those parts most lucrative to ourselves, most fatal to Spain.[3]

Egmont's optimism that the Falklands, in the south Atlantic, could ever seriously form the key to the whole Pacific Ocean might have seemed totally irrational, except that it was shared by Choiseul. His principal interest in Les Malouines was as a springboard for future French action on the western, or Pacific, seaboard of America, with particular interest in the coastline of California. The unquestioning assumption that such geopolitical absurdities might be achievable in the face of all known hazards still has the power to amaze.

The second British expedition, mounted in secrecy, landed at Port Egmont in January 1766. Despite a search, the French colony was not spotted. Only at the end of that year, when British ships again returned for the southern summer, was the small French port finally discovered. Following a rather edgy confrontation with the settlers of Port Louis, the British captain delivered a warning to leave, and departed to report back to England. The stage was set for higher-level confrontation.

While these time-lapse events were gradually shaping the attitudes of the French, Spanish and British governments, they were also complicating the Manila ransom negotiations which ran on throughout 1765. At the beginning of the year, Rochford in Madrid, reporting on discussions with Grimaldi, showed that the Spanish government was in a hurry neither to advance that particular issue nor to concede any ground on it. Continuous correspondence between London and Madrid showed that the governments were interested principally in securing adherence to the terms of the Treaty of Paris. Since Manila was only relevant in terms of being restored to Spain, it was only a sideshow; and the ransom was only a small part of this sideshow. The requests of the East India Company for repayment of debts incurred by the Company in administering civil government in Manila only served to confuse the issue, as did the question of the fate of the *Santissima Trinidad*. The Spaniards were in any case determined to blame the whole issue on the dead Archbishop Rojo, and his inexperience in committing himself to a line of conduct for which he had no real authority.

Both governments were now concerned with more important bones of contention and wider trade issues. They would have been happier to allow the Manila ransom to be forgotten immediately, but were prepared to keep it alive as a negotiating counter. Thus it was kept in a state of uneasy animation during 1765 and into the next year, particularly in England where it was used as a convenient weapon by opponents of Grenville's lacklustre government.

Some tangible consolation came to Draper when he was appointed colonel of the 16th Foot in succession to his old friend the Hon. Robert Brudenell, brother of James Brudenell, his fellow-ADC to the Duke of Marlborough nine years previously. His appointment would have needed the approval of the Duke of Cumberland, now in the last year of his life though still only in his forties. Cumberland had devoted much time and energy after the end of the war in trying to alleviate the hardships of those who had served under him and was active in dispensing colonelcies to 'his family' where possible. His approval indicates that his irritation with Draper from years ago had been forgiven.

Draper retained his colonelcy for about a year, before receiving the King's permission to exchange it with Lieutenant-Colonel James Gisborne in return for Gisborne's half-pay, as Colonel of the recently disbanded Irish Regiment, the 121st. This sort of 'trading' arrangement was common practice in the army at the time and evoked no comment when Gisborne took over the colonelcy of the 16th in March 1766. If Draper had been able to foresee how soon the probity of the arrangement would be called into question by the sharp pen of Junius, he might have resisted the opportunity to improve his meagre income. At the end of the year, he received the even more tangible honour of the Knighthood of the Bath, gratifying to him personally but also as a tribute to the merit of the whole Manila expedition. His coat of arms included the motto *Vicit, Pepercit* ('He conquered, he spared') to mark his feelings about Manila.

Cornish, his fellow commander, who had taken no further command after his return from Manila, was granted a baronetcy in the following month. Shortly afterwards he became MP for Shoreham, which he continued to represent until his death in 1770, by which time he had also been promoted to Vice-Admiral. Despite his later jibe that he would never again accept joint command with a senior officer who negotiated in Latin, Cornish maintained regular contact with Draper and they were both involved early in 1766, cooperating with the Company, in the submission of a memorandum to the King seeking to speed any decision about the ransom. The document was presented to the King at a time when he was distracted by yet another ministerial crisis. Grenville's ministry, bedevilled since its formation in 1763 by its prolonged mishandling of the provocations of the maverick 'libertarian' politician John Wilkes, was replaced in July 1765 by a government headed by the taciturn, amiable, Marquis of Rockingham.

The King had nominated him reluctantly, recognising that he was unlikely to be able to handle the problems beginning to surface from the reaction of the American colonists to Grenville's Stamp Act. In justifying their opposition to the Act they enunciated the principle of 'no taxation without representation' and thereby focused on the broader issue of Parliament's right to legislate for the colonies. The first aggressive steps had been taken on the road to independence.

Rockingham was not sufficiently heavyweight to deal with a crisis of this magnitude. Political attention became focused once again on the possibility that William Pitt, whose absence from office since his resignation five years earlier had somehow increased his stature, might be persuaded to join a ministry of which he could be the effective leader. In the debate on the Stamp Act in the House of Commons in January 1766, which opened the way to its repeal shortly thereafter, he overwhelmed the House with a passionate appeal against the Act and in favour of colonial liberty.

As so often in Pitt's longer speeches, he covered other subjects of current concern, among these the Manila ransom and its continued denial by Spain, en passant paying tribute to Sir William Draper as 'Manila's gallant conqueror, basely traduced into a mean plunderer, a gentleman whose noble and generous spirit would do honour to the proudest grandee of this country'.[4]

Pitt was called to form a new ministry in July 1766, and became the Earl of Chatham. His term of office was, however, to prove almost disastrous, as he was almost immediately afflicted by lengthening periods of profound depression. Handling of government business became uncoordinated and within months of Chatham taking office, ministers were given, or took, the opportunity to promote their own policies in the absence of any dominating guidance.

Among the young ministers feeling their way through this muddle was the Earl of Shelburne who, as Secretary of State for the South, had inherited the problem of Spanish negotiations. Shelburne was then only twenty-nine, but his intellectual maturity was equal to the task of coping with Choiseul and Grimaldi who had assumed that Pitt's return to power could trigger the war for which they were preparing but were still unready.

Chatham instructed Shelburne to insist on immediate settlement of the outstanding claims of Britain against France and Spain. Shelburne, though anxious to maintain the spirit of the Treaty of Paris, informed Prince Masserano in London as early as August 1766 of the justice of the Manila claim in a pugnacious memorandum. Choiseul and Grimaldi chose to react coolly and, as Chatham's illness gradually paralysed the London government, the possibility of direct confrontation receded. Lord Rochford was moved from Madrid to be ambassador in Paris where his experience would be available at the focus of the real decisions.

The formal decision to link the Manila ransom dispute with that of the Falklands was taken by the Cabinet in October 1766. It followed the British refusal to accept a Spanish offer in July to submit the Manila issue to an arbitrator, the Spaniards having suggested King Frederick of Prussia as an arbitrator who would not be suspected of automatically siding with Spain. The British had refused this offer as compromising the dignity of the Crown; thereby stalling the proposal and incidentally adding to Frederick the Great's lingering resentment of Britain's attitude towards relations with himself and Prussia since the end of their wartime alliance.

Choiseul saw advantage in linking the two issues as a means of further protracting the negotiations. By November, the British were proposing that evacuation of Port Egmont would take place only after the Manila ransom had been paid and Spain had conceded to the British the freedom of navigation in the Southern Seas. The French then suggested that resolution of the problem could be achieved through British abandonment of the Falklands in exchange for payment of the ransom, subject to France's arbitration on the final amount. Shelburne insisted that there could be no arbitration either on the principle or the amount, but that its full payment would be accepted as a set-off for the immediate abandonment of the settlement at Port Egmont. There, for a few months, matters remained poised.

The London government's persistence in pursuing the Manila ransom was partly explained by the continuous pressure exerted by the East India Company. The Company, principally as a result of Clive's conquests, had moved to the forefront of political attention. Misgivings about the Company's transformation from a purely trading organisation to a quasi-sovereign entity, exercising power over large areas of India, had been gathering strength since the end of the war. As these complex matters were directly related to the guaranteed annual payment of £400,000 per year to the Government, the Company's views on matters such as the Manila ransom could not be ignored.

Clive himself had encapsulated the Company's overall attitude to the Manila venture in a letter he sent from the Cape of Good Hope on his return journey to India in January 1765, having received news of further trouble on the Indian coast:

> The Manila expedition has certainly proved a very unfortunate
> one for the East India Company, since it had given rise to a very
> powerful rebel, whom we have not yet been able to subdue with all
> our force on the coast of Coromandel, who has cost us not only the
> lives of numbers of private men but also of many gallant and brave
> officers.[5]

The Company was still years away from presenting its final bill for the Manila venture but was determined to maintain pressure and haggling over accounts between the Treasury, the Company and the representatives of the victors continued during 1766.

Continued public interest in Indian affairs was given an extra dimension of human tragedy during that year by the reporting of the trial and execution of the Comte de Lally in Paris, and the publication of his *Memoirs* in English. His misfortune had been protracted over the four years since he had arrived back in France in 1762 following his final defeat at Pondicherry. He had reached Paris to find himself being made a scapegoat for the collapse of French power in India. He was consigned to the Bastille, where he languished for three years while a Court of Enquiry was prepared. During his incarceration, he had time to write a full account of, and justification for, his actions in India. Even accepting that they were written as an apologia, referring to himself in the third person, they make painful reading. The long recital of all the hazards he faced in trying to coordinate the French ground forces, Admiral D'Aché's fleet, and the *Compagnie des Indes* bear a direct similarity to those faced by Cornish, Draper and the East India Company.

Lally's tale is one long shout of anger at his fate; though his adversaries argued that he made it inevitable through his own inadequacies. He accurately pinpointed the crucial importance of the French navy in the whole campaign, and in casting doubt on D'Aché's capabilities sought to share the blame with the Admiral. His accounts of the various phases of the French collapse were intermingled with constant repetition of the incompetence of a system which made no real provision for the payment of troops, or continuity of supplies. Most of his officers had to dig into their own pockets to stem the steady trickle of deserters, while the civil authorities at Pondicherry did almost nothing to assist the Royal French forces:

> It looks in a word as if during Count Lally's station in the Indies he, the Comte D'Aché, and M de Leyrit served three different masters. Count Lally could do nothing without the other; he could do nothing without money to pay his troops, and ships to favour their operations.[6]

He ended by describing the extreme ill-health he had suffered during the final months before the fall of Pondicherry, and the attempt by the *Compagnie* to have him assassinated as he was about to leave Pondicherry.

Lally's apologia was not sufficient to avert a fate which may in any case have been decided in advance on the cynical assumption that it would cause less trouble to blame the disaster on one of the Irish 'Wild Geese' than to make a scapegoat of an admiral from an old French family. The Court of Enquiry led to Lally being attainted, and subsequently convicted of having betrayed the interests of the King of France, his dominions, and the *Compagnie des Indes*. D'Aché was acquitted. Lally was shortly afterwards publicly executed in Paris, a handkerchief stuffed into his mouth to prevent him making any last declaration.

It was a humiliating death for a brave general who, for all his faults, had acted honourably in the service of his adopted country. The only natural justice to emerge eventually from this discreditable episode was that Voltaire, incensed by the wrong done to Lally, gave all the support of his intelligence and energy to Lally's son in his attempt to vindicate his father's reputation. In May 1778, twelve years after the trial and execution, as Voltaire lay on his death bed, news reached him from Lally's son that the King had annulled the judgement and cleared the general's reputation. Voltaire roused himself to dictate his last letter:

> The dying man revives on hearing the good news; he affectionately embraces M. De Lally; he sees the King is the defender of justice; he will die content.[7]

Lally's execution and the publication of his *Memoirs* stimulated considerable comment in London. Sir William wrote to the *Public Advertiser* agreeing with Lally's assertion that the lack of support received from the French navy on the Coromandel coast had been the crucial factor in his eventual defeat. Draper was writing from Clifton where he spent much of the year, enjoying some of the minor fruits of his knighthood and fame. He was presented with the Freedom of the City of Bristol in June 1766 at a ceremony in the Guildhall and also elected an Honorary Member of the Society of Merchant Venturers of Bristol in the same year. Like all semi-retired military figures he could not resist the habit of exercising authority, even if only at a local level, and shortly after his election to the Venturers was appointed as conservator of Clifton Down.

It appears that both he and Caroline were content to spend much of their time enjoying the rustic quietness of Clifton, their decision possibly dictated

10. Christopher Anstey (1724–1805), poet and author of the New Bath Guide in 1766, which brought him wide literary acclaim. He was a lifelong friend of William Draper, and their daughters were close in childhood. Anstey composed the epitaph to the 79th regiment, as well as Sir William's epitaph in Bath Abbey.

by his comparatively slender means. His house, Manila Hall, was the first place in which they could lead an undisturbed domestic life with some degree of comfort. Among their guests were his friend the poet Christopher Anstey who stayed at Clifton with his wife while composing the *New Bath Guide*, which, on its publication in 1766, brought Anstey immediate fame as a witty commentator on current social follies.

Both William and Caroline also found time to have their portraits painted by Thomas Gainsborough at Bath, shortly before the painter moved permanently to London. While Sir William's portrait is typical of the public depiction of a military figure displaying a degree of vanity and self-satisfaction, that of Caroline is more expressive of a reflective and private individual pondering her own thoughts.

She may simply have been wondering how her husband was going to pay for the two portraits. His half-pay from the swap with Colonel Gisborne, his pay as Governor of Yarmouth, and the residue of the £5,000 from the East India Company would still have left him a far from rich man. Although he and Caroline still had no children he had all the expenses of a household to maintain, and little prospect of any addition to his income. The Manila ransom issue was therefore to him, as to all his fellow survivors, a matter of direct personal importance.

During the latter part of 1766, as if to round off a phase in contrast to the melancholy fate of the Comte de Lally, his great adversary Stringer Lawrence finally retired, having survived twenty years of service in India and deservedly earned for himself the later appellation of 'Father of the Indian Army'. Lawrence returned safely to England and lived until 1775, dying only a few weeks after the suicide of his great protégé, Lord Clive. In the days when honours were sought by, and given to, so many men of lesser calibre and achievements it was strange that Lawrence never received public recognition for the contribution he had made to British settlement in India. The East India Company at least acknowledged its debt to him in the monument erected in Westminster Abbey, bearing the crisp inscription:

> For Discipline established, Fortresses protected, Settlements
> extended, French and Indian Armies defeated, and Peace restored in
> the Carnatic.

Lawrence, in retirement, though he made no public utterances on the subject, would have followed with detached interest the denouement of the Manila ransom issue, not least in justifying his sustained misgivings about the merit of the whole venture.

18

PUBLIC AND
PRIVATE CONCERNS

During 1767, the issue of the Manila ransom was allowed to slide into a diplomatic limbo from which it has never returned. There was no announcement to pinpoint the fact that the British and Spanish governments had reached a point where further discussions seemed fruitless, nor did either government officially concede that they had. The issue was simply allowed to recede into the past, overtaken by more pressing and more important concerns.

Breaking of the linkage between the Manila and Falklands issues marked an important point in the process. On 1 April, as agreed between Choiseul and Grimaldi, Bougainville formally handed over his settlement at Port Louis to the sovereignty of the Spanish, in the person of the Captain General of Buenos Aires.

The cession of the new colony from France to her ally allowed Choiseul to shift from his role as possible mediator on the Falklands and Manila issues to that of protagonist for Spain. More directly, it strengthened Spain's hand. There was no longer any need to balance payment of the Manila ransom as a quid pro quo for Britain quitting Port Egmont. Spain could now lay claim to sovereignty over the whole group of islands, which they immediately called Las Malvinas, without any matching concessions.

Some fast diplomatic footwork followed. Choiseul persuaded the Spaniards not to press their protests about the British presence at Port Egmont. Masserano in London informed the British government that Spain had no intention

157

of paying the ransom, but did not press the Spanish case on the Falklands. Shelburne, despairing of ever getting satisfaction on the Manila issue, judged the lack of further protests about the Falklands as compensation of any further claims about Manila. He found himself in a position where there was more to be gained than lost by allowing the issue to die an unannounced death.

Shelburne then manoeuvred the East India Company, during wider discussions, into becoming resigned to the reality that the ransom was never going to be paid, while leaving it free to seek compensation from the Spanish for the sums disbursed by Drake's administration on behalf of the Spanish in Manila.

This finally allowed Shelburne to brief the new Ambassador to Madrid, Sir James Gray, in June 1767 that when he arrived *en poste* in Madrid later in the year he should treat the Manila controversy as 'of minor consequence', while going through the formalities of 'strongly insisting on the undoubted rights of our subjects to the money remaining due'.[1] This instruction was not of course a matter of public knowledge. In Britain the subject could, and still did, arouse passions, particularly among those still nursing hopes of some final payout.

The *Scots Magazine* in particular kept the issue alive for its readers, and in October 1767 published a letter from a Madrid correspondent, coinciding with the arrival of the new British ambassador:

> Our politicians are at a loss to know what will be the result of
> the demand made by the British Ambassador for the payment of
> the Manila ransom. If the English court are really in earnest it is
> generally thought by those who pretend to be conversant with our
> court affairs that the Spanish court would rather pay it than venture
> another war with Great Britain. All I can say in this affair is that it
> should be immediately insisted upon ... If one may add this thought,
> I believe one or two ships to back the above demand would be more
> powerful intercessors.[2]

This appeal for a display of gunboat diplomacy to stimulate Spain's flagging interest alluded also to the expulsion of the Jesuits, a subject of intense current interest in Spain and the rest of Europe. The Jesuits had long held great spiritual and temporal power in Spain and their mission to spread Catholicism had been a main engine of Spain's imperial expansion. William Draper, in his *Plain Narrative* of the Manila expedition, had unquestioningly spelt out that:

> Manila ... is maintained by the Crown of Spain at the request of the
> Church for propagating the Christian faith ... for which they have
> a large annual allowance from Mexico, for the maintenance of their
> public officers and clergy, and for the support of their convents;
> they are also indulged with ships built and navigated at the King's
> expense to bring the said allowance in money: these ships go laden

with merchandise (a still further indulgence allowed them) from
Manila and Acapulco and return with money.[3]

This ecclesiastical and trading power rankled with Charles III of Spain to
the point where, in April 1767, a Royal proclamation suddenly banned
the Jesuits from Spain and its overseas settlements. The resultant furore
occupied statesmen, diplomats, and churchmen all over Europe, and puts into
perspective the context in which the Manila ransom issue was sent into a state
of suspended animation.

Public concern over any ransom settlement began to diminish in Britain
amidst more pressing worries over the ragged state of Chatham's ministry and
worsening friction with the American colonies. Although the administration
was nominally under the control of the Duke of Grafton, Chatham remained
the dominant presence, even when isolated by his deepening depression. His
absence from day-to-day work of government became increasingly a subject
of open debate and public comment.

The combative John Wilkes, still a thorn in the side of the Government and
enjoying his self-serving exile in France, published a pamphlet addressed to
Grafton casting strong doubts on Chatham's ability to continue as a minister.
This in turn produced a letter to the *Public Advertiser* in May 1767, strongly
defending Chatham and signed with the initials 'W. D.', a thin disguise for the
fact that the letter had been written by Sir William. His defence of Chatham
was then rebutted by the pseudonymous 'Poplicola', who concluded:

> I cannot admit that because Mr Pitt was respected and honoured a
> few years ago, the Earl of Chatham deserves to be now; or that a
> description which suited him in one part of his life must be the only
> one applicable to another.[4]

The fact that 'Poplicola' was an early pseudonym for the brilliant young
Philip Francis, son of Sir William's friend in Bath, the Reverend Philip Francis,
was relevant to the suggestions within two years that Philip Francis might be
identified as Junius, the anonymous scourge of the Government.

In the vacuum created by Chatham's illness, factional tensions began to
multiply, with Grafton unable to control the centrifugal momentum of his
colleagues. The paralysis of the Government over this period extended into
diplomatic channels, and the last positive move by the British to press the
Spanish government about the Manila ransom was in December 1767. Gray
wrote to Shelburne that:

> In a conversation I have had with the Marquis of Grimaldi on the
> Manila ransom I find the minister strongly confirmed of the injustice
> of our demand ... I am convinced that all discussion of this affair
> will only produce idle talk and continual altercations ... I have

therefore determined to present an office demanding payment of what remains.[5]

The final Spanish refusal came in February 1768 when Gray reported that Grimaldi's response to his 'office' was that Spain had no intention of paying the ransom because 'Article 21 of the Treaty of Paris had annulled all our claims to payment'. There was no further mention of the subject in diplomatic correspondence between Madrid and London. Six years of wrangling had been won by the King of Spain.

On a more mundane level, the Treasury and East India Company were still haggling over details of accounting, while the Treasury was also resisting the claims of some of the officers of the 79th who had had to cope with local crises in Manila in a way which could not be reconciled or probably even understood by the bureaucrats.

Realisation that all was possibly lost would not have seeped through to Sir William and his co-survivors for some months. During the time that Grimaldi was preparing his final rebuff to the ministry in London, Sir William was at Clifton, enjoying an exchange of gifts and poems between Christopher Anstey and himself. The poet, his friend from Eton days, sent Sir William a gift of Cottenham cheeses from his Cambridgeshire home accompanied by a long poem which included the lines:

> Something to eat I'll have you know it
> Is no small present from a poet
> And though I've took some little pains
> In weaving my Pindaric strains
> You're welcome, if my verse displeases
> To damn my book and eat my cheeses.[6]

The poem goes on to refer to the 'law's unjust delay' in giving the conqueror his reward, hoping that the muse will provide some consolation.

Anstey's gift brought a response from Sir William at Manila Hall in January 1768, in the form of a letter and accompanying poem. These are the sole surviving expressions of the genial side of his nature, and give an insight into the warmer dimensions of his character:

> In return for your very kind present I send you some very bad ones.
> I had a mind to try if, after 24 years interruption, I could again put
> my thoughts into metre; therefore you will wonder not so much
> at their mediocrity, as that I could write at all, since which I have
> hammered out a few for your perusal. To atone for which I beg your
> acceptance of some claret, not to bribe your approbation but as a
> kind remembrance of my friendship towards you and yours; as I
> can assure you with much truth and sincerity there is no man living

that I love and honour more than yourself. Your poetical talents are now so much admired that besides my private satisfaction I have a public vanity in boasting that the author of the *New Bath Guide* is my particular friend; that he has composed under my roof. Let me not despair of enjoying that happiness again ... Mrs Anstey is so interwoven with your happiness and so deservedly makes the chief part of it that to desire your company is to request hers of course. Caroline joins me in this request; her house is now very pretty but she cannot think it completely ornamented until you promise to grace it once more with your companies. By the 20th I shall be at General Peirson's in Hill Street, it would add to my pleasure to find your family in town ... Adieu, your affectionate friend.[7]

The accompanying poem of more than 100 lines opens with thoughts expressing Sir William's continuing dismay at his and Caroline's childless state in comparison with Anstey's large family. He alludes to 'the learned Glynn giving no hope'. Robert Glynn was then a fashionable apothecary and Fellow of King's Cambridge, who would doubtless have had more than his fair share of patients concerned with problems of fertility when venereal disease was so rife and effective cures so rare. Sir William's three daughters by his second marriage some years later indicate that the problem must have been more with Caroline than himself, but that in their ignorance they shared their dismay.

He goes on to suggest that:

> If it can amusement give
> Hear how your friend has learned to live
> His sword (its barbarous use forgot)
> Becomes the cook-maid's harmless lot
> To toast your cheese and scrape the paring
> Is all the merit it can share-in
> Manila's ransom quite forgetting
> It asks no more another whetting.
> By downy peace and rest undone
> Othello's occupation gone
> The squeaky fife and noisy drum
> No more shall drag him from his home
> No circumstance of glorious war
> Tempt him to mount Bellona's car
> His gentle spirit-lulling wife
> Comforts his mild decline of life ...
> Fortune alas begins to spread
> His thin grey mantle upon my head
> And with his much too serious play
> Steals beauty, manhood, wit away ...

> Contentment, peace, conjoined to health
> Supply the place of wretched wealth
> Hence more true joy my bosom warms
> Than e'er was felt from conquest's charms.

The poem takes the opportunity to express his thanks to Ligonier whom he obviously regarded as perhaps the foremost of his patrons and benefactors:

> Scarce Ligonier you more can know
> Whose heart with goodness taught to flow
> Sighs for occasions to bestow
> Fair Fortune's smiles; of human kind
> The friend to merit never blind.

The old Field-Marshal would probably never have seen this tribute to his talent for choosing young commanders of potential merit. He had finally retired with an earldom in 1766, aged eighty, and lived until 1770, his memories stretching back to the distant days of service under the great Duke of Marlborough in the early years of the century.

He was succeeded as Commander-in-Chief by the Marquis of Granby, heir to the Duke of Rutland, a dashing cavalry general who was deservedly the most popular soldier in the country. Granby's popularity arose not so much from his wartime exploits in Germany as because he had generously helped many of his impoverished soldiers after the war in setting up as publicans. The large number of pubs still named after the Marquis of Granby perpetuate his generosity.

Granby was much less of a political animal than Ligonier had been and was more at ease in the army messes or clubs than as an active politician. As an appointee of Chatham he nonetheless shared the growing concern that Chatham's illness was producing a dangerous sense of drift. Grafton's ministry was seen to be unable to deal with the many urgent problems of the day, not least those presented by the libertarian Wilkes, whose return to England had inflamed debate on the vast questions of parliamentary reform and political corruption.

Chatham finally resigned as Lord Privy Seal in October 1768, his first really decisive action in eighteen months. During his illness, his principal contact with the outside world had been his admirable wife, Hester, sister of George Grenville and Lord Temple, the only woman in British history to have been the sister, wife and mother of three Prime Ministers, though none formally bore that title. Hester had brought stability to Pitt's political and private life throughout the years of his greatness. A woman of outstanding intelligence and blessed serenity she shielded him from obtrusive pressures during his periods of illness, coping with all his correspondence and showing unruffled courtesy in the face of unceasing demands for her intercession with her agonised husband.

An example of her role as tactful interlocutor was the brief exchange of letters between herself and Sir William during June 1768, one of the many months in which Chatham was incapable of response on his own behalf. Sir William had written to Chatham seeking the statesman's approval to put a long adulatory inscription to Chatham on an obelisk he was erecting in his garden at Clifton. The idea would not have seemed strange to Chatham who had himself raised a similar monument in the grounds of his own house at Burton Pynsent in Somerset to its previous owner Sir William Pynsent.

Hester Chatham replied tactfully:

> Sir, My Lord continuing so much indisposed as to be quite unable to write is obliged to commit to me the pleasure of acknowledging the honour of your letter. He desires me to say he is truly touched with the too favourable and partial sentiments of one who is himself so justly the admiration of his country, and so distinguished an instrument of its glory. He begs me to add, as nothing can or ought to make him so proud as the testimony of Sir William Draper's private friendship, that he hopes Sir William will give him leave most earnestly to entreat that of an inscription so infinitely partial the last four lines alone may remain as conveying the honour he is so ambitious of. He trusts that Sir William will have the goodness to grant and to pardon the liberty of this request.[8]

The last four lines of the proposed inscription stated that the monument had been placed there as a testimony of private friendship and a monument of public honour. Draper responded to the Countess:

> I am honoured with Your Ladyship's letter. Lord Chatham shall be obeyed; but it is the first time in my life that I could almost wish to disobey his commands. I shall be most truly sorry if his delicacy has been offended by the former part of the inscription as it spoke only the sentiments of every person in the three kingdoms unconnected with faction, and the envy, malice and rage of party quarrels; nor will I scruple to affirm that it spoke the sense of every nation in Europe, even of those who have had the greatest reason to dread his superior genius and abilities, and have so severely felt the consequences.[9]

Hester Chatham continued the correspondence by asking Sir William to send a copy of the full text as:

> My Lord is not a little unhappy not to have in his private drawer, for his children hereafter, a composition of so much beauty dictated by the partiality, and written with the hand of, Sir William Draper;

which my mistake put into the letter to you. Give me leave to add the extreme interest I take in that paper and how sensibly I should share in the obligation if you would have the goodness to send it back to me.[10]

On returning it to Lady Chatham, Sir William added that its Latin text had been corrected and improved by Dr Barnard of Eton, whose 'wholesome severity had pruned the prolixity and luxuriances' of the proposed inscription.

Behind the courtesy of this exchange of compliments probably lay both Chatham's and Draper's understanding that the monument was not only an expression of gratitude for past recognition but of hope for further opportunity. The general was then still only forty-seven, fit enough to be a regular tennis player at Whitehall and in need of the income which a further period of active service would provide. Chatham, despite his illness, remained the commanding figure in the nation's political life. If he recovered his health, and it was assumed that he would, he might once again be called to further greatness as a war leader. Draper had much to bid for in his timely reminder to Chatham.

Indeed, within a few months of their exchange the likelihood of serious challenges to the Government's authority in America brought Sir William's name forward for a possible command in America. The policy for revenue collection in the colonies introduced by Charles Townshend had posthumously aroused a storm of opposition. Britain was beginning to suffer from the fact that the American colonies no longer needed the protection of the home government against the French.

The Government in London, via Lord Hillsborough, first holder of the new post of Secretary of State for the Colonies, decided it would be necessary to increase the royal forces in America. Knox, his Under-Secretary, writing to Grenville on 27 September 1768, commented:

> [T]he rendezvous of the troops is I learn at Halifax where there were three regiments collected, and the detachments from the Southern colonies which had arrived at New York were ordered from thence to Halifax; but whether they are to proceed directly to Boston or to await the arrival of the regiments from Ireland I do not know. I should think the latter, from an application having been made to Sir William Draper to go out with them to command the whole, but it seems the purpose was afterwards changed with regard to him … It is said a plan of accommodation had been proposed by Lord Chatham which will render all military proceedings unnecessary, and on that account it was not thought expedient to send Sir William with the troops.[11]

Chatham resigned a month later, his 'plan of accommodation' being absorbed into the wider attempts being made by Grafton's ministry to cope with the situation. Troops were eventually sent to Boston where their garrison presence contributed to popular disaffection as proof of British readiness to exercise arbitrary power.

Chatham's resignation had followed that of Lord Shelburne a few weeks earlier. In the subsequent reshuffle, a Cabinet post was given to Lord Rochford, promoted from his duties as Ambassador in Paris. Taking up his duties, Rochford brought the long experience of dealing with Spain and France, and his appointment was the *coup de grâce* to any further chances of the Manila ransom issue being resuscitated.

As if to confirm the certainty that the issue was now finally buried in the minds of the Spanish, James Harris, later 1st Lord Malmesbury, reported from the embassy in Madrid of his attendance at Charles III's court at Aranjuez on 29 April 1769 that 'Anda was there and kissed hands upon being appointed Commander of the Philippines and Captain General.'[12] The guerrilla leader had finally been accorded the dignities he had done so much to deserve, and the honour paid to him by his king was itself enough to signal that Charles III had never deviated from his intention of resisting all pressures to pay the ransom.

With Chatham and Shelburne departed, Grafton soldiered on, having lost the only two original minds in his Cabinet, in deference to the King's wishes and with a majority of his Cabinet members in favour of a coercive policy towards the American colonies.

In the lull before the storm in America, and in the diplomatic calm over Europe, Grafton's ministry was principally concerned with coping with the domestic political fallout of the Wilkes saga. The Falklands situation hardly impinged on the scene – and yet the Spanish government had already set in train the next initiative which was to lead to a full-scale diplomatic crisis within two years, a planned foray by the Captain-General in Buenos Aires, Bucareli, to expel the British. Because of the long lead-times and seasonal changes, his expedition only sailed in December 1769, and news of his foray took a further six months to reach England in mid-1770 to trigger a diplomatic crisis.

At the time that Bucareli was preparing for his Falklands venture, another small expedition was passing Buenos Aires en route to the South Seas and the epic discovery of Australia. Captain James Cook, in command of *Endeavour*, rounded Cape Horn in December 1768 on his way to the immortality of identifying the last unnamed continent. That honour, denied to him by his own obstinacy, could have belonged to the ubiquitous Alexander Dalrymple. He had returned to England from the Indies in 1765, seeking further support from the East India Company for new ventures. Publication of his *Account of the Discoveries in the South Pacific before 1764* led to his being proposed as leader of the forthcoming voyage whose principal objective was to observe the transit of Venus in the Southern Ocean in 1769. Dalrymple, however, still a Company servant, insisted on being given a commission as a captain in the Royal Navy, such as had been granted to Halley a century earlier. This demand was totally rejected by the First Lord of the Admiralty, Lord Hawke, who declared he would sooner have his right hand cut off than sign such a commission. So James Cook was given the command, while Dalrymple returned to the Indies and further research which led to his appointment years later in 1795 as the first hydrographer to the Admiralty; by which time his youthful explorations round the Sulu Sea, the China Coast, the Philippines and Manila must have seemed in the distant past.

While Dalrymple was thus absorbing the disappointment of being denied command of the *Endeavour* voyage, his fellow-enthusiast for the Manila expedition, William Draper, was undergoing a much more public humiliation as victim of the dismissive pen of Junius.

IV

LATE CHALLENGES
AND DISMAYS

11. *John Manners, Marquess of Granby (1721–1770),*
Commander in Chief at the time of the Junius Letters and earlier
a dashing cavalry commander. His generosity towards troops
after the end of the Seven Years War resulted in many public
houses around England being named in his memory.

19

JUNIUS CHALLENGED

The real identity of Junius, writer of the fiercest political invective of the eighteenth century in the *Letters of Junius*, has never been revealed. It was remarkable enough that he managed to avoid being pinned down in the years between 1768 and 1772 during which the seventy *Letters* appeared in the *Public Advertiser*, where the letters were the most urgent topic of London's political and social life. It is even more remarkable that the whole of the subsequent Junius 'industry' of historians, memoirists, graphologists and generations of literary detectives have been unable to arrive at any agreed conclusion. Most remarkable of all was that Junius, whoever he was, could resist the temptation of revealing his identity, even posthumously.

The principal purpose of the *Letters* was to shed savage light on the incompetence and malpractice of the Government of the day; to rebuke where rebuke was merited, even if that involved the King; and to measure the public figures of the day against standards from which they were lamentably departing. Junius, by the quality of his style and the depth of his inside knowledge of politics and government, could only have come from a tiny list of possible candidates.

In the furore caused by the *Letters*, the names of no fewer than fifty political figures were mentioned as the possible author, ranging from Chatham, Temple, George Grenville and Edmund Burke, through Horace Walpole, Edward Gibbon and Lord Chesterfield to mavericks like John Wilkes. Over the years, this widely varied list shrunk to four, and although evidence pointing towards the two most probable suspects, the Earl of Shelburne or Philip Francis, is more convincing than that towards Earl Temple or Hugh Boyd, nothing is certain. The mystery still remains to be solved.

Earl Temple, the most senior by age and experience, brother of George Grenville and brother-in-law of Chatham, has been suggested more for his affiliations and confidence in his own importance as a quarrelsome political heavyweight than for any evident talent. Shelburne, in contrast to Temple, had both talents and motive. Although still young, his recent tenure of office as a Secretary of State had given him experience and deep insight into the weaknesses of his erstwhile colleagues. His forced resignation from Grafton's ministry had given him the motive to seek revenge. He knew that his talent and ambition could lead to his return to office – as they did – but that anonymity as the author was essential to keep open that option. He had the choice either of biding his time, or using his talents and insider knowledge to hasten the collapse of a government he held in contempt. The short gap of three months between Shelburne's resignation in October 1768 and the first of the major Junius *Letters* in January 1769 could have been coincidental, but the timing was significant.

Philip Francis, who at the time of the *Letters* was about thirty, had already accumulated experience beyond his years as a diplomat, ministerial secretary, linguist, amanuensis to Pitt, and writer. He was a protégé of Henry Fox and of John Calcraft, who was a great friend of his father the Reverend Philip Francis, himself an active commentator. Calcraft, involved in some intrigue as always, was currently helping to create a coalition which might topple Grafton's discredited ministry. He maintained close relations with Philip Francis who was himself disenchanted with his post as First Clerk at the War Office which had yet to result in any significant promotion. Francis had the talent, motive, and a strong streak of malicious wit to arm him for a role which he had already undertaken under different pseudonyms.

Hugh Boyd, the last of the probable candidates, was a young Irish lawyer whose wit and talents had quickly earned him entree into literary and political circles in London. He was a frequent contributor to the *Public Advertiser*, a member of Edmund Burke's circle, and sufficiently well informed to equip him for the task of assailing the Government from the shelter of anonymity.

Whichever of the four may have been Junius, and it might not have been any of them, he was certainly not breaking new ground. The tradition of political invective and satire had flowered throughout the century. The advent of cheap printing and wider distribution had resulted in an explosion of newspapers, magazines and pamphlets accessible to the whole population; while the absence of libel laws and the general contentiousness of the age ensured a constant flow of public controversy. The practice of writing under a pseudonym, or initials, was widely accepted not least because it protected the writer from challenges to a duel from professional bounty hunters seeking revenge on behalf of aggrieved parties.

Junius, using that name, had written to Chatham a year before the first of his public letters, and one or two letters from Junius published at the end of 1768 failed to arouse any particular response. It was his letter of 21 January 1769 which created a public furore, not only because it attacked senior members of the Government with relentless vigour, but also because it drew an immediate response from a respected non-political figure, Sir William Draper.[1]

The attack opened along the lines that 'the situation in this country is alarming enough to rouse the attention of every man who pretends to a concern for the public welfare,' and that 'it is the pernicious hand of government, which alone can make a people desperate ... We need only mark how the principal departments of the state are bestowed, and look no farther for the true cause of every mischief which befalls us.'

The attack then fell on specific targets: on Grafton as First Lord of the Treasury; North as Chancellor of the Exchequer; Hillsborough and Weymouth as Secretaries of State. Junius then turned his fire on the Marquis of Granby, as Commander-in-Chief, for no reason other than that he was a member of the Government. Granby had little pretension to being a political figure, nor any intention of tackling the rampant inefficiencies of the army system. His undoubted stature and popularity would normally have left him impervious to the scratches of a political dart-thrower:

> It has lately been a fashion to pay a compliment to the bravery
> and generosity of the commander-in-chief, at the expense of his
> understanding. They who love him least make no question of
> his courage, while his friends dwell chiefly on the facility of his
> disposition. Admitting him to be as brave as a total absence of
> all feeling and reflection can make him, let us see what sort of
> merit he derives from the rest of his character. If it be generosity
> to accumulate in his own person and family a number of lucrative
> employments; to provide, at the public expence, for every creature
> that bears the name of Manners; and neglecting the merit and
> services of the rest of the army, to heap promotions upon his
> favourites and dependants, the present commander-in-chief is the
> most generous man alive. Nature has been sparing of her gifts to
> this noble lord; but where birth and fortune are united, we expect
> the noble pride and independence of a man of spirit, not the servile,
> humiliating complaisance of a courtier ... And if the discipline
> of the army be in any degree preserved, what thanks are due to
> a man, whose cares, notoriously confined to filling up vacancies,
> have degraded the office of commander-in-chief into a broker of
> commissions ...?

In the canon of contemporary insults, this would hardly have caused comment, particularly since it was embedded within an attack on ministers of greater importance. Junius moved on from Granby to stab at Hawke at the Admiralty and Mansfield as Lord Chief Justice.

This first *Letter* made no points which could not have been made by the small army of scribes always ready in London to hire their talents to the highest bidder. There were no revelations from an obvious insider, no damaging facts exposed and, most important, no absolute need for a response.

Onto this dangerous ground, uninvited, ventured Sir William, with a response limited to the defence of Granby. He had obviously discussed it in advance with the Reverend Philip Francis in Bath, for Francis, writing to his son Philip from there on 28 January said:

> My love to Mr Calcraft. Tell him he is to expect a very spirited and honourable defence of L--- G----y from our friend Sir W-----m D----r. I truly honour him for it.[2]

There is no evidence that Granby was ever consulted by Draper before he sent his response. Although they were contemporaries at Eton and Cambridge, members of White's, and would have known each other as senior officers, their military careers had never been close enough to make them brother officers. They were both attached to the Duke of Bedford's broad political faction and, in defending Granby, Sir William might have felt that he was somehow repaying a debt of gratitude to Bedford. He could also have thought that by coming unasked to Granby's defence he would have earned the gratitude of his Commander-in-Chief. He might have been lured into responding to Junius through his vanity, as a Fellow of King's, in believing that he might outwit the anonymous scribe. He might simply have felt that the honour of the army demanded a reply and that he was prepared to risk delivering it. Whatever his motives, his undoubted courage invited and attracted the ensuing personal disaster.

In his reply to Junius, Sir William, writing under his own name in a style as florid and lengthy as that of Junius, limited himself to defending Granby, but dangerously aroused Junius's ire by diverting him from more important targets to concentrate on others in whom he had no real interest but who now had to be dismissed before he could return to the main line of his attack.

Sir William, opening his response with the assertion that it was 'the duty of every good citizen to stand forth and undeceive the public when the vilest arts are made use of to defame the brightest characters', went on:

> A very long, uninterrupted, impartial, I will add, a most disinterested friendship with Lord Granby, gives me the right to assert that all Junius's exertions are false and scandalous ... Can a man, who is described as unfeeling, and void of reflection, be constantly employed in seeking proper objects on whom to exercise those glorious virtues of compassion and generosity? The distressed officer, the soldier, the widow, the orphan, and a long list besides, know

that vanity has no share in his frequent donations; he gives because he feels their distresses. Nor has he ever been rapacious with one hand to be bountiful with the other; yet this uncandid Junius would insinuate, that the dignity of the commander-in-chief is depraved into the base office of a commission broker; that is, Lord Granby bargains for the sale of commissions; for it must have this meaning, if it has any at all. But where is the man living who can justly charge his Lordship with such mean practices ...?[3]

Going on to say that Granby is next attacked for being unfaithful to his promises and engagements he asks:

Where are Junius's proofs? Although I could give some instances, where a breach of promise would be a virtue, especially in the case of those who would pervert the open, unsuspecting moments of convivial mirth into sly, insidious applications for preferment, or party systems, and would endeavour to surprise a good man, who cannot bear to see anyone leave him unsatisfied, into unguarded promises. Lord Granby's attention to his own family and relations is called selfish. Had he not attended to them, when fair and just opportunities presented themselves, I should have thought him unfeeling and devoid of reflection indeed. How are any man's relations and friends to be provided for, but from the influence and protection of the patron? It is unfair to suppose that Lord Granby's friends have not as much merit as the friends of any other great man: if he is generous at the public expense, as Junius invidiously calls it, the public is at no more expense for his Lordship's friends, than it would be if any other set of men possessed those offices.

It was an interesting proof of the accepted rules of contemporary patronage that Sir William should spell out, with no embarrassment, the rhetorical question, 'How are any man's relations and friends to be provided for, but from the influence of the patron?' The question did not even evoke a response from Junius, though it touched on the very core of the army system.

Sir William finished his defence on the professional military point that Granby's period as Commander-in-Chief had not led to a 'mouldering away' of the army, accusing Junius of 'strong assertions without proof, declamation without argument, and violent censures without dignity or moderation'.

The Reverend Philip Francis, writing to his son from Bath on 5 February commented in a PS:

I really honour Sir William as I know the motives of his writing. *Quis non defendit, alio culpante.* I wish his letter had been shorter.[4]

Sir William probably shared that thought a few days later when Junius returned to savage his challenger, addressing him directly:

> Your defence of Lord Granby does honour to the goodness of your
> heart. You feel, as you ought to do, for the reputation of your friend,
> and you express yourself in the warmest language of your passions.
> In any other cause, I doubt not, you would have weighed cautiously
> the consequences of committing your name to the licentious
> discourses and malignant opinions of the world. But here, I presume,
> you thought it would be a breach of friendship to lose one moment
> in consulting your understanding; as if an appeal were no more than
> a military *coup de main*, where a brave man has no rules to follow,
> but the dictates of his courage. Touched with your generosity, I freely
> forgive the excesses into which it has led you ...

> You begin with a general assertion that writers such as I are the real
> cause of all the public evils we complain of ... A little calm reflection
> might have shown you that national calamities do not arise from the
> description but from the real character and conduct of the ministers
> ... if commerce languishes, if public credit is threatened with a new
> debt, and your own Manila ransom most dishonourably given up, it
> had all been owing to the malice of political writers ... But it seems
> you are a little tender of coming to particulars. Your conscience
> insinuated to you, that it would be prudent to leave the characters of
> Grafton, North, Hillsborough, Weymouth and Mansfield to shift for
> themselves; and truly, Sir William, the part you *have* undertaken is at
> least as much as you are equal to.[5]

Having thus contemptuously signalled the level at which he intended to continue the exchange, Junius launched into a series of rhetorical questions and jibes about Granby's conviviality, and the current state of the army, none of which, even if answered, would have added to Granby's reputation. Turning from matters of genuine public concern, Junius then impaled Sir William himself:

> Permit me now, Sir William, to address myself personally to you,
> by way of thanks for the honour of your correspondence. You are
> by no means undeserving of notice; and it may be of consequence,
> even to Lord Granby to have it determined, whether or no the man,
> who has praised him so lavishly, be himself deserving of praise.
> When you returned to Europe, you zealously undertook the cause
> of that gallant army, by whose bravery at Manila your own fortune
> had been established. You complained, you threatened, you even
> appealed to the public in print. By what accident did it happen, that

in the midst of all this bustle, and all these clamours for justice to
your injured troops, the name of the Manila ransom was suddenly
buried in a profound, and, since that time, an uninterrupted silence?
Did the ministry suggest any motives to you, strong enough to
tempt a man of honour to desert and betray the cause of his fellow-
soldiers? Was it that blushing ribband which is now the perpetual
ornament of your person? Or was it that regiment, which you
afterwards (a thing unprecedented among soldiers) sold to colonel
Gisborne? Or was it that government, the full pay of which you are
contented to hold, with the half-pay of an Irish colonel? And do you
now, after a retreat not very like that of Scipio, presume to intrude
yourself, unthought-of, uncalled-for, upon the patience of the public?
Are your flatteries of the commander-in-chief directed to another
regiment, which you may again dispose of on the same honourable
terms? We know your prudence, Sir William, and I should be sorry
to stop your preferment.

This series of questions, all loaded with malice, could only have come from
someone familiar with the sequence of events since the Manila expedition.
Sir William must now have realised that he was trapped; either reduced to
silence with his reputation and honour undermined, or forced to respond to
an opponent more menacing than he had foreseen.

The Reverend Philip Francis, writing to his son a day or two after the
publication of this letter, by which time Sir William's plight was as widely
known in Bath as in London, said:

Poor Sir William. I am glad he is gone to Clifton where he may
eat his own heart in peace. So sensible to friendship, what he must
suffer in his feelings for his own reputation. When he repeated some
passages in his letter to me I bid him prepare his best philosophy for
an answer. But who is this devil Junius? ... Poor Sir William.[6]

The thought apparently never crossed the mind of the Reverend Francis that
his own son could well have been Junius. It seems also that Draper never
conjectured that his antagonist might have been the younger Francis, though
he must have been tantalised by Junius's allusion to his retreat at Clifton, and
to his vanity in always wearing the ribbon of the Order of the Bath.

Draper's presence in Clifton, at a time when he might have wished to
be closer to events in London, could well have been explained by the fact
that, on 7 February, Caroline made her will, although she was not to die for
another seven months. The will, a very simple one, left everything to 'my dear
husband Sir William and his lawful heirs', thus expressing the generous hope
that he might in time produce children by another wife. The witnesses to her
will were his niece Anna Collins, wife of Navy captain Richard Collins who

commanded *Weymouth* at Manila, and one of her Drummond in-laws who helped her financial affairs.[7] The 'sweet spirit-lulling' Caroline would then have been near her fortieth year of a life of fragile health.

Sir William meanwhile chose the courageous option of replying to Junius on 17 February. He returned to his defence of Granby and in trying also to salvage his own reputation he gave a subjective insight into the events of the previous decade and the accepted military mores of the time:

> Junius tells me, that, at my return, I zealously undertook the cause of the gallant army by whose bravery at Manila my own fortune was established; that I complained, that I even appealed to the public. I did so; I glory in having done so, as I had an undoubted right to vindicate my own character, attacked by a Spanish memorial, and to assert the rights of my brave companions. I glory likewise that I have never taken up the pen but to vindicate the injured. Junius asks by what accident did it happen that in the midst of all this bustle, and all these clamours for justice to the injured troops the Manila ransom was suddenly buried ... I will explain ...

> The several ministers who have been employed since that time have been very desirous to do justice for two most laudable motives, a strong inclination to assist injured bravery, and to acquire a well-deserved popularity to themselves. Their efforts have been in vain. Some were ingenuous enough to own, that they could not think of involving this distressed nation in another war for our private concerns. In short, our rights for the present are sacrificed to the national convenience; and I must confess that although I may lose five-and-twenty thousand pounds by their acquiescence to this breach of faith in the Spaniards, I think they are in the right to temporize, considering the critical state of this country ... Lord Shelburne will do me justice to own that, in September last, I waited upon him with a joint memorial from Admiral Sir S. Cornish and myself, in behalf of our injured companions. His lordship was as frank upon the occasion as other secretaries had been before him. He did not deceive us by giving any immediate hopes of relief.[8]

Sir William thus confirmed that as late as September 1768 he and Cornish still entertained hopes that the ransom might eventually be paid, probably not knowing that Gray in Madrid had already abandoned hope. At least Shelburne had been honest enough to hold out no real chance for satisfaction.

Draper then finished by referring directly to his own position, rejecting in detail the implications that he had been bribed by honours and appointments to keep silent on the Manila ransom, and ending 'If this be bribery; it is not the bribery of these times.'

Junius had a need to gratify some fury aroused by the hapless Sir William and returned to the attack later in February, turning his knife on the embarrassment Sir William had caused to Granby, and going on to savage Draper's reputation even further:

> After selling the companions of your victory in one instance, and after selling your profession in the other, by what authority do you presume to call yourself a soldier. The plain evidence of facts is superior to all declarations. Before you were appointed to the 16th regiment, your complaints were a distress to government; – from that moment you were silent. You insinuate to us that your ill state of health obliged you to quit the service. The retirement necessary to repair a broken constitution would have been as good a reason for not accepting, as for resigning the command of a regiment ... In exchange for your regiment you accepted of a colonel's half-pay (at least 220 l. a year) and an annuity of 200 l. for your own and Lady Draper's life jointly ... And is this the losing bargain, which you would represent to us, as if you had given up an income of 800 l. a year for 380 l. ? Was it decent, was it honourable, in a man who pretends to love the army and calls himself a soldier, to make a traffic of the royal favour, and turn the highest honour of an active profession into a sordid provision for himself and his family? It were unworthy of me to press you farther. The contempt with which the whole army heard of the manner of your retreat, assures me, that as your conduct was not justified by precedent, it will never be thought an example for imitation.[9]

The depth of Junius's knowledge about the relatively unimportant details of Sir William's financial arrangements as well as the procedures relating to half-pay could have been known to either Philip Francis or Shelburne, as indeed to others in government, but it needed a well-informed advocate to simulate outrage about a practice so commonly in use, the sale and transfer of commissions. When Junius said 'your conduct was not justified by precedent' he was simply ignoring the reality around him. Gisborne's arrangement with Draper had aroused no comment at the time it took place; it was so common as to be unremarkable; but Junius had the forensic skill to examine it as if it were some new virus.

Junius finished his letter to Sir William with a question as to whether, in receiving his half-pay, he took an oath that he did not actually hold another office of profit under the Crown. The question related to Sir William's governorship of Yarmouth, and its implication of perjury could not be ignored. The tone of Sir William's short reply[10] matched the words about his life and conduct being put on the rack, as in refuting the implication of perjury he went into details of his financial arrangements. Recitation of the details of Sir William's sparse income would not have proved too embarrassing in an age when there was a general obsession about money and no reticence in discussing it, but the brevity of the letter indicated a writer dismayed by recognition of his own folly in embarking on his challenge. His dismay must have become almost intolerable when Junius produced yet another letter in March casting doubts both on the General's motives and conduct in relation to his own half-pay transaction. Junius ended his serpentine demolition of Sir William's case by bidding him farewell:

> And now, Sir William, I shall take my leave of you for ever. Motives
> very different from any apprehension of your resentment make
> it impossible you should ever know me. In truth, you have some
> reason to hold yourself indebted to me. From the lessons I have
> given you, you may collect a profitable instruction for your future
> life. They will either teach you so to regulate your conduct, as to
> be able to set the most malicious enquiries at defiance; or, if that
> be a lost hope, they will teach you prudence enough not to attract
> attention to a character, which will only pass without censure when
> it passes without observation.[11]

Sir William could only have been devastated by the dismissive finality of Junius's leave-taking. He was left not only with taking the blame for causing embarrassment to Granby but with the difficult task of restoring himself to the esteem in which he had been held before his imprudent intervention. Both in relation to the Manila ransom, and to the later colonelcy of the 16th Foot, he had given Junius the opportunity to raise unnecessary questions, and in doing so called into question his own judgement both as an individual and as a senior officer still fit for future command.

The exchange of letters with Junius simultaneously produced correspondence from other writers, one signed 'An Half Pay Subaltern'. His letter called upon Sir William to 'stand forth in the behalf of the much distressed Officers now upon half pay'. Sir William queried, in the *Public Advertiser* of 1 May, how a 'person out of Parliament who has long retired from the great World … can be of much use to those gallant and distressed gentlemen to whom I have the greatest obligation'. He went on to make a crucial revelation; one that hitherto had never been mentioned; that Archbishop Rojo had tried to bribe him after the conquest:

> I here most solemnly declare, that I never received either from the
> East India Company, or from the Spaniards, directly or indirectly,
> any *present or gratification*, or any circumstance of emolument
> whatsoever, to the Amount of Five Shillings, during the whole course
> of the expedition, or afterwards, my Legal Prize Money excepted.
> The Spaniards know that I refused the Sum of Fifty Thousand

Pounds offered me by the Archbishop, to mitigate the terms of
the Ransom, and reduce it to Half a Million, instead of a whole
one. So that, had I been disposed to have basely sold the Partners
of my Victory, Avarice herself could not have wished for a richer
opportunity.[12]

The revelation that he had resisted the temptation of such an enormous bribe
– which would have put him in the same league as the victors of Havana – at
least served to muffle any further criticism. He guarded his silence during
the summer of 1769, enveloped in the chagrin of a soldier suffering from
self-inflicted wounds. The misery of that summer was compounded by the
death of Caroline at Clifton early in September after thirteen years of happy
but childless marriage. She was buried at St Augustine the Less at Bristol,
leaving him isolated at Clifton with the additional burden of contemplating
how much his public debacle might have weakened her resolve to live, with its
damage to her Beauclerk family pride.

20

JUNIUS
REVISITED

Junius, having despatched the unfortunate Sir William to the outer edges of the battlefield, then concentrated his full attack on the Government, particularly the Duke of Grafton as First Lord of the Treasury. Grafton, an easygoing aristocrat more interested in racing than politics, was simply not equipped either by nature or talent to handle the restlessness caused simultaneously by John Wilkes and Junius on top of the Government's other problems.

The *Letters* addressed to Grafton during the rest of the summer of 1769 deserve to be read in full to do justice to their glittering and accurate malice. Grafton and other senior figures in the Government avoided the mistake of trying to respond to Junius, but their silence was itself used by him as proof of the validity of his accusations. Behind the sharpness of the style lay the strength of a perceptive mind accurately focusing on the Government's mishandling of the key issues.

Junius was not alone in fomenting an atmosphere of political unrest. Licence rather than liberty seemed the order of the day and, in the absence of effective libel laws, the newspapers and magazines were only too willing to print any outrageous libels which came their way. There was a constant demand for wider circulation of the more notorious publications, which printers were only too eager to satisfy. Early in September 1769, Junius took the initiative of republishing a collected series of the *Letters*, including his earlier exchanges with Sir William.

Almost unbelievably, the General could not resist the urge to defend his conduct once again, and put himself on the rack for a final exchange of four letters. He opened by coming straight to the point which distressed him most:

> Having accidentally seen a *republication* of your letters wherein you have been pleased to *assert* that I had sold the companions of my success; I am again obliged to declare the said assertion to be a most *infamous* and *malicious falsehood*, and I *again* call upon you to stand forth, avow yourself, and *prove* the charge.[1]

Protesting that the colonelcy of the 16th had not bought his silence, he then challenged Junius to reveal his identity, implying he would be prepared to fight a duel to defend his soldier's honour. Junius, in response, expressed surprise at the whole issue being aired again, and logically countered the General:

> Had you been originally and without provocation attacked by an anonymous writer, you would have had some right to demand his name. But in this cause you are a volunteer ... After voluntarily attacking me under the character of Junius, what possible right have you to know me under any other? Will you forgive me if I insinuate to you, that you foresaw some honour in the apparent spirit of coming forward in person, and that you were not quite indifferent to the display of your literary qualifications? ...
>
> Your appeal to the sword, though consistent enough with your late profession, will neither prove your innocence, nor clear you from suspicion. Your complaints with regard to the Manila ransom were, for a considerable time, a distress to government. You were appointed (greatly out of your turn) to the command of a regiment, and *during that administration* we heard no more of Sir William Draper ... Your solicitations were, I doubt not, renewed under *another* administration. Admitting the fact, I fear an indifferent person would only infer from it, that experience had made you acquainted with the benefits of complaining ...
>
> Take care, Sir William, how you indulge this unruly temper, lest the world should suspect that conscience has some share in your resentments. You have more to fear from the treachery of your own passions than from the malevolence of mine.[2]

Junius meanwhile, in an entirely separate *Letter*, launched a fierce attack on the Duke of Bedford. He, though still formidable as a Whig heavyweight, no longer held any office and was suffering from advancing age and the recent death of his only son, the Marquess of Tavistock, in a hunting accident.

Bedford at the time was believed to be manoeuvring for return to high office and for additional ministerial posts for his political faction.

Junius was out to undermine this effort. He used the Duke's role as chief negotiator of the Treaty of Paris to reawaken the rumours which had circulated at the time – that Bedford had been bribed by the French. He moved on to sneer at the Duke's political gyrations and current bid for power, going on to chide him as a person incapable even of showing sorrow at the death of his son. Though the virulence of the attack on such a political heavyweight added to the furore surrounding Junius, there were few prepared to rush to the Duke's defence. An imperious figure, he had quarrelled at one time with all his political friends, allies and adversaries; and his strong opposition to Wilkes's libertarian posturings, as well as to wider freedom for American colonists, had earned him the hostility normally reserved for more ruthless politicians. Also, Junius's letter contained so much that was close to the truth, or at least current gossip, that it would have required a skilled and calm advocate to restore some balance on behalf of the Duke. The last thing Bedford needed was another overheated response from Sir William Draper on his behalf.

Sir William wrote again on 7 October, attempting to reject Junius's vague accusations against the Duke but with an equal vagueness which did nothing to nail the lies, and came up with the two-edged suggestion that:

> Potent as he is, the Duke is amenable to justice; if guilty, punishable. The parliament is a high and solemn tribunal for matters of such great moment. To that be they submitted. But I hope also that some notice will be taken of, and some punishment inflicted upon, false accusers, especially on such, Junius, who are *wilfully false*.[3]

Following this bizarre notion, which would have done little to comfort the Duke, Sir William at least ended with an accurate forecast that the long-term effect of Junius's letters would be of less profound importance than seemed likely at the time of their publication.

Within a week, Junius came back with a *Letter*, not addressed to Sir William but to the printer of the *Public Advertiser*. He produced a dismissal which must have been as enjoyable for him to write as it was painful for Sir William to read, and which even in extracts still has the power to convey how completely he had overcome his imprudent adversary:

> If Sir William's bed be a bed of torture, he has made it for himself. I shall never interrupt his repose ... Leaving his private character and conduct out of the question, I shall consider him merely in the capacity of an author, whose labours certainly do no discredit to a newspaper.

We say, in common discourse, that a man may be his own enemy, and the frequency of the fact makes the expression intelligible. But that a man should be the bitterest enemy of his friends, implies a contradiction of a peculiar nature. There is something in it, which cannot be conceived without a confusion of ideas, nor expressed without a solecism in language. Sir William Draper is still that fatal friend that Lord Granby found him. Yet I am ready to do justice to his generosity; if indeed it be not something more than generous, to be the voluntary advocate of men, who think themselves injured by his assistance, and to consider nothing in the cause he adopts, but the difficulty of defending it.[4]

He referred back to the General's outrage at his remarks about Bedford's alleged lack of feeling on his son's death, and contrived to score a point which proved not least that he was familiar with Sir William's family life:

Had *he* been a father he would have been but little offended with the severity of the approach, for his mind would have been filled with the justice of it. He would have seen that I did not insult the feelings of a father, but the father who felt nothing. He would have trusted to the evidence of his own paternal heart, and boldly denied the possibility of the fact, instead of defending it. Against whom then will this honest indignation be directed, when I assure him, that this whole town beheld the Duke of Bedford's conduct, upon the death of his son, with horror and astonishment? ... After all, as Sir William may possibly be in earnest in his anxiety for the Duke of Bedford, I should be glad to relieve him from it. He may rest assured that this worthy nobleman laughs, with equal indifference, at *my* reproaches and Sir William's distress about him.

Having again dismissed Draper's points in favour of Bedford he ended with his final expression of contempt:

I have a heavier charge against Sir William Draper. He tells us that the Duke of Bedford is amenable to justice; – that parliament is a high and solemn tribunal; and that if guilty he may be punished by due course of law; and all this, he says, with as much gravity as if he believed every word of the matter. I hope indeed, the day of impeachments will arrive, before this nobleman escapes out of life; – but to refer us to that mode of proceeding now, with such a ministry, and such a house of commons as the present, what is it, but an indecent mockery of the common sense of the nation? I think he might have contented himself with defending the greatest enemy without insulting the distresses of the country.

His concluding declaration of his opinion, with respect to the present condition of affairs, is too loose and undetermined to be of any service to the public. How strange it is that this gentleman should dedicate so much time and argument to the defence of worthless or indifferent characters while he gives but seven solitary lines to the only subject which can deserve his attention, or do credit to his abilities.

The 'solitary lines' had been remarks about the present state of the Government, but even if they had been more forceful they would have done nothing more to protect Sir William from ending as the victim of his own misplaced courage or vanity. There was no escape from this public humiliation, and no safe retreat from the lines of print which were to haunt him for the rest of his life.

The only consolation he could possibly have gained from his impetuous foray, a sort of verbal parallel to his sally years before from the Fort at Madras, was that it never led to any subsequent queries about the validity of his own case or the merits of his actions. He may have been acknowledged as architect of his own misfortune, but no worse. His willingness to engage Junius was broadly taken as proof that he had nothing to hide, and the lashing he had brought upon himself was ultimately not justified by examination of the truth behind the arguments.

Whoever Junius was, he was obviously close enough to the details of the ransom affair to relish the chance of venting his wrath on the very person who had caused all the aggravation in the first place. There are few supplicants as annoying as those with a seemingly just cause about which nothing can be done. Junius's evident concentration on the task of demolishing a lightweight military opponent suggested that he had a deep personal involvement, and pleasure, in savaging the general.

Lord Shelburne, having endured years of inconclusive haggling with the Spanish and French on post-expedition matters would have enjoyed the opportunity, if indeed he were Junius, of expressing his frustrations. Similarly, Philip Francis, both from his experience at the War Office and because of Sir William's closeness to his father, was well placed to strike with malicious authority and seems to have been a writer quite prepared to override the normal dictates of family friendship in search of advantage.

Hugh Boyd's qualifications for being identified were less convincing than those of either Shelburne or Francis, but he had apparently come to know Sir William in 1769 when they regularly played tennis at Whitehall, he then aged twenty-three against the General's forty-eight. An anecdote in Boyd's biography sheds light not only on the possibility that Boyd might have been Junius, but also on the generous quality of Sir William's nature:

Some months after the letters of Junius were published collectively Boyd met Sir William at the tennis court where, both being great tennis players, they often used to meet. Sir William observed that though Junius had treated him with great severity he now looked upon him as a very honest fellow and that there was no man with whom he would more gladly drink a bottle of old Burgundy. Boyd took no apparent notice of this observation but after playing tennis until a late hour he proposed to Sir William that they might dine together at a favourite tavern. The knight readily consented to this proposal and he enjoyed his Burgundy while Boyd had the inward satisfaction of doing justice to his candour as well as his wishes.[5]

Anecdotes being notoriously unreliable as evidence, this says less about Boyd possibly being Junius than about the resilience of the soldier in the aftermath of his misfortune as well as his ability to play tennis at an age when so many of his contemporaries had succumbed to the ravages of gout.

In the wake of Junius's sweeping dismissal, Sir William was given some public support from his old friend Christopher Anstey, who produced for the *Cambridge Chronicle* on 24 October a consoling poem including the lines:

Draper whose early fortitude and truth
First warmed my soul with friendship's generous flame
Say what avails it in adventurous youth
Thou led Britannia's sons to deathless fame.[6]

Despite his preoccupation with his savaging at the pen of Junius and his mourning the death of Caroline, Sir William did not withdraw into a self-absorbed melancholy, however embarrassed he might have felt. He found time to be involved in helping to mend a rift within the Townshend family during those months, which again showed how closely attached he was to the family.

The rift, with attendant elements of farce, centred around Audrey Townshend, sister of his brother-officer Viscount George Townshend. Audrey had been estranged from her family because of a runaway marriage to a Captain Robert Orme, a worthy young officer but of no fortune, and below the expectations of Audrey's mother Lady Townshend.

The estrangement had been made much worse earlier in 1769. Audrey's involvement in an unseemly fracas at the Pump Room at Bath, during the election of a new Master of Ceremonies, had been the subject of a widely circulated cartoon called *Female Intrepidity*, bringing shame to the Townshend family. Mrs Harris, mother of the future Earl of Malmesbury, reported on the affair:

There has been a most violent combustion at Bath. I am not clear as to the particulars, but there was a prodigious riot last Tuesday night in which the ladies joined as well as the gentlemen. Mrs Hill, our acquaintance, and Mrs Orme, Lady Townshend's daughter, had a fight and Mrs Hill was knocked down; in short things were carried to such a pitch that the Mayor, his brethren, and a number of constables entered the room. The Riot Act was read three times, 'tis said the last reading was to the ladies only.[7]

Although Mrs Orme's mother, Lady Townshend, herself continued to lead a notoriously rackety life, her daughter's involvement in a brawl, albeit in the fashionable surroundings of the Pump Room, compounded her mother's anger with her daughter. Sir William, as a friend of the family, appears to have acted in the role of conciliator, for, in October, Audrey Orme, writing to her forgiving sister-in-law the younger Lady Townshend, said:

> I have long wished for an occasion to write to you, but the restraint of all my family, except that of my poor brother Charles, was so great that it deterred me from making any other application, but Sir William Draper was so feeling and humain as to have at heart a family reconciliation filled me with joy at his account of your great benevolence, compassion and good will … and I also beg of you, dear madam, to use all your influence upon my brother to forgive me and my children [8]

Sir William's intervention produced a partial reconciliation, but the older Lady Townshend never fully forgave her daughter for her runaway marriage.

While these more personal involvements took up much of his time, Sir William was still involved in the slow postscripts to the Manila expedition circulating around the recesses of the Government and the East India Company. The Company, having finally given up hope over the ransom, had calculated by 1768 that its disbursement on the expedition had been over £200,000; and it looked to the Treasury for reimbursement in agreement with the original terms of the expedition. It looked, as with so many others dealing with the Treasury before and since, largely in vain.

The directors were well aware that the Grafton administration was tottering under the triple burdens of the Wilkes upheavals, the later Junius letters which were an agony for Grafton as an individual as much as a minister, and the increasingly fractious situation in America. On 10 December 1769, Junius wrote his infamous *Letter* addressed directly to the King. It attacked George III initially as victim of the incompetence of his self-seeking advisers and ministers, but then called upon him to face up to his kingly responsibilities. The King's wrath at being impotent in the face of such provocation hastened the collapse of the Government early in the next year, its problems exacerbated by the political resurgence of Chatham who had recovered his mental stability during the year since his resignation and now looked upon the hapless Grafton as a deserter from the principles for which Chatham had chosen him.

The year 1770 was thus to open in an atmosphere of yet another political crisis, the domestic problems being overshadowed by those in America, and those of the Falkland Islands about to take everybody by surprise. The presence of royal troops in Boston was arousing tensions in and around that city, and a growing awareness in both British and colonial circles that firm and intelligent action was urgently needed from the London government if the whole American situation was not to slide out of control.

It was a time when a semi-retired general, still possibly in line for active command, might easily justify a reconnaissance visit to America on the grounds of performing some vague duty, especially if that duty could take him away from the scene of his recent dismays. So it was no great surprise when Sir William booked a passage to South Carolina from Bristol, sailing in October 1769, only a few weeks after the last of his exchanges with Junius. Now a widower, he departed with the vague suggestion that he would be involved in assessing recruiting possibilities in that Southern state. The *Gentleman's Magazine*, probably closer to the truth, commented, 'The recovery of his health is probably his only motive, though his enemies have ascribed it to other views.'

21

AMERICAN CONNECTIONS

For the remaining quarter of his life, Sir William was involved in events which flowed from the drift to war between Britain and the American colonies. His professional interest in America as a possible opportunity for renewed command was given a personal dimension as he married into one of the great Loyalist clans of New York, the De Lancey family, and thereafter was close to all the consequences of the War of Independence.

On leaving England for Charleston at the end of 1769, he still nursed hopes of some official post but the gossip in London that he was to be appointed Governor of South Carolina had no real basis and he was still there in March 1770 when Philip Francis' young cousin, Alexander MacKrabie, who lived in Philadelphia, writing to Francis about Junius, noted:

> Junius is the Mars of discontents. His Letter to the King is past all endurance as well as compare. The Americas are under no small obligation to him for his representation of them.
>
> I will do them more justice than he does by declaring that his production is not very favourably received among them. Sir William Draper is arrived in South Carolina. I have read all *that* correspondence and never before met with such cutting satire.[1]

The Junius *Letters* had aroused as much interest and speculation in America as in England, bringing the General's name into more prominent circulation. As a respected military figure, in touch with recent events in London, Sir William would anyway have been guaranteed an interested reception wherever he went. As challenger to Junius, however badly savaged, he came with added *réclame*.

He travelled to North Carolina in May where the governor William Tryon was yet another contemporary from the 1st Guards. Tryon was then in the process of creating a new residence in New Bern, the state capital, which came to be known as Tryon's Palace. He dedicated the residence to Sir William and in the portico is still a Latin inscription composed by Draper during his stay with his friend.

He arrived in New York in late spring. The city then hardly stretched farther than the confines of the Battery and Wall Street, with Greenwich village a cluster of farms and mansions some distance to the north. His host in the city was General Thomas Gage, Commander-in-Chief of the British forces in North America, who had been a contemporary in the 48th Regiment a generation earlier. Gage had had more than twenty years of service in America, being appointed to his present command in 1764. He had married into the close-knit New York community of prominent landowners, professional men, merchants and traders, and his wife Margaret Kemble was a daughter of the linked families of van Cortlandt and De Lancey.

These dominant families, an interrelated mingling of British, Dutch and French stock, were beginning to be put under the strain of divided loyalties as the source of their influence, attachment to the Crown, was increasingly the focus of dispute. Divergent attitudes on the political future of the American colonies were putting old alignments to the question and the provincial aristocracy of New York was as much affected by the tensions as their more voluble countrymen in Massachusetts.

Among this small group was the De Lancey family, into which Sir William was to marry within months of arriving in New York. The De Lancey 'interest', one of the major political forces in New York from early in the century until the War of Independence, included James de Lancey as Chief Justice and Lieutenant-Governor of New York. His brother, Oliver, was a successful merchant and politician, a Member of the Assembly and a major landowner. He retained the military link with the royal forces which he had forged during the Seven Years War when he raised troops and commanded the provincial contingent in the Ticonderoga campaign. His connections with the British establishment had been reinforced some years earlier through the marriage of his sister to Admiral Sir Peter Warren, whose prize money from naval actions in the West Indies had enabled him to buy enormous estates on Manhattan Island.

Oliver de Lancey apparently took Sir William on a visit to Ticonderoga, north of New York, to visit the site of the battle in which De Lancey had fought and Draper's friend Roger Townshend had been killed. De Lancey was only three years older than Sir William and their shared interests brought them close enough for the General to be accepted into the family when he proposed to and married Oliver's daughter Susannah. She, one of the older of De Lancey's six children, was then aged around twenty-five. The disparity in age between herself and her husband Sir William, then approaching fifty, would have been no bar to what would have been a match agreeable to both sides: for her the status of being the titled wife of a military celebrity with the prospect of a comfortable life in England and possibly a family; for him a new companion who might be a mother for his longed-for children and an eventual beneficiary of some of the De Lancey fortune. They were married in New York's Trinity Church on Wall Street in October 1770.[2]

Their thoughts on the future would have been brought into sharper focus earlier in that year when British troops in Boston fired into a riotous throng, killing five. Although New York remained peaceful, the turmoil was not far below the surface. There was a strong awareness of approaching crisis.

Susannah Draper, when she set out on her voyage to England shortly after their marriage, must have left her family in New York sensing that she might never again see them in the same pleasant state of stability and comfort. Sir William probably also came to recognise over the next year or two that by marrying an American, even from a strongly Loyalist family, he might be risking his chances of being given a senior command in America should armed conflict break out. His occasional public writing came to show how preoccupied he was in trying to reconcile these divergent loyalties.

During the year of his absence from England, the political landscape had again shifted. At the end of January 1770, the harassed Grafton had finally resigned to make way for Lord North, who was to stay in power for the next ten years during all the disasters in America. Chatham, who was largely responsible for the ousting of Grafton, had subsided to the role of elder statesman. In that year, Ligonier and Granby had also both died, the Field-Marshal by then in his eighties, but Granby much younger.

The major political excitement of 1770 had not, however, been yet another change of ministry but news of the seizure by Spain of Port Egmont in the Falklands and the expulsion of the tiny British settlement. By the time news reached England, both Spain and France had decided that they should avoid the catastrophe of a premature war. Compromise was made easier when Choiseul, the French Foreign Minister was dismissed by King Louis XV, reluctant to support Spain if she unilaterally declared war with Britain.

Charles III of Spain was pressed to seek compromise and, before the end of the year, Spain agreed to evacuate Port Egmont and allow the British settlement to return, though without prejudice to Spanish claims to sovereignty. The later rumour of a secret agreement by which Britain pledged to withdraw from the Falklands after a discreet interval has never been verified by any documentary evidence. The evacuation of Port Egmont by the British some years later was dictated simply by economy, rather than being a concession on sovereignty. So the question of sovereignty was left floating and unresolved, with all the consequences which have continued over two centuries to the present.

Resolution of this immediate crisis brought relief throughout Europe. Lessening of tension, however, inevitably reduced the leverage which other unresolved conflicts such as the Manila ransom might exert. The end of the Falklands crisis effectively rang the death knell for the Manila issues; all that remained for discussion over the next two or three years were vexatious details of accounts.

The East India Company had also accepted reality. The formal decision that it was no longer prepared to press for the Manila ransom money was set out in the Minutes of the Court following a meeting on 6 February 1771, only a month after Sir William arrived back from America. By then Admiral Cornish had been dead for some months and he was represented at a meeting at India House by a nephew, Samuel Cornish, who had captained the *America* on the Manila expedition as Samuel Pitchford,

The Minutes noted:

> The Court being acquainted that Sir William Draper and Captain Cornish (representative of the late Admiral Cornish) were desirous of conferring with the Court respecting the sum to be stipulated for the ransom of Manila, and that it was requested that the Court would join the claimants in a petition to Parliament in support of their claims ... and the Court entering upon consideration of the matter ... it was deemed improper for this Court to join in the said application to Parliament ... and these gentlemen, being introduced, were acquainted with the Court's sentiments therein and the said resolution of the Court having been read to them they withdrew ... It was then resolved that it would not be proper to join in a petition to Parliament on the subject of the Manila ransom.[3]

In short, the Company was telling Sir William and Captain Cornish that the issue was being buried. The two military figures must have felt dejected as they withdrew from India House into Leadenhall Street. The high hopes of eight years ago had finally come to nothing.

Sir William's chagrin that there was no longer any hope of ransom money would have been counterbalanced by his joy later in the year when Susannah produced the first of their daughters. The *Annual Register* recorded her birth on 21 August 1771 – although she seems hardly to have survived beyond infancy.

His own professional standing was finally accorded its recognition when, early in the following year, 1772, he was promoted to Major-General, having held the ambivalent rank of 'Brigadier-General in the East Indies only' for the past ten years. He had probably worried that his involvement with Junius might have reduced his chances of this substantive rank and his exchange with Colonel Gisborne could also have been a hindrance. This was confirmed in a letter he received from Lord Barrington, Secretary at War, in May:

It is a long established and good rule that officers who have voluntarily exchanged to Half Pay should not afterwards be employed or promoted in the Army. The King has today made one exception. He thinks the Conqueror of Manila be exempted from the general rules which are disadvantageous to him and might prevent his doing future service to his country. In short, Sir William Draper is included in a promotion of Major-Generals. I most sincerely wish you joy.[4]

The satisfaction of being accorded this mark of George III's personal esteem was enhanced in the following month when the King attended the installation of fifteen Knights of the Bath at a ceremony in Westminster Abbey. This unusual gesture marked the King's acknowledgement of the contribution made to the nation's life made by the fifteen, not least the trio whose careers had been so closely connected with India; Lord Clive, Sir Eyre Coote and Sir William.

The *Gentleman's Magazine*, reporting the event, noted, 'The Knights in their surcoats, mantles and spurs, met in the Prince's chambers at Westminster Abbey, each attended by three esquires.' Sir William's three were Robert Fell, George Ayscough, and John Fitzwilliam. Fell was the senior surviving officer of the 79th, with the exception of George Monson, and had survived all the post-expedition turmoil in Manila. George Ayscough was a maverick figure who at one time had been in the Guards and was currently a minor playwright. General John Fitzwilliam was another military contemporary.

The Knights celebrated their investiture by giving an evening party and ball over which the newspapers enthused:

At night there was a most magnificent supper and ball at the Opera House Haymarket, at the expense of the new Knights, to which were invited the nobility and foreign ambassadors, and almost every person of distinction in town ... The entertainment was universally confessed to have been the most magnificent and superb yet seen within the Kingdom. The company was more select at this than at any former assembly of the kind and seemed to express the warmest tokens of approbation and pleasure ... The ladies seemed selected on account of their beauty as well as their rank.[5]

No record survives of how the cost of this splendid evening's celebration may have been divided, though it was likely that Lord Clive, enriched far beyond the capacity of his fellow knights, and generous as well, would have contributed a disproportionately large sum.

Sir William seemed as usual, despite Susannah's putative wealth, short of money, and would have been gratified later in the year when she was granted a pension of £300 per annum. The pension was not only useful in itself, but a further mark of royal favour and a reminder that the embarrassment of the Junius episode could now slide into the past. Indeed, Junius himself had written his last major *Letter* a few months earlier, in January 1772, after which he abandoned his attempts to force political change by strength of sarcastic malice.

Shortly after the June investiture, Sir William's friend and former regimental agent, John Calcraft, died suddenly at the early age of forty-six, busy as ever with his political machinations. Any sense of loss for Sir William from the death of his contemporaries would have been reduced by the birth of his second daughter in August 1773. She was christened Anna Susannah Ethelreda, the third name unusual and again suggesting some connection with the Townshend family in being the names of both Lady Townshend and her daughter Mrs Robert Orme. At the time of her birth, Sir William was offering his 'elegant house and gardens' for sale in *Felix Farley's Bristol Post*. The advertisement ran from May until October 1773, describing the house as 'very well furnished, the gardens enriched with the finest fruit trees, a large hot house, two coachhouses with stabling for seven horses, and excellent cellars'; but apparently no purchaser was found as the advertisement was withdrawn after several months. The expense of spending time both in Clifton and London must have been a strain on his modest resources.

His need to be in London was the purely practical one of being visible around military and club circles to remind his peers of his availability. His earlier military patrons, Cumberland and Ligonier, were now dead, Chatham was in the shadows of retirement, Bedford had also died in the previous year. With no major patron he had to rely on his own visibility to sustain any further chance of the active employment which alone would guarantee him an income large enough to meet his commitments.

He was also still involved in the final attempts to extract recompense from the Treasury or War Office, as well as the Admiralty, for individual officers who had suffered financially from the Manila expedition. In 1773, the petition from Sir Samuel Cornish and Sir Eyre Coote was still grinding round the system, grumbling about the unfair distribution of booty at Pondicherry, a victory now eleven years in the past, and various individual officers, particularly the naval captain Brereton, were receiving disappointment at the hands of the Treasury.

All these problems, touching directly on the pockets of serving officers always pressed for money, were made worse by the fact that there was simply no administrative or statutory framework within which to solve trilateral disputes involving the navy, army, and the East India Company. In these grey areas, where self-interest could be masked as national interest, it was hardly surprising that issues remained unresolved for many years, and often were never resolved. Individual officers seeking redress were always conscious that the whole system was weighted against them. Sir William must often have felt grateful for the supposedly interim draft for £5,000 which he had extracted from Dawsonne Drake before he left Manila. If he had not received that, he might never have received anything.

He had resigned himself by 1773 to the knowledge that nothing further could be done to gain recompense for any of the forces involved in the expedition. Even with his many past and present contacts he was unable to make any more headway against the obduracy of the Government or the Company, and awareness of failure left him with an abiding sense of injustice.

He did not, however, decline into a melancholy retirement, and nor could he afford to. He spent as much time in London as in Clifton, and was also still closely connected with the expanding world of cricket. In recognition of his interest, he was invited in February 1774 to be Chairman of the 'Committee of Noblemen and Gentlemen of Kent, Hampshire, Surrey, Sussex, Middlesex and London', to revise and define the Laws of Cricket,[6] probably because he was the senior amongst the group who were active players themselves or raised teams to play in their names. The Duke of Dorset, twenty-nine, and the Earl of Tankerville, thirty-one, present on that evening, were both keen players as was Sir Horace Mann, the young nephew of Horace Walpole's correspondent of the same name. The Reverend Charles Paulett represented Hambledon, the club in Hampshire regarded traditionally as the 'birthplace of English cricket'. The Committee met at the Star and Garter tavern in Pall Mall, often mentioned in William Hickey's *Memoirs* as one of his favourite haunts, not least for the quality of its wines.

Unlike modern committees, this gathering seems to have met only once, and it says much for the common sense of its ten members that most of the rules formalised during that one evening have endured to form the basis of the game ever since. Within the space of a few convivial hours, the Committee produced definitive rules on size of bat and ball, bowling crease and popping crease, bowlers, batsmen, wicket-keepers and umpires. The only rules which have disappeared over time were those on betting which was largely the dynamic for the increasing popularity of the game. The only important point left unresolved by the committee was the number of stumps which stayed at two for some further years.

Members of the committee remained prominent in the growth of cricket and were involved in the progress of the White Conduit Club, which in 1787 changed its name to the Marylebone Cricket Club. Christopher Morris, the historian of King's, Cambridge stated that Sir William, had he not died in the same year, would have been appointed first President of the MCC, though in fact that position was not formally established until much later, in 1825. It would have appealed to the clubbable side of his character.

Sir William's and Susannah's life was also enriched again in August 1774 with the birth of their third daughter, Phila Augusta, at Clifton, named after her maternal grandmother Phila de Lancey. Susannah Draper would not have felt completely cut off from her family in America as her brother, Oliver, then aged twenty-five, was in England as a captain in the 17th Dragoons. But Oliver's imminent departure with his regiment for service in America would have reminded them all of their vulnerability in the face of greater events.

News of the Boston Tea Party in December 1773 had reached England early in 1774 and stunned Westminster. The attempt by the Government to help the East India Company out of a financial crisis by enabling the Company to export tea direct to America had backfired. Lord North's government compounded the crisis by overreacting in the following months. As part of the measures against Massachussets, General Gage was moved from New York to Boston in May 1774 accompanied by four regiments. Gage was perceptive enough to warn North that if the situation deteriorated to the point of armed struggle the British forces would be seriously overstretched. Gage found his authority undermined by the canard that his American wife was always ready to leak his plans to her countrymen. It was the sort of rumour which would have reached London and may have been relevant to the fact that Sir William,

12. Philadelphia de Lancey, sister of Susannah de Lancey who became Draper's second wife in 1770. Seemingly they bore a strong family resemblance, although no portrait of Susannah survives. Phila de Lancey became wife of Stephen Payne-Galwey.

also with an American wife, was passed over for command in America. He was certainly under active consideration for, in October, Horace Walpole was writing to George Conway:

> I can tell you still less of America. There are two or three more ships going there, and Sir William Draper as second-in-command.[7]

Within a month, Walpole was also reporting, 'Sir William is writing plans for pacification in our newspapers.'

Perhaps these 'plans for pacification' might have led the Government to judge that Draper lacked the capacity for ruthless action required by the Government in view of his American connections. Yet, in his desire to search for an amicable compromise in America, he was at one with a large number of more thoughtful debaters. During 1774, he wrote constantly on the subject to the *Public Advertiser* and, towards the end of the year, the publisher presented in a single pamphlet his *Thoughts of a Traveller upon our American Disputes*, written under the pen name Viator.[8]

It was no great landmark in the voluminous output during the prelude to the War of Independence, but illustrates the anguish felt by many in those years as they were being forced to choose between equally unwelcome options.

'I must confess to be one of those who wished that the grand question of our legislative right to tax the North Americans had never been agitated,' Sir William opened, aligning himself with the great majority of his readers. In touching upon the many advantages which America enjoyed as 'the seeds of a mighty empire', Sir William conceded the mistakes of Parliament's 'ebb and flow'. He then posed the question:

> What steps must we take, when it is thought dangerous to proceed, disgraceful to retire? ... If among so numerous a people not one will acknowledge our lawful power of taxation, prudence ought to tell us that we are pursuing too dangerous a system in order to support this power ...

> Let both parties listen to the calm and dispassionate voice of reason and moderation. Let the Americans modestly point out their grievances, whether real or imaginary. The deliberate wisdom of the Legislature may then consider how far to proceed, and where to stop; what points may be given up with grace and dignity, and in what points the interests and dignity of our country and the majesty of government must be maintained with unabating firmness and resolution.

Sir William was well aware that the chances of either side being prepared to listen to the calm and dispassionate voice of reason had already passed, with the noise of confrontation growing louder. His thoughts on 'unabating firmness and resolution' were those of the soldier rather than the politician or the diplomat. He suggested, strangely for a soldier, that naval power alone would be effective in enforcing this obedience and that the royal troops should be withdrawn as 'they are too numerous for ambassadors, and too few for soldiers.' The right of the mother country to tax the colonies was defended, but not as one that should be imposed by force.

His *Thoughts* were only those of an articulate writer without executive responsibility, and punctuated with some unworkable ideas. At one point he questioned how long the Americans would remain a people if they were to give 'freedom to their Negroes'. This implied threat caused outrage when the *Thoughts* were published in America, and Benjamin Franklin, writing to a friend in England from Philadelphia, commented sarcastically:

> The humane Sir William Draper, who had been hospitably
> entertained in every one of our colonies, proposes, in his Papers
> called the Traveller, to excite the domestic Slaves, you have sold us,
> to cut their masters' throats.[9]

Sir William's broad plea for unity, worthy and disinterested though it was, suffered the fate of being rapidly swept away by the tide of stronger currents. In America its most lasting effect was probably little more than to remind hotheads that he was connected by marriage to the De Lancey family, whose known dedication to the Loyalist cause was about to be put to the test.

22

DOMESTIC GENEROSITIES

While Sir William was pleading for a spirit of national generosity towards the Americans, his personal capacity for generosity was being shown towards the suddenly notorious Eliza Draper, wife of his cousin Daniel Draper, a member of the Bombay Council of the East India Company.

The literary and social scandal caused in London in 1775 by the posthumous publication of Laurence Sterne's *Letters from Yorick to Eliza* and *The Bramin's Journal*, which earned Mrs Draper the nickname of 'the Immortal Eliza', now seems difficult to comprehend, particularly in comparison with the real scandals abounding at the time. There was an air of silliness about the whole episode, and bogus sentimentality in Sterne's 'recounting the miserable feelings of a person separated from a lady for whose society he languished'. But he, the literary lion, author of *Tristram Shandy*, was then a figure of compelling interest.

Eliza Draper, daughter of a family with long links to the Company, was married very young in Bombay to Daniel Draper who was considerably older than herself. After bearing three children, two destined to die young, she came to England on leave in the autumn of 1766 where at the house of Sir William James, Chairman of the Company, she had briefly met the ageing Sterne. He was captivated by the guileless exuberance of the still-young Eliza, with whom he exchanged letters until her return to India to rejoin her husband in the following spring. The whole brief liaison seems to have been totally blameless, significant only in inspiring Sterne to produce the anguished letters which were embodied in the two publications. Sterne himself had died in 1768, so that he and Eliza never met again.

In Bombay, following her return, she continued to lead the leisurely but constrained life of a wife of a senior Company servant. Daniel was hardly a suitable companion for a lively woman still in her twenties, preoccupied with his work but still finding almost as much time for his housekeeper as for his wife. Finally in January 1773, distraught after yet another altercation with her husband, who also had much to endure, she made good her escape in a manner whose romantic style was soon common gossip in India and England. She reportedly lowered herself at night by rope down to a waiting boat on the nearby shore to take refuge on a naval ship, the inappropriately named HMS *Prudent*, with the connivance of Commodore Sir John Clarke. She made her way to London where she was received in literary circles and had her portrait painted by the fashionable Richard Cosway. She, and her daughter Betsy, were sustained by regular income from her husband Daniel, who stayed on in Bombay, accepting her departure with some equanimity.

Eliza allowed Sterne's widow to go ahead with publication of *Letters to Eliza*, moved probably as much by vanity as literary enthusiasm. Their publication added to Sterne's posthumous reputation although their overheated

*13. Eliza Draper, Sterne's 'Immortal Eliza',
runaway wife of William Draper's cousin
Daniel, who died at the general's house in
Clifton in 1779 aged only 34. Her monument
survives in Bristol Cathedral.*

style now makes them almost unbearably sentimental. Eliza, perhaps un-expectedly, acquired a distasteful notoriety and in the aftermath of the stir caused by the book and its links with her abandonment of her husband, de-cided that it would be wiser to leave London for a time. She seems to have been offered, and accepted, refuge at Sir William's house at Clifton. She was almost the same age as Susannah, the General's wife, and would have been a lively addition to the household.

At the time of Eliza's arrival Sir William must have been sharing the feeling of Herodotus that 'The worst pain a man can have is to know much and to be impotent to act.' As America and England stumbled towards the War of Independence, he knew that the lives and fortunes of his wife's family were increasingly at risk. His chances of being given some command in America seemed to have receded. His need for increased income with a young family became ever more pressing. Yet he was enduring the fate of being no more than an onlooker at events which directly affected him but about which he could do nothing.

Within sight of his house at Clifton, the port of Bristol was, almost more than London, immediately and deeply affected by the war triggered by the first shots at Lexington and Concord in April 1775. Trade with the American colonies was of critical importance to Bristol and the prospect of a long disruption spelled economic disaster. Bristol's two members of Parliament were in the forefront of debate in attacking Lord North's lack of a spirit of conciliation. Of the two, Edmund Burke was already recognised as a formidable parliamentary figure; the other, more closely connected with Bristol's trading community, was a merchant from New York, Henry Cruger.

Cruger was close to Sir William's divided loyalties because his brother in New York, John Harris Cruger, was married to Susannah Draper's sister, Anne de Lancey. John Harris Cruger was shortly to become one of the outstanding Loyalist commanders in New York, initially as second-in-command to his father-in-law Oliver de Lancey. Even before the war had started, there had been a flow of American refugees into Bristol, and their numbers increased as the war extended. They were a constant source of disquieting news as the accuracy of General Gage's predictions about British troops being overstretched became more obvious by the month.

Susannah Draper had the particular worry of knowing that both her father and brother were involved in the fighting in New York State. Her brother, Oliver de Lancey, had gone across as a captain in the 17th Dragoons, the only British cavalry regiment present in America throughout the War of Independence. Susannah's father, Oliver de Lancey, who had been Colonel-in-Chief of the Southern Military district of New York since 1775, had raised a brigade of 1,500 Loyalists as soon as hostilities began, and his three units, known as De Lancey's Battalions, were constantly involved in the fighting. De Lancey himself, promoted to brigadier, remained in New York and became the senior Loyalist officer with the British army in America. His troops were involved in support of General Howe in the autumn of 1776 when Washington's small army was forced to quit New York and Manhattan Island.

The initial success of Howe, and two other young major-generals Henry Clinton and John Burgoyne, was sufficient to defer any plans for their replacement. As news filtered back to England of the early and deceptive successes of British arms, it must have seemed depressingly obvious to Sir William that he was not going to be favoured with any command in America.

He was possibly pinning his hopes once again on another real chance – further command in the East Indies, this time for the vacant post of Commander-in-Chief reporting to the Governor-General, Warren Hastings, based in Calcutta. The opportunity had arisen following Hasting's appointment to fill the new post of Governor-General of India, reporting to a Supreme Council of four. Two members appointed to this new body were the durable George Monson, and, more surprisingly, Philip Francis.

Francis' nomination to the Council was seemingly mysterious. He had sought nomination via his earlier contacts at the War Office, but his claims to preference were tenuous at best, and the fact that this post, worth the enormous salary of £10,000, was eventually awarded to him had generated rumours that he was being paid hush-money to cease his writing as Junius. He had reached Calcutta in 1774 and almost immediately begun the long struggle with Hastings which was to lead to the Governor-General's eventual impeachment.

The question of appointment of a new Commander-in-Chief arose in 1776 and the Court of the Company favoured appointing Monson, whose long experience in India made him admirably qualified. Before he could be appointed, however, Monson resigned from ill health in September and died in India in the same month. The news of his death did not arrive in London until well into the next year, after discussions between Lord North and the directors had identified Sir Eyre Coote as the preferred candidate if George Monson could not be persuaded.

Lord North reporting to the King in April 1777 noted:

> Lord North ... has already sent the names of Major-General
> Mackay, Lord Adam Gordon and Sir William Draper to the
> Directors as persons who would willingly serve in the East Indies.
> They objected to gentlemen of North Britain for Commands-in-
> Chief, and to Sir William Draper as too volatile; and wish to have
> Sir Eyre Coote again at the head of their army if Colonel Monson,
> after he has heard of his succeeding to the command of the army
> should persist in desiring to come home ... Sir Eyre Coote will, I
> dare say, wish for the situation and, if accepted by the Directors, will
> apply again to His Majesty for leave to serve the Company.[1]

The fact that the directors of the Company were sufficiently self-assured to dictate to the King whom he should nominate as Commander-in-Chief for their service indicates the continuing ambivalence between the Government and the Company. The added fact that they were able to reject the two senior Scots mentioned as candidates shows how long antipathy towards the Scots had lingered after the Jacobites had ceased to be a source of sedition.

The objection to Sir William was at least direct, concise and, from the Company's viewpoint, understandable. For the past fifteen years, whatever his military record, he had been a source of irritation to the Company. Even the most sanguine director would have hesitated to recommend him as Commander-in-Chief. Nor was it necessary to dip back into the past to reawaken memories of Manila; only two years earlier the Company had presented its final bill to the Treasury for reimbursement for the expedition and the matter was, as usual, still under discussion.

It was hardly surprising that the directors, given the option to choose from other candidates, would reject the one about whom they probably felt a mixture of embarrassment and annoyance. It was much easier to bypass Sir William with the label of 'volatility', and leave it at that. They opted for the safe hands of Eyre Coote, who went back to India, assuming command at Calcutta in 1779. He immediately found himself involved in the quarrelling between Warren Hastings and Philip Francis. He sought relief in being needed urgently in the field and repeated all the old battles around Madras and Wandiwash until his major victory over Hyder Ali at Porto Novo in 1781. Even this triumph was not sufficient to bring peace to the region and Coote soldiered on, until his sudden death in 1783.

Sir William's disappointment at not being given command in India, assuming that he was well aware of the possibility, was mollified by his promotion to Lieutenant-General in August 1777 on the same day as Eyre Coote. But though he might have retained his competitiveness in terms of seniority he was still without active command, and even less likely to get it after Burgoyne's spectacular defeat at Saratoga in October.

Saratoga, the first substantial American victory of the war, was not just a military disaster. Its wider repercussions were immediate as the European powers, particularly France, recognised that Britain's military incompetence had presented them with an opportunity for restoring the balance of power. The new French king, Louis XVI, at once extended official recognition to the 'United States' and opened talks towards commercial and military alliance.

The crisis in London caused by the disaster at Saratoga was the stimulus for the last great parliamentary speeches by Chatham between November 1777 and May 1778. Chatham, who had remained consistent in his views over the essential justice of the American position, still hoped that total severance could be avoided. His plan was to repeal all contentious legislation, and withdraw most of the British forces. Rockingham and the younger Whigs favoured giving the Americans their independence as soon as possible and negating France's intention of coming to their rescue. Lord North's ministry struggled to cope with this mounting crisis.

In the comparative calm of New York the De Lancey family had however suffered greatly in November 1777, when the family mansion at Bloomingdale was attacked and burnt down by insurgents under cover of darkness. Bloomingdale was situated in the country outside New York, in an area now occupied by Central Park, and beyond the protection of any garrison patrols. It was an ideal target for patriot fighters who regarded Oliver de Lancey and his Loyalist battalions as no better than auxiliaries of the hated British redcoats. News of the burning of her family home would have reached Susannah early in 1778 to add to the tales of woe from the increasing number of loyalist refugees settling in Bristol, many complaining that they met with a cold reception on arrival in Bristol from inhabitants in favour of the American rebellion. Susannah Draper and Henry Cruger, both New Yorkers but each in different ways prominent in Bristol, would have found themselves on either side of the divide of loyalties; Cruger as a radical, Susannah as the daughter of an outstanding Loyalist and wife of a British general who might still be called to some command in America.

The pace of international events quickened in the early months of 1778. France and America signed a defensive alliance in February. Lord North, faced with the appalling prospect of an extended war involving France and Spain, announced that he was prepared to repeal all legislation applicable to America since 1763. The huge volte-face was too late. In the following months there was pressure for Chatham to be recalled as the only statesman with sufficient stature to restore stability and authority. But his dramatic last speech in the Lords in April and his death a few weeks later seemed to embody the anguish of a nation unable to avoid the consequences of its own folly.

The void left by his death was not filled by immediate crises, but it was a dispiriting time, as governments and people adjusted to the fact of renewed war. For Sir William it was doubly so. In August 1778, his wife Susannah died, not yet in her mid-thirties, and leaving him with their two daughters, aged only five and four. Earlier in the same month, Eliza Draper had also died, aged only thirty-four. It is impossible to know the exact cause of their deaths, so close together, although contemporary doctors and medicine were capable of converting any serious illness into a lethal crisis within days. Typhoid fever was rife throughout that summer. It appears that neither Eliza nor Susannah had time to make a will, which suggests that their illnesses had been sudden and overwhelming.

Eliza had not obviously been ailing, as there is a typically lively and silly letter of hers to John Wilkes, in the Wilkes correspondence, dated 22 March 1778, suggesting a continuing correspondence and exchange of books.[2] It says much for Eliza's continuing ability to charm that she should have captured and retained the interest of Wilkes at a time when he was still the centre of public attention, having just been elected Lord Mayor of London, and finally retaken his seat as a Member of Parliament after the seemingly endless disputes with successive governments.

It seems also that Eliza had not lost the affection of other admirers for there remains a mystery as to which of them paid for her monument in Bristol Cathedral. Sir William seems unlikely to have been the donor, since at the time of Eliza's death he was much more preoccupied with Susannah's simultaneous death. He was also in considerable financial difficulty probably because of a dramatic fall in Susannah's fortunes as the war took its toll on the De Lancey family fortunes.

Some rather elusive confirmation of his difficult situation at that time is referred to in the *Memoirs of Sir Philip Francis*, which noted:

> Among Sir Philip's miscellaneous papers are copies by himself of letters of a melancholy description which passed in that year (1778) between Sir William and Maria Hart an actress who had lived with him and who solicited pecuniary assistance, which Draper laments his inability, from extreme poverty, to afford her. He describes his situation as very miserable ... Francis appears to have relieved the supplicant.[3]

Maria Hart was of course Polly Hart, Sir William's mistress from thirty years earlier. Her career as an actress had never brought her much more than a common-law marriage with the actor Samuel Reddish, who had died a year or two earlier, and poor Polly was obviously reduced to seeking help from any of her old admirers, and particularly Sir William.

If Philip Francis, as the *Memoirs* suggest, did provide for the unfortunate Polly, it must have been via correspondence from Calcutta because in 1778 he was not only heavily engaged in his quarrels with Warren Hastings but was also involved in a scandal with the sixteen-year-old wife of a Swiss officer in the service of the Company. She was an enterprising girl who went on to much greater things when she eventually became the mistress and then wife of the French statesman Talleyrand.

Polly's plea to Sir William must have been a reminder of more carefree days. His account at Drummonds for the year 1778 confirms his lamentations about being hard-pressed, and Susannah's death would have added to his problems in cutting off the pension of £300 per annum which she had been receiving since 1772. He was thus faced with the most urgent need of providing for the upbringing of his two daughters, Anna Susannah and Phila, a dilemma which could only be solved by a return to active service.

In the midst of all this gloom he must have been immensely relieved when, in May 1779, he was notified of an appointment which would go some way towards satisfying both his professional and financial needs – being designated as Lieutenant-Governor of the strategically important island of Minorca in the Balearic Islands.

23

FINAL CALL TO ARMS

Minorca during the eighteenth century had an importance comparable to that of Malta during the Second World War. Its magnificent natural harbour made it the key to naval supremacy in the Mediterranean, and throughout the century it had been changing hands as the fortunes of war dictated. Its loss to the French in 1756 led not only to the disgraceful court martial and execution of the scapegoat Admiral Byng but also to a national sense of shame in Britain. This in turn had opened the way for William Pitt to take effective leadership of the wartime government with all the consequences which flowed thereafter.

Under the Treaty of Paris in 1763, Minorca had been restored to British control, a concession which rankled with both France and Spain. The island went back to its soporific garrison life, but remained a strategic objective for both the allies in the Family Compact. It was inevitable that it should become the focus of military attention in the event of renewed hostilities.

The Saratoga disaster tempted France and Spain to consider a major pre-emptive strike. In April 1779, the two countries signed a new treaty committing Spain to declare war on England. The French had conceived a grand re-enactment of the Armada involving both the French and Spanish fleets, whose combined force would overwhelm the British in the Channel as a prelude to invasion by the French army. In return for this invasion plan Spain was to receive French help in recovering Minorca and Gibraltar.

Through the summer of 1779, the British fleet was on the alert in the Channel for the arrival of the combined fleets. The need for every available ship would explain the long lead-time between Sir William's appointment to Minorca and his arrival there with reinforcing troops in February of the following year. The invasion scare lasted for months as the French and Spanish fleets laboriously assembled, made rendezvous, and finally anchored in full view of Plymouth in August, causing great alarm in the south of England.

A combination of weather, victualling problems, sickness, and the harassing skill of the British fleet under Admiral Hardy eventually forced the massive fleet back to Brest early in September. Plymouth remained on the alert, both to the precarious state of the British ships drawn up around the Scillies and to its own inadequate defences should the town be attacked. A correspondent writing from there in September reassured his recipient, 'The town is not quite defenceless … Sir William Draper will have the command for a short time, and then it is to be invested in General William Havilland.' By October, it was clear that the invasion scare was over, and the Spanish by devoting their naval strength to the Channel had lost the opportunity of striking first at Gibraltar and Minorca. Reinforcements could now be safely despatched to both these outposts from England.

Sir William, apart from his temporary duties in charge of the Plymouth garrison and militia, had also been involved in assembling the troops going with him to Minorca. As well as his military duties, he was making arrangements for his household in the event of long absence. He leased Manila Hall to his nearest neighbour, William Gordon, a Bristol merchant with whom he remained in touch during his time at Minorca. His two daughters, now motherless, were left in the care of his cousin, Anne Collins, wife of the naval captain Richard Collins. She, who had now been a member of Sir William's household for some years, would have been a family guardian to the two young girls, most probably in Bath.

Before his departure to Minorca, Sir William wrote to Charles Jenkinson at the Treasury in June, suggesting that he might be considered for a more important command than Lieutenant-Governor of Minorca. Jenkinson replied that he had put Draper's letter to the King, who had been pleased to receive his offer of further services and commended his zeal but made no further comment. Sir William was by then fifty-eight, and if there were more interesting commands to be distributed they would more surely go to the younger generation of officers who had gained experience in the war in America.

Despite their preoccupation with the invasion scare, the newspapers and magazines in the summer of 1779 continued to lighten their columns with less weighty matters. *Town and Country Magazine* ran a long 'Tête-à-Tête' series of juxtaposed portraits of couples who were easily identifiable as topics of current London gossip. In July, two engraved busts were featured, entitled 'The Manila Hero and Mrs P---s', the first being Sir William, the other a Mrs Potts.[1]

The long introductory text leading up to the liaison, mentioned earlier in regard to his amorous forays at Versailles, shed more light on his early years in which as a penniless young officer he was making his way towards promotion.

The text opened:

> We have the uncommon pleasure of introducing our hero who is at
> once a scholar and a gentleman. He has distinguished himself for his
> bravery, judgement and skill as an officer; as a writer he has given
> sufficient testimonies of his abilities and learning which have done
> honour to his profession.

The writer then alluded to the course of Sir William's military career and his
damaging encounter with Junius:

> From this time Sir W-----m has contented himself with a private
> station and no way intermeddled with party or politics. His chief
> amusement when in town is tennis, a game he has invariably
> attached to since youth ... His acquaintance was not only cultivated
> by men of mere rank; there was not a man of science or a favourite
> of the muse who did not strenuously solicit being introduced to the
> Manila Hero; among the number of those may be placed the late
> Lord Chesterfield, Lord Lyttelton, Dr Johnson, and many more.
> Even those who differed from him in political principle could not
> refrain from testifying the highest approbation of his literary talents
> and polite address, as he was a scholar without the least tincture
> of pedantry and the polished man of the world without either the
> frivolity or classical ignorance which accompanies that character.

The 'Tête-à-Tête' then introduced Mrs Potts, a clergyman's daughter, whose
petulant good looks, wild hair, and healthy cleavage testify to the writer's
assurance that 'she was not deficient in those personal attractions which more
certainly captivate a transient beholder.' She had married a Mr Potts, 'a capital
dealer in the Manchester manufactures', but unable to bear his insane jealousy
had broken away in accepting his offer of £100 per annum for maintenance.
A number of indiscreet affairs had followed until:

> In the person of the knight she found a man whose sentiments were
> entirely congenial with her own; his first advances were so polite
> and strictly consistent with decorum that she was at first staggered
> what construction to put upon them. He at length however came to
> an explanation and she was rather too far to recede with propriety
> before she found herself incapable of rescinding such declarations as
> had voluntarily escaped her. Our hero was a man too much of the
> world not to avail himself of the partiality she had testified but in so
> prudent and secret a manner there is scarce one of her acquaintances
> who does not imagine the correspondence between the Manila Hero
> and Mrs P----s to be of the sentimental kind.

The opaque quality of the allusions leaves questions unanswered. Since the liaison was the subject of London gossip in the summer of 1779, it could well have started after Susannah Draper's death the previous year. Why then the need for prudence and secrecy? Or perhaps before? And how did Sir William, justifiably pleading financial hardship, manage to keep Mrs Potts in bearable comfort in London? And what happened to Mrs Potts after his departure for Minorca? She hardly looked the placid woman who would waste much time waiting around for the uncertain return of an ageing and impoverished general. Their attraction for each other was probably as ephemeral as the gossip in *Town and Country*.

This gossip would certainly have arrived in Minorca at the same time as the new Lieutenant-Governor in February 1780, giving him an added touch of metropolitan scandal which might have grated on those he was joining.

His journey to Minorca had been characterised by yet another of those quarrels without which no military career seemed replete. He and the reinforcing troops stopped en route to Minorca at Gibraltar, where they arrived safely after Admiral Rodney had broken the blockade of the fortress. The redoubtable General Eliott, Governor and Commander-in-Chief of Gibraltar, knowing that relief was only a pause before a much greater assault, made the most of the opportunity presented by the arrival of reinforcements destined for Minorca. He simply pulled rank, and hijacked them.

Sir William reported the row to Charles Jenkinson who had become Secretary at War, from Gibraltar just before he sailed on to Minorca on 28 January 1780, and Jenkinson acknowledged the letter in May saying:

> I am sorry that General Eliott thought it proper to detain what was designed for you. We are however fully satisfied that you and the Governor will do everything that can be done, and am on that account under no apprehension.[2]

Jenkinson, and the War Office, should have been apprehensive. To commit two military commanders to the same post with overlapping responsibilities is rarely advisable. To post two old generals to that command is to raise the chances of explosive confrontation. To place Sir William Draper and Lieutenant-General the Hon. James Murray in joint command facing the prospect of a siege was to make that explosion virtually certain. The appointment could only have been sanctioned by a War Office determined to find active employment for senior officers and resigned to the idea of their perpetual quarrels. Both men over the years had given ample advance warning that their strengths and weaknesses were too similar to allow much room for manoeuvre. Somewhere in the process of bringing them together lurked a malicious sense of humour.

James Murray, then aged sixty, was a veteran of forty years service. He had commanded the left wing of Wolfe's army at Quebec, and had stayed on in Quebec to repel the French counter-attack and siege in the following year.

He nursed a grievance that his role in both battles had been given insufficient recognition, exacerbated by the criticism he attracted for the harshness of his government of Quebec between 1760 and 1763. His subsequent appointment as Governor of Canada, during three years when he was faced with a range of intractable problems, involved him in an inquiry by the House of Lords in London. This absolved him from charges brought by British settlers, but left him with an increased burden of anger. After leaving Canada he served in Ireland, was promoted Lieutenant-General in 1772, and two years later was designated Lieutenant-Governor of Minorca. Since the titular Governor never went to Minorca, Murray was effectively in charge from the start of his posting.

He would normally have expected his governorship to last for a few comfortable years in an undemanding backwater, manned largely by veteran semi-invalid troops and naval base personnel. He, a soldier of undeniable integrity, had reluctantly accepted the fact that traditionally the perquisites of the Governor's office, as well as judicious trading, were expected to swell his income. In 1779, fearing the possibility of a French invasion, he had sent his ailing and childless wife, Cordelia, home to England where she died soon after arrival. In 1780, he had married his second wife, the young daughter of the British Consul in Majorca. The commitments of late parenthood had increased his sense of involvement with Minorca, which was now as much a family home as a military posting. The last thing he would have welcomed was a war which brought Minorca into the front line. The arrival of another old warhorse, Sir William, could only have irritated him even more.

As so often in that period, there was a long hiatus after war had been declared. In June 1779, Murray arranged for the evacuation of his wife, and their infant daughter, to Leghorn. The Spanish were concentrating their forces on Gibraltar, and the French had made no offensive move. The following months of inactivity were devoted to improving the fortifications around Fort St Philip, the great ramparts of which dominated the harbour beyond the capital Mahon. This pause should have given Murray and Draper time to establish the parameters of their authority, but in the absence of any clear guidance from London, the position remained ambiguous.

The calm rolled on into 1781. The Spanish siege of Gibraltar was getting nowhere, and the defiance of the garrison caused the French and Spanish to decide that Minorca should be captured as a prelude to a final attempt on Gibraltar. Accordingly, on 20 August 1781, Spanish forces, 8,000 strong, under the command of the French Duc de Crillon, landed on the island and moved largely unopposed towards a siege of Fort St Philip.

De Crillon's force took Mahon without resistance, and was soon joined by French reinforcements which brought his combined strength to around 16,000. The overwhelming size of this force was to an extent irrelevant, since the key to the conquest lay solely in Fort St Philip. Its commanding position effectively kept open the harbour to any friendly ships bringing in supplies or reinforcements. A direct assault would have been unbearably costly. The allied

14. Fort St Philip, Minorca, at the time of the siege of 1781–1782, guarded the entrance to the great harbour and anchorage of Mahon.

army set about the laborious business of building artillery batteries to reduce the Fort by attrition.

The British garrison was almost ridiculously small, numbering some 2,000. There were only two British regiments of infantry, the 51st and 61st, both of which had deteriorated during their eleven years on the island. They were supported by two battalions of Hanoverian troops, and a mixed collection of artillerymen and armed seamen. There was no realistic hope that they would be reinforced in any significant numbers, since Eliott in Gibraltar had already commandeered those reinforcements.

In September, Murray showed his fighting mettle by personally leading a sortie from the Fort, similar to that which he had led from Quebec in 1760, and Draper had made from Madras, both twenty years earlier, attacking de Crillon's headquarters, destroying one battery and capturing 100 prisoners.

The progress of the siege was delayed while de Crillon, despairing of reducing the fortress, secretly offered Murray a bribe of a million sterling to surrender. The similarity of that sum to the Manila ransom would have touched Draper's ironic sense of humour. Murray spurned the insult, writing back to de Crillon on 16 October:

> [W]hen your brave ancestor was desired by his sovereign to assas-
> sinate the Duc de Guise he returned the answer that you should have
> done when you were charged to assassinate the character of a man
> whose birth is as illustrious as your own or that of the Duc de Guise.
> I can have no further communication with you except in arms.[3]

De Crillon replied, 'Your letter restores each of us to our place; it confirms the high opinion I always had of you.'

By the end of November, de Crillon had decided that the fortress could only be overcome through a blockade. His artillery and sapper troops had been so cautious in constructing their works that they were laughed at by the emaciated British troops in the fort above who shouted that they should be sent to school to learn to stand up to fire.

De Crillon managed to stop all supplies getting into the Fort, and by good fortune had demolished one of the Fort's magazines containing six months' provisions. Thenceforward it was simply a matter of time for deprivation to take its course. For the next seven weeks, until February 1782, the garrison had no alternative but to endure the ravages of hunger and sickness, cooped up in the crowded casements of the Fort.

As if the defenders had not already enough to endure, the friction between their commanders had grown worse over the months. Although they were both in the same enormous complex of buildings, Murray as Governor was in St Philip's Castle, while Sir William was in the Fort. This made it sensible for them to communicate by letter.

The specific cause for the break in their relations appears to have been brought about by Sir William's seemingly reasonable initiative of ordering some of the cannons to be deployed in sinking a small Spanish ship which had strayed within range, as early as mid-October. Murray issued an order the same day to the effect that the commander of the artillery could only accept orders directly from the Governor, 'who is eternally vigilant', and any requests for such orders must be referred to him. It was hardly surprising that Sir William should take exception to this order. Indeed Murray would probably not have issued it had he been on better terms with his Lieutenant-Governor. They were both seriously at fault in finding themselves unable to set an example of easy cooperation in circumstances where it was desperately needed.

Immediately after the order was issued to the garrison on 15 October, Sir William complained to one of the captains:

> that he was deprived of all command by the order, which was such
> an affront shown to him so serious that he would insist on a General
> Court Martial to decide who was in the right or wrong in regard to
> that as well as other things. That a General officer on the staff, and
> in his position here, to be obliged for permission to fire a gun was a
> thing unheard of, and extremely insulting to him.

The basic absurdity of the situation was that two senior generals should be sharing responsibility for a motley garrison of two thousand immobilised troops, most of them now beginning to suffer the effects of scurvy. Their obstinate reluctance to trim their own sense of importance and honour to the realities of the blockade would have been farcical had it not been tragic.

Although their relations deteriorated thereafter, as late as January they were corresponding on immediate military needs. The usual discussion of ravelins, glacis, covered ways, batteries, mines, etc, showed that they were both still prepared to pay more attention to their professional duties than to their personal differences.

On 16 January, however, Murray started his letter with the words which brought about their final rupture:

> I wish to avoid all altercation with you at present; I and I alone am responsible to my King and Country for the defence of this place. Every attempt to take the command of the garrison from me will be ineffective.[4]

Sir William's reply was equally provocative;

> I deny Sir that you alone are responsible for the defence of this place; my commission as Lieutenant-Governor tells me to take this island, its fortifications, forts and castles under my charge. I therefore require you to call a Council of War to consider a situation according to the rules and practices of our profession ... I must decline acting if you refuse this ... your insinuation that I am trying to take the command from you is false and infamous.

Murray was not going to be manoeuvred into the formality of calling a Council of War, and replied the same day:

> As you declined the execution of the command I assigned to you and will not obey your Governor it is better for the service that you should be taken at your word. Such an example of disrespect and contempt of a Governor is inexcusable at all times in the present situation of affairs here. I think it cannot be justified, and therefore Colonel Pringle will take command of the outer British lines, and Colonel De Luisiy that of the Hanoverians; the King is to determine whether you or I is right with what regards his service. As to personal abuse I shall do justice to myself, when the proper time arrives.

Six days later, Murray sent another missive:

> The Governor presents his compliments to Sir William Draper. When Sir William declined acting and the Governor consented he should not, it was never meant by the Governor that Sir William should be put under arrest; the Governor only meant to lay the whole affair before the King ... and it cannot be supposed that it was ever the

Governor's intention to confine Sir William, although he agrees to
his not acting as Lieutenant-Governor.

The bizarre interchange finished with Draper acknowledging Murray's words
by confirming:

I have only to say I am perfectly indifferent to your mode of
proceeding. I depend upon nothing but the justice of my cause.

The only mitigating factor in these deplorable jousts was that they did
not involve any casualties sacrificed as offerings to the obstinacy of either
commander. By January, the long-suffering soldiery probably regarded the
quarrels of their senior officers as yet another infliction to be borne along with
malnutrition, scurvy and the occasional French bombardment.

By the beginning of February 1782, the garrison was so reduced that only
600 men were fit for duty, and of these no fewer than 500 were suffering from
scurvy. Murray, in his dispatches which still continued to filter through to
London noted:

Such was the uncommon spirit of the King's troops that they
concealed their disorder and inability rather than go into hospital;
several men died on guard after having stood on sentry, their fate not
being discovered till called upon for relief.

Accepting the inevitable in due course, Murray capitulated after a parley on
5 February, the details of which took another nine days to arrange, including
the concession that the garrison could march from the Fort with flags flying
and drums beating.

On the morning of 14 February, the remnants of the garrison, 600 soldiers,
200 seamen, 120 artillerymen and 45 Corsicans, Jews, Turks and Moors
marched from the Fort. A contemporary historian wrote:

A spectacle so very tragical and at the same time so glorious to
the sufferers was perhaps never before seen as when the miserable
remains of the brave garrison of Fort St Philip marched out with
the honours of war. The Spanish and French armies were drawn
up opposite to each other and formed a line for the passage of the
emaciated, worn down and decrepit soldiers who were followed
by the artillery and the seamen. The scene became truly interesting
when the battalions arrived at the place appointed to lay down
their arms. He must have been devoid of every noble feeling who on
this occasion would not have felt a pang for these heroic veterans
who exclaimed with tears in their eyes that 'they surrendered their
arms to God alone' and at the same time appeared to derive great

consolation from the opinion that the victors would not boast of their conquest in taking a hospital.[5]

As the garrison marched out, no fewer than 660 men were left inside incapable of moving through illness or wounds. During the siege, a total of just forty-nine had been killed, with 149 wounded. Scurvy had claimed many more lives. The survivors were conducted to the small port of Alcor to await transports as prisoners of war.

Despite the bravery and endurance of the whole garrison, the fact remained that Minorca had fallen, and de Crillon was free to move his forces to concentrate on the more important fortress of Gibraltar. It was a major loss for Britain, and the commanders would have been well aware that the defeat would be directly compared with the loss of the island twenty-six years earlier. The ghost of Admiral Byng was probably also hovering in their thoughts.

In the knowledge that an inquiry into the disaster was likely in London and that news of his altercations with Murray had already reached London, Sir William, as early as 5 February had sent a marker for his case to Jenkinson:

> I have the great misfortune to find myself a prisoner of war by an infamous capitulation made without my knowledge or consent. I console myself with the reflection that it has not happened through any fault of mine; my appeal is to the whole garrison. Sickness certainly contributed something, but pride, passion, arrogance, presumption, ignorance and fear conspired much more to deprive His Majesty of this fortress.[6]

Pride, passion and arrogance had been shown as much by himself as by Murray, but Sir William had been deeply at fault in allowing his sense of self-importance to distort his order of priorities. Whatever his personal feelings about Murray's erratic qualities these should have been kept under control by the need to display unanimity to the troops under their joint command. Retiring into a huff was not a substitute for leadership.

Both Murray and Draper, in accordance with the terms of the capitulation that officers in bad health could return to England travelled back overland through France, though Murray spent some time at Leghorn with his family. They would have arrived back in London to find that the political landscape had suddenly changed through the resignation of Lord North. He had finally left office in March 1782 after the news of Cornwallis's surrender to Washington at Yorktown in November 1781 had signalled the loss of the war in America.

North's departure and the perceived scale of the disaster in America completely overshadowed the news of the loss of Minorca. Whereas its fall in 1756 had been crucial to the outbreak of a major war, now it was almost a sideshow. Horace Walpole put both events in context, writing to Horace

Mann who, as ambassador to the Grand Duke of Tuscany, had been the main conduit of information between Minorca and London during the siege:

> The total revolution in the ministry ... you will not be surprised we have been occupied with that event ... we have not run into any great heats on the loss of Minorca. It has made no more impression than if the King had lost his handkerchief. For Minorca we are satisfied with the encomiums showered on General Murray by the Duc de Crillon. We know poor Draper was mad, and we have no more curiosity.[7]

Sir William's reappearance in England coincided with the return of Lord Shelburne to power, his main priority to direct negotiations towards an acceptable peace. These negotiations were channelled principally through the American representative in Paris, Benjamin Franklin.

Sir William, passing through Paris on his way back to England in late March, was oddly able to play a small role in accelerating the moves towards negotiations. Even though he was a 'prisoner of war' on parole, he had a conversation with the French Foreign Minister, the Comte de Vergennes. It was apparently arranged for him by none other than his old acquaintance the Comte d'Estaing who, writing to Vergennes on 1 April 1782, said that Draper had 'departed perfectly content' and that d'Estaing had wished him luck as 'a channel of peace'.[8] He also mentioned in his letter that he had advised Draper, unsuccessfully, not to proceed with his plan for bringing charges against Murray.

The conversation between Vergennes and Draper must have been more than an exchange of pleasantries. On 5 April, Shelburne, writing to George III, mentioned:

> I have been surprised since I took up my pen with a letter from Mr Franklin. I immediately sent for Lord Cholmondeley who tells me much of the disposition to peace and refers to a conversation which Sir William Draper had upon the subject with M. De Vergennes. I have sent to desire to see Sir William tomorrow morning and I have appointed to see Mr Oswald [the secret British negotiator] this evening that he may be ready in case it should be thought fit to sound Dr. Franklin.[9]

Shelburne's position in relation to France had been strengthened by the epic resistance of Gibraltar to de Crillon's siege, and Admiral Rodney's victory over the French at the Battle of the Saints which re-established British control over the Atlantic.

In the Indian seas the French had been unable to regain their former naval power and it was a strange irony that the ageing Sir Eyre Coote, still in command of the Company's forces, should have had his death hastened when his ship was chased into Madras by a French cruiser in April 1783 before news of the peace reached the Indies.

There had been no plans to restage the expedition to Manila during that period of hostilities as a diversion against Spanish forces elsewhere. By then only two senior officers from the 1762 expedition were still alive, William Draper and Admiral Sir Richard Kempenfeldt. By an odd coincidence, Kempenfeldt was drowned in August of that year, 1782, when his flagship, the *Royal George* suddenly sank in Spithead with the loss of 800 lives. Kempenfeldt would have found little consolation in achieving immortality through the indifferent poems and songs dedicated to this tragedy.

In the same month, Sir William was effectively putting an end to his own military career by pressing on with his decision to initiate court martial proceedings against Murray. Both were now back in England, neither willing to concede the justice of his own case or leave unquestioned the slur on their honour as commanders.

24

COURT MARTIAL

In the eighteenth century, the court martial of a senior officer was not the rare event it has since become. It was accepted as a routine method for exploring failures in command rather than a trial on criminal charges. It was often the only channel by which senior officers could clear their names or vindicate their actions. Because so many senior officers were also members of Parliament, the court martial had also become a medium for indirect attacks on the government of the day or the paying off of old scores.

The chance of being involved in a court martial at some time in his career was looked upon as a normal professional hazard by any officer in the army or navy. This likelihood ran in tandem with the freedom to publicise or protest about one's case in pamphlet or newspaper column with total disregard to the concept of a fair trial. There is a rich mine of outrage, invective, special pleading and insult in the accumulated mass of writing produced by aggrieved officers during the period, most of it linked to courts martial or some other form of enquiry.

The fact that Sir William should prefer charges against General Murray was not in itself sensational. Murray could equally easily have made charges against Sir William, not least for insubordination. Murray's reputation was not, however, under question, despite having lost Minorca. The praise accorded to him by the Duc de Crillon was sufficient evidence of his valour, and the knowledge that he had rejected a bribe of one million pounds had added to his reputation. He would have had little to prove in bringing charges against Sir William and whatever his faults of impetuosity and arrogance he was not a vindictive man. He would probably have been content to let the matter

15. Gillray's cartoon of the 1782 Court Martial depicting both Draper and Murray attesting before the court at which all the senior officers would have known each other well. Above Murray's head is inscribed 'Matrimony'. Draper stands with both hands on the barrier with a composed expression.

drop, with his own honour intact and Sir William's behaviour discounted as a mental aberration.

Sir William could on the other hand justifiably feel that his honour and reputation had been impugned, and could only be salvaged by a robust presentation of his case to be aired in public and judged by his military peers.

Courts martial were seen by the public, which followed them closely, to be somewhere between an entertainment and a useful guide to the mysteries of command and control in the armed services. The courts were expected to have elements of theatre, and as they usually proceeded at an extremely slow pace could be a source of gossip and enlightenment over a number of months.

Sir William, immediately after his return to London, stuck to his intention of bringing Murray to a court martial. The subsequent accusations by Murray's biographers that he had gone round London bad-mouthing Murray before the latter's return from Minorca and Leghorn seem to have been dubious, since Sir William considered himself still a prisoner of war on his parole and wrote in those terms to Lord Sydney, the Secretary at War, from Bath in May 1782:

> I am extremely sorry that my situation as a prisoner of war puts it
> out of my power to offer my services to His Majesty ... if any cartel
> take place to free me from this odious and humiliating engagement

there is no part of the globe to which I will not go with the utmost
goodwill to endeavour to be of use to Him. Having been informed
on my arrival that it was not customary for prisoners to appear at
Court I quitted Town with much anxiety that I could not personally
throw myself at His Majesty's feet and thank him for the numerous
instances of his goodness to me.[1]

Horace Walpole, writing to Mann in August 1782, kept him in touch with the
early moves by Sir William:

who some weeks ago preferred a complaint against General Murray,
but the Judge Advocate General said it was not sufficiently specific.
I believe he has now given one less general, but the cause cannot be
tried yet for the want of Colonel Pringle who was hostage for the
transport vessels.[2]

Pringle was back in England by the autumn and his reappearance enabled
Walpole to write in October, 'Sir William persists in bringing General Murray
to a court martial, of which he will probably make nothing,' and a month
later was adding:

You have seen I suppose in the newspapers the articles preferred
against General Murray by Sir William Draper who has certainly
attacked his weak side, his judgement. It threatened to be a most
tedious trial ... but it is interrupted for the present by Sir William
falling ill. I have long determined not to concern myself with Courts
Martial which I do not understand and it is unjust for so ignorant a
person to pronounce on men whose honour is at stake.[3]

This last sentence must be one of the very few occasions on which Horace
Walpole ever expressed reluctance to pronounce on anything, though he
added, with his usual wit, 'were a lawyer to be tried his character is of no
consequence – at worst he could be made a peer.'

The Court finally assembled in November 1782, presided over by Generals
Sir George Howard and Studholme Hodgson. Howard was probably selected
because, as a former Governor of Minorca, he should have been familiar with
the island. Sir Charles Gould, Judge Advocate-General, conducted the court
which consisted of twelve lieutenant-generals, and three major-generals. All
of them would have personally known both plaintiff and defendant and felt
a mixture of embarrassment and irritation at having to be involved in the
whole affair. Two in particular, Thomas Gage and George Lane Parker, had
been in constant touch with Sir William over many years, Parker not least
in proposing Draper for membership at Brooks's in 1764. It also says much
about the superfluous numbers of senior officers at the time that no fewer

than seventeen generals could be spared for the three months needed for the hearings and verdict.

The verbatim evidence of the trial, recorded by Gurney the renowned shorthand writer, rests in 700 pages in the National Archives. It still manages to impart a sense of the claustrophobic pressure endured by the whole garrison during the two months of the siege, with plenty of time for small issues to become magnified to absurd proportions.

The twenty-nine charges levelled against Murray were a mixture of attacks on his handling of events before, during, and after the siege, some of specific military incompetence, but most of a varied nature involving allegations of waste of public money and stores, extortion, rapacity and cruelty. Sir William weakened his chances of getting the court to concentrate on the key issue – the demarcation of his authority – by putting forward a rag-bag of other accusations.

The Court sat intermittently from November 1782 to January 1783 in the Horse Guards. Gillray's cartoon, *The Court Martial*, drawn during one of the days of the trial, illustrates the cosy nature of the proceedings. Some of the seventeen generals felt no concern about dozing or attending to other paperwork. Contemporary accounts described Murray as 'looking very broken, but with all the remains of a very stout man'; while Sir William was 'looking very well and in the flower of his age, his star very conspicuous and his arm always carefully disposed so as never to eclipse it'.

To justify the large number of charges, Sir William explained in evidence that:

> I informed General Murray ... that I would certainly bring him to
> a General Court Martial for his order of October 15th, as being
> destructive to the public service, as well as most injurious and
> disgraceful to my own character as a general officer. In General
> Murray's answer, produced in Court, he challenged me to investigate
> his whole conduct from the time of my arrival.[4]

Hence the multiplicity of charges, the crucial one – whether or not the Lieutenant-Governor had the right to order the use of artillery pieces without referring to the 'ever-vigilant' Governor – becoming obscured in wider and less relevant issues. Much questioning was devoted to the charge that Murray had abused his civil powers by seeking to raise his cut on all the local auctions. The bizarre amount of time devoted to this charge confirmed yet again that the division of the spoils of office, and opportunity for privateering, were never far from the minds of senior officers, whatever the other calls of duty.

The court delivered its verdict at the end of January. Murray was fully and honourably acquitted of all the charges preferred against him with the exception of two; the trivial one of interfering with auction dues, and the crucial one of issuing his Order of 15 October 1781, derogatory to his

Lieutenant-Governor. On these he was sentenced to be reprimanded. On the proceedings being submitted to him, the King was 'pleased to approve of the zeal, courage and firmness with which General Murray had conducted himself in the defence of Fort St Philip, as well as that of his former long and approved services'. The King also dispensed with the reprimands and further expressed his concern that an officer like Sir William Draper should have 'allowed his judgement to become so perverted as to bring such charges against his superior'.

The court was worried that because of the exchanges between the two in Minorca there might still be an occasion for a duel. They ordered Sir William to sign an apology to Murray drafted by the court, which he did, as he said, 'because he had been so ordered'.

Murray, just to complicate matters, then refused to accept the apology in its drafted form. He wrote to Harry Conway, who by then had become a Field-Marshal and Commander-in-Chief, saying that he would rather resign his regiment than accept the draft but as he had a wife and three children, with another on the way, asked Conway for a pension for her of £300 per annum. Conway, backing the court, tried to persuade him to accept the apology but failed to do so. Absurdly, Murray was then put under arrest, until he finally acquiesced.

Walpole commented to Mann:

> The sentence was a strange one; yet I imagine calculated to prevent very desperate consequences between a madman and a very hot-headed one. Of the 29 charges they pronounced 27 trifling; and on the other two which do not seem very grave they reprimanded Murray; and then ordered accuser and accused to apologise to each other. Draper, though the great Bedlamite, obeyed; Murray would not utter all that was enjoined and was put under arrest. It seems that Draper, during the siege used even in writing most harsh expressions to his commander. Pains are taken to mollify the latter and reconcile him to submission; there I must leave their history till I know how it ends.[5]

It continued for a few more months, as the published proceedings of the court failed to include Sir William's rejoinder to Murray's defence although it had been read before the Court. In 1783, to redress what he felt to be an imbalance of the record, Sir William published a pamphlet entitled *Observations on the Hon. Lieutenant-General Murray's Defence*, justifying his effort by stressing that 'these few observations to the public will set many facts in a very different light. No public war is intended.'[6]

The tone of the pamphlet, including letters exchanged between Sir William and other officers during the siege, at least disproved Walpole's gibe about Draper being the great Bedlamite. The arguments were reasonable and calm, free from any personal rancour and expressive mostly of a sense of bafflement that his action should have been so misrepresented:

> General Murray has also taken great pains to make the Court and the public believe that the cause of our dissension originated with me; I have served in three great wars; let him or his emissaries produce a single instance in either where His Majesty's service has suffered by my want of temper or moderation ... Even after the insults and disgrace I had suffered, whenever he would condescend to ask my opinion I gave it to him honestly and in writing.

Even allowing for exaggeration in some of Sir William's original charges, Murray seems to have made some curious decisions during the siege which any fellow officer of the same seniority might reasonably have queried. One was to sink a serviceable navy frigate, so that its crew of thirty could be added to the garrison, despite the protests of the Royal navy captain, Lawson, who would have seen a court martial staring him in the face. In pursuing this question Sir William also revealed that no fewer than 1,100 of his men had been hijacked by Eliott at Gibraltar:

> A vessel, [the frigate] valued at fifteen thousand pounds is sunk to gain thirty hands to the garrison; they were dear recruits. The General Murray privateer could have been navigated by ten hands only. Had the Governor dispatched these vessels for Gibraltar we were sure, if they were not taken, to have a supply of men, because it was in General Eliott's interest to have sent them; for he could not be attacked until our fate was determined; as long as we held out, the siege of Gibralatar would not be undertaken; General Eliott took 1100 men from me, which were under my command, and designed for our garrison; he would not have denied a part of them on so just a requisition.

The reference to the 'privateer General Murray' was to a ship rather than to the general. Apparently Murrray had shares in a privateer named after himself, although, with foresight more typical of a modern tax-evading entrepreneur, had placed the shares in his wife's name. He had also, before the siege, suggested Draper's involvement in his enterprise via shares allotted in the names of Sir William's daughters, a temptation which the penurious soldier seems to have resisted, thus enabling him to claim the high moral ground when he queried:

> The Court has been through the motive for introducing the names of my daughters as having shares in the General Murray privateer; it has been proved that I had no concern in it, either directly or

indirectly; but can that Governor be said to have no concerns in privateers fitted out by him with government stores and men, when he exacts arbitrary dues upon all private goods?

Sir William finished with an exposition of the case lying at the core of the dispute, the confusion around the limits of the authority shared between himself and Murray, posing a final question: 'I leave to the court to decide if the man who gives an affront, or he who receives it, sows the seed of dissension in a garrison, is the aggressor or the sufferer most to blame?'

The pamphlet did not trigger any further airing of the issues. The verdict of the court that several of the charges had been ill-founded was enough to undermine any thoughts that great national issues were, or had been, at stake. Yet the court martial, in reprimanding Murray on the charge of derogating his Lieutenant-Governor, touched upon an issue of military importance and the Court might have served a more useful purpose if it had gone any way to clarifying the exact balance of responsibilities in such situations.

A curious postscript to the affair, which at least showed that Sir William was not alone in tangling with Murray, followed immediately after the court martial. A Mr Sutherland brought an action against Murray for his illegal suspension from the office of judge of the Vice-Admiralty Court in Minorca. Murray had offered to reinstate Sutherland on his making an apology. The matter had been referred home, and the King had approved Murray's action; but a jury found that Murray had acted arbitrarily and unreasonably, awarding damages against him for the large sum of £5,000. This would have spelt disaster to the old general burdened with four young children. He was, however, able to enlist the aid of friends in Parliament who provided for him from the public purse. Murray lived on until 1794, and one of the four children himself went on to become a major-general.

The court martial verdict coincided with completion of the peace process, and in consequence marked the end of the military careers of both Murray and Sir William. Both were now over sixty, and in the imminent peace there would be no more need for their services. For Sir William there were to be no more opportunities or disappointments like Manila or Minorca.

25

CHIMERA
RENEWED

The Treaty of Versailles of September 1783 finally brought peace between England, France and Spain, as well as independence to the United States of America. Under the Treaty, Minorca was formally ceded to Spain, while Gibraltar, which had resisted the epic siege, remained in British hands. The agreements between England, France and Spain were of limited importance in comparison with formal recognition of the United States of America, a landmark whose long-term implications could hardly have been grasped by most contemporaries.

On a more immediate level, the Treaty of Independence represented a conclusive disaster for the active Loyalists in America. They could no longer take comfort from the hope that a British victory would restore their fortunes or justify the sacrifices they had made over the previous eight years. Peace brought them face to face with the cold reality that they were to be virtually abandoned by the mother country.

The British Government under Shelburne, anxious for quick disengagement from the American morass, chose to compensate active Loyalists, many of them now refugees in England. The Government had not realised that it would be receiving at least 3,000 claims for support. In July 1783, Parliament established a commission to process Loyalist claims, but the hope that it could finish its work within a year soon turned out to be unrealistic, as each claim had to be scrutinised on the basis that it was likely to be, and usually was, grossly exaggerated.

The De Lancey family was closely involved with the work of the Commission in London, all having been forced to quit New York in 1783. Susannah Draper's father, General Oliver de Lancey, was among those who had suffered most, having been included in the New York Act of Attainder of 1779 by which all his property was confiscated. When New York was evacuated by the British at the end of the war, the family had no other choice but to go into exile and accept the consequences of having been on the losing side.

James de Lancey, cousin of Oliver, represented the exiles of New York in London, on the Board of Agents. Months of quibbling turned into years. The Prime Minister, William Pitt the Younger, successor to Shelburne, finally decided in 1785 that only £150,000 should be distributed among all those claimants whose cases had already been reported. It seemed scant compensation to those who had lost everything through their loyalty to the Crown, but the British Government was itself in dire straits through the immense expenditure involved in eight years of attempting to sustain British rule in America.

General Oliver de Lancey had submitted his claim in May 1784, invoking the support of senior British military figures to vouch for his contribution to the Loyalist effort. At the time of his claim he was living in Beverley, Yorkshire with his wife and daughter Charlotte, on a tiny income. His total claim amounted to around $390,000 but, in the end, he had to settle for the paltry sum of $25,000. The days of splendour at Bloomingdale must have seemed already far in the past, and De Lancey had died by the time the claim was finally settled. His widow and daughter lived on in Beverley, and were joined there by his other daughter Anne who had also come to England in exile with her husband John Harris Cruger.

It was one of the strange ironies of Loyalist involvement that Cruger's brother Henry, the MP for Bristol, who throughout the war had remained a constant spokesman at Westminster for American secession was soon welcomed back in America while still remaining an MP. He eventually became a member of the New York Senate, while John Harris Cruger had to live out the restricted life of an exile in Beverley.

James de Lancey, in his work for the claimants, divided his time between London and Bath, and would have been in frequent touch with Sir William, who had retired to Bath after the Minorca court martial. Draper had by then sold Manila Hall, and had suffered the death of his younger daughter Phila Augusta before she was ten.

Despite support from relations, he was still in a parlous financial state and during 1784 was trying to enlist some sympathy from his residual contacts in government. In March he was writing from Brompton Row in London to Lord Sydney, now Secretary at War, seeking to establish whether it might be possible for him still to draw some salary as Lieutenant-Governor of Minorca:

> [T]he events of the last war have been peculiarly fatal to me as an individual. I am a sufferer in various shapes. My wife's fortune of

£6000 to be paid out of General de Lancey's American estate is forfeited to the rebels. My hopes of the Manila ransom are done away ... I lose a thousand per annum as Lt-Governor of Minorca. As I am very conscious of the necessities of the state as well as my own perhaps it may appear improper to solicit a continuation of my income as Lt-Governor but as I am so unequal to the rank and honour which His Majesty was pleased to confer upon me in my more prosperous days (unless I have some appointment) ... my state is a burden to me ... I have no pretensions but from actual and personal exertions. Political merits I have none, having industriously avoided that path ... I have not the honour of being acquainted with the Minister [William Pitt], His Noble Father was pleased to consult and employ me and to rank me in the number of his friends. Do not give me reason to say that I have outlived them all.[1]

Later that same month he was writing again to Sydney seeking some sort of acknowledgement of his request:

My rank gives me the usual privilege of an audience from His Majesty but I am so circumstanced that I *cannot* go to St James's; for as His Majesty was pleased to deny me the satisfaction ordered by the General Court Martial on General Murray's trial I conceive him to be greatly displeased with me; of course I have not presumed to approach the throne since that time, so that it in some sort obliges me to this form of solicitation.[2]

Neither letter produced any positive response during that summer, and in September he again approached Sydney, finishing with the plea:

All I ask is to be put on such a footing as may enable me to end my days in decency and comfort. I am sixty three years of age and cannot be long a burden on the public. I am humbled indeed. This letter is a proof of it; having been honoured with the command of a conquering army and with the thanks of the House of Commons it is with great pain that I find myself obliged to assure your Lordship that I am below the convenience of a post chaise or a horse. I am literally *sur le pavé*.[3]

Similar letters were equally unproductive. The Government, overburdened by a massive national debt, was in no position to find increased pensions or employment for a large number of superannuated senior officers. As some form of compensation, Sir William was nominated to a mixed board of land and naval officers set up in April 1785 to review the defences of Portsmouth and Plymouth. Apart from this equivalent of 'light duty', Sir William had to accept the inevitability of half-pay and oblivion. He spent most of his time in Bath for the remaining three years of his life. In being hard-pressed for cash he was at one with most of his fellow senior officers, and he still had a network of contacts, not least from among his relations who looked upon him as the most distinguished member of the family.

His cousin Daniel, who had just retired as a rich man from the East India Company, still maintained friendly contact, probably in gratitude to Sir William for having given shelter to his runaway wife Eliza and her daughter Betsy in the wake of the Laurence Sterne scandal. Daniel Draper kept in close enough touch with Sir William to be chosen as executor of the will of the General's daughter Anna Susannah. The Drummond family also appear to have ensured that their one-time brother-in-law should not have to endure real poverty, and in 1785 George Drummond, nephew of Caroline Draper, extended Sir William a loan of around £1,500.

The General also still kept in touch with current events, and in 1786 was consulted by his long-standing friend and possible tormentor Philip Francis, now Sir Philip, who had returned from India and was deeply involved in the early moves for impeachment of the Governor-General Warren Hastings. Francis had sought Sir William's opinion as to whether it would be correct for him, Francis, to be included among the managers of the impeachment. Francis, the following year in Parliament paid tribute to Sir William and the advice he gave in saying, 'The honourable person I consulted is no more ... but those who knew Sir William Draper I am sure will acknowledge that there could not be a stricter and more scrupulous judge of points of honour than he was.' It would be interesting to know whether Francis, if he was Junius, had been tempted to share that secret with his most obvious victim when he consulted Sir William about the Hastings impeachment, shortly before the General's death when he must have been showing signs of impending mortality.

Sir William died in Bath on 8 January 1787, in his sixty-sixth year, 'sincerely lamented by all who had the pleasure of his acquaintance'. Both the *Gentleman's Magazine* and the *Bath Journal*, in reporting his death, made certain with their usual frankness that their readers should be aware of his surviving daughter's prospects, the first commenting that 'she survives her father with an ample fortune from her maternal relations,' the second, more specifically, that 'he has left an only daughter, about 14 years old, adorned with every desirable accomplishment. She has a fortune above £20,000, lately bequeathed to her by a relation.' Both these details of her inheritance sit oddly with her father's much-discussed poverty, and the possible source of her inheritance. However, she was undoubtedly well provided from whatever source.

The Times on 18 Jan 1787, ten days after Sir William's death, produced a long 'Characteristic Sketch', obviously written by a friend who had known him over the years. It referred to:

his unhappy propensity to play, in which he was not successful, and conducting himself at the gaming table with that liberal spirit which he manifested on all and every occasion of his life he became frequently involved in difficulties which checked the current of his humanity, narrowed the circle of his comforts, and embittered his days.

It also, with candour typical of the period, mentioned that 'the death of his second wife was accompanied with the loss of a most amiable daughter, the offspring of an illegitimate passion, but whose virtues had rendered her as dear to Lady Draper as to her father.' There was no further clue to as to the age of this daughter, or indeed to this added dimension to Sir William's life, but it seems that she had been part of his life before his second marriage. Her acceptance by Susannah, and earlier by Caroline, points to domestic generosity on all sides.

Sir William was buried at Walcot Church, Bath, and his connection with Bath is marked in the Abbey with a tablet and Latin inscription composed by his oldest friend Christopher Anstey, noting the highlights of his career and hailing him as an energetic leader and a kindly man.

The administration of his estate confirmed at least his concerns about virtual penury; since he left no will in the knowledge that there was nothing to leave. Administration of his affairs was granted to three creditors, the founding partners of the London bankers Cox and King's. Richard Cox, then aged seventy, had been appointed agent for the First Foot Guards as far back as 1758 by the then colonel, Ligonier, and would have known William Draper as a young captain. Cox had probably been swayed more by ties from the past than hope for the future when he granted the loan against Sir William's bond.

The burden of paying off Sir William's debts now lay on the young shoulders of Anna Susannah who, as a minor, could at least defer responsibility for some years. She, aged fourteen, was now an orphan; having lost her mother at five, her sister Phila a few years later, and finally her father. The only figure in her young life who had been constantly present was her much older cousin, Anna Collins, whose husband, the naval captain Richard Collins, had himself died in 1780. Like so many of her contemporaries, she had grown up at a time when sudden death in the family was considered normal, but this could not have diminished the loss experienced on the death of her beloved father. Her only future consolation was that as an heiress she would not be short of suitors.

Her chances of leading a lively few years after her father's death were greatly enhanced by being placed under the guardianship of Viscount Duncannon and accepted into his family. Duncannon, heir to the Earl of Bessborough, was husband to Lady Henrietta Spencer, sister of Georgiana, Duchess of Devonshire. The two sisters shone at the centre of London society in the 1780s and their extended families shared their reflected light. The Duncannons, and their four children, the youngest of whom, Caroline, was to become notorious years later as Lady Caroline Lamb, lived between Cavendish Square and

Roehampton. It is not immediately apparent why Duncannon should have agreed to be guardian to Anna Susannah Draper, who was eight years older than his eldest child. It seems that Duncannon – 'a man of most amiable and mild manners' – was sufficiently friendly with Sir William to give his orphaned daughter a place in the Duncannon family group assuming that as an heiress it would not be long before she left again as a bride.

Within three years, that assumption was a reality. In 1790, at St Marylebone Church, close to the Duncannon home in Cavendish Square, Anna Susannah, at seventeen years still a minor, was married by special consent of her guardian Duncannon, to John Gore. He, aged twenty-two, was from an old Somerset family with estates near Bristol and was obviously an acceptable match for the young bride, as the witnesses of the marriage were Duncannon himself, and her young uncle Oliver de Lancey who was shortly to be promoted to Deputy Adjutant-General.

Anna Susannah might reasonably have hoped that her marriage would bring some settled and fruitful years. She was to be cruelly disappointed. In July 1792, only two years after their marriage, John Gore suddenly died. He was buried in the tiny church of the Somerset village of Christon which still contains a memorial tablet placed there in his memory by his 'disconsolate' wife. The nineteen-year-old orphan was now already a childless widow, with many reasons to feel disconsolate.

She herself only survived her husband by one year, dying suddenly at Hotwells near Bristol in 1793 at the age of twenty, still on the threshold of adult life. She had taken the precaution of preparing a will, its details tying together the residual strands of her family life, as well as shedding light on the indebtedness of her father after his lifetime of military service, directing that:

> [T]he sum of six thousand pounds in the Funds be applied solely
> towards the debts contracted by my late father, Sir William Draper
> ... and for the proper application of the said sum I appoint as
> trustees Daniel Draper of St James's Street Westminster, and
> Benjamin Ashe of Oxford Row, Bath.[4]

The appointment of Daniel Draper, her father's rich cousin, as a trustee confirms the closeness of the contacts maintained over the years. The other trustee, Benjamin Ashe, had been an officer in the Company since 1768 and his wife Mary was a daughter of Sir William's sister Anne Moore.

Among Anna Susannah's bequests was one of £500 to her cousin William Howe de Lancey, who had just become a Lieutenant in the 16th Dragoons, and fifty pounds to Christopher Anstey, 'as a slight memorial of my gratitude to his attention to my father's memory'. All the remaining sums were bequeathed to Mrs Anne Collins who had been so close to her since the time of her birth. Lamentably in a codicil, she desired *most particularly* that Mrs Collins should 'collect all my papers, letters, pocket books etc and burn them all herself and that all the papers to and from the Countess of Bessborough are to be returned to her'. Thus in a self-absorbed but not unusual gesture she virtually wiped out all trace not only of herself but of the whole network of her personal and family relationships.

Anna Susannah's early death and her directions for the burning of the family papers thus severed any connection with the Manila venture. Yet by a strange coincidence that connection was carried into the next generation via the De Lanceys. William Howe de Lancey, her young cousin and small beneficiary of her will, was serving four years later as Aide-de-Camp to Colonel Arthur Wellesley, the future Duke of Wellington, when as colonel of the 33rd Regiment he had recently arrived with his regiment in Calcutta. Almost immediately after their arrival it seemed likely that Wellesley might be entrusted with command of another expedition formed to re-enact the seizure of Manila.

Hostilities with Spain had become likely since Spain's decision in 1796 to drop out of the coalition against revolutionary France, and in India there was suddenly discussion of an opportunity to mount an expedition similar to that of 1762. Wellesley, writing from Calcutta to his brother Lord Mornington in April 1797, discussed the possibility of commanding the large force being assembled, in terms of his own suitability for such a daring operation in comparison with any of the other likely candidates.[5] In the letter, he also echoed the feelings of William Draper, expressed almost forty years earlier, that such a command 'would make my fortune. Going upon it at all will enable me to free myself from debt; therefore you may easily conceive that I am not very anxious for a conclusion of a peace at this moment.' It seems likely that his enthusiasm for the Manila project had probably been stimulated by young De Lancey, passing on recollections given to him by his uncle, Sir William.

The expedition set out from India, including Wellesley though not under his command, but never got farther than the island of Penang. Having landed there in September 1797, the troops were immediately recalled by Lord Hobart, the Governor of Madras who was (echoes of Stringer Lawrence) worried about the activity of the French around Pondicherry, and the threatening attitude of Tippoo Sultan. Wellesley returned to India with his regiment to set out on the campaign which was to take him forward to the great pinnacles of his later career.

Cancellation of the expedition at Penang was the last military offensive planned by Britain against Spain in the Pacific region. Manila subsided into the peaceful calm of a commercial backwater for a further century as patterns of trade changed. Its isolation within the waning authority of the Spanish empire resulted in the virtual abandonment of its fortifications. The cannon still on the ramparts when the Americans landed in 1898 to absorb the whole of the Philippines into the American sphere of influence were those which had been in place to resist the British fleet 130 years earlier, in 1762. By then they were decorative rather than functional.

By then, also, the memory of the unique conquest of Manila had long faded in the shadow of greater events. The last tribute to Sir William had surfaced in the *Gentleman's Magazine* in 1799, when it carried a letter from a correspondent who had found a copy of the *Madras Courier* of October 1788 which had a Memoir of Sir William, almost certainly written by the then proprietor, Hugh Boyd, his tennis-playing friend, who twenty years earlier had been suspected of being Junius.

The Memoir traced Sir William's achievements, but the writer was more interested in him as an individual than as a military monument, concentrating as he did on the General's personal qualities:

> Relying solely on his own merits he aspired after the highest prefer-
> ment and succeeded by mere dint of superior worth. That courtesy
> which distinguished his demeanour sprang not so much from stud-
> ied politeness as from a mild and gentle heart. He possessed manly
> sense and dignity which are the issues of a liberal mind polished by
> the hand of freedom. He distinguished himself by the most intrepid
> courage as well as by that affable disposition which gains the hearts
> of soldiers and qualify a man to shine in a military light ...

> He had a mind capable of forming great designs and of executing
> them with surprising celerity, and with all that a patience that could
> wait the favourable moment for their ripening ...

> His philanthropy was great – numberless are the instances of the
> benevolence of his heart and the bounty of his hand. His only
> surviving child was zealous in rendering, by every tender office and
> mark of affection the warmest filial affection could suggest, the
> evening of his life serene and pleasing ...

> In short, if unshaken loyalty, intrepidity of mind and tenderness of
> heart all united in an eminent degree can distinguish a character, that
> of my late lamented friend Sir William Draper is by these qualities
> discriminated from others. His life was gentle and the elements so
> mixed in him that nature might stand up and say to all the world
> 'This was a man'.[6]

It was somehow appropriate that this last tribute to Sir William should have been printed in Madras. As the place which he had helped to defend in 1758, and from which he set out on his unique expedition in 1762, it had played a major role in his life.

The tribute disappeared into the recesses of libraries, leaving as the only other tangible memorials to Sir William the Gainsborough portrait which now hangs in the De Young Museum in California, the tablet in Bath Abbey, and the monuments on Clifton Down.

Manila Hall went thereafter to the Miles family, pioneers of banking in Bristol. In 1882, Sir Joseph Weston, then Mayor, bought the Hall and sold part of its grounds as building plots. The following year, he sold the Hall itself to a French Roman Catholic sisterhood, the Dames de la Mere de Dieu, as a school, which it remained until it was demolished in the early 1900s.

The nuns, perhaps disliking the idea that the monuments in the garden had been placed there to commemorate events in which the French were clearly losers, ordered their removal. They would have been lost forever had it not been for the efforts of a local antiquarian, Dr John Beddoe, who organised a private subscription to save them. The cenotaph to the vanished 79th Regiment, and the obelisk to William Pitt, Earl of Chatham, were re-erected on Clifton Down where they still stand today.

NOTES

ABBREVIATIONS USED

ADM	Admiralty Papers, Public Record Office
AMS	Additional Manuscripts Collection, British Library
B	Minutes of East India Company Directors (Court Books), OIOC
BL	British Library
BM	British Museum
BoL	Bodleian Library
BRO	Bristol Record Office
CO	Colonial Office Papers, Public Record Office
Documents	Documents Illustrating the British Conquest of Manila 1762–1763, ed. N. P. Cushner Camden Fourth series Vol. 8
E	General & Miscellaneous Correspondence OIOC
H	Home Miscellaneous Series, OIOC
L/MAR	Maritime Department Records, OIOC
OIOC	Oriental and India Office Collections, British Library
Orme MSS	Orme Manuscripts Collection OIOC
PRO	Public Record Office
RA	Royal Archives, Windsor
SP	State Papers, Public Record Office
T	Treasury Papers, Public Record Office
TNA	The National Archives: Public Record Office
WA	City of Westminster Archives
WO	War Office Papers, Public Record Office

CHAPTER 1. UNCERTAIN OPPORTUNITIES

1. William Draper's life as Squire of Beswick in Holderness is covered in Reynard's *Hunting Notes from Holderness* (1914) and McCausland's *Old Sporting* (1948). On an income of £700 a year Squire Draper, who survived until 1745, raised seven sons and three daughters. His portrait, painted around 1730, is in a private collection in Yorkshire.

2. BRO: Customs House Officers Affidavits 1702–35, 'Ingleby Draper, Kingswayter (sic), sworn before Mr Mayor 29 December 1715'.

3. BRO: Parish Registers of St Augustine the Less. The church, almost adjacent to Bristol Cathedral, was demolished after being blitzed in the Second World War. Ingleby Draper's tombstone inscription, and that of his wife Mary, had been recorded by a Bristol historian as far back as 1816.

4. OIOC: Court Minutes of the East India Company 1729.
5. OIOC: Bombay Mayor's Court 1736.
6. OIOC: Bombay Marriage Registers.
7. TNA: PRO: WO 25/21. Commission Book March 1744: 'William Draper, gent, to be Ensign in Lord Henry Beauclerk's Regiment'.

CHAPTER 2. STEPS TOWARDS VISIBILITY

1. Postings of the 48th and changes in colonelcy of the regiment are covered in Lt-Col. Russell Gurney's *History of the Northamptonshire Regiment*.
2. George Townshend, who became Field-Marshal 1st Marquess Townshend, was the eldest son of Charles 3rd Viscount Townshend and his wife Audrey Harrison, daughter and heiress of Edward Harrison of Balls Park, Hertford, one time Governor of Madras. Audrey, or Ethelreda, Harrison was a scandalous figure, known in London as the 'Lively' Lady Townshend. Her Harrison family connections suggest that she was in some way related to Mary Harrison, mother of William Draper, though the exact relationship remains obscure.
3. *History of the Northamptonshire Regiment*, p. 17.
4. TNA: PRO: WO 25/21: May 1746, 'William Draper, gent, to be Adjutant to our 1st Regiment of Foot Guards commanded by our Most Dearly Beloved son, William Augustus, Captain-General'.

CHAPTER 3. PLEASURES OF PEACE: CALL TO COMMAND

1. King's College, Cambridge: Archives.
2. Beckles Willson, *The Life and Letters of James Wolfe*, p. 191.
3. BL: *Town and Country Magazine*, July 1779, 'Histories of the Tête-à-Tête Annexed, or Memoirs of the Manila Hero and Mrs P---s'. Account of Sir William's life and achievements, as well as alluding to his current liaison with a Mrs Potts. The text is accompanied by two bust portraits in oval frames.
4. H. T. Waghorn, *Cricket Scores, Notes etc from 1730–1774*.
5. Horace Walpole, *Memoirs of the Reign of George II*, ed. Brooke, Vol. II.
6. Drummond's Bank, *Archives*. Draper's account was handled by Drummond's from 1751, until a year or two after his death in 1787.
7. *The Times*, 18 January 1787.
8. C. E. Vulliamy, *Mrs Thrale of Streatham*; James Clifford, *Hester Lynch Piozzi*. Polly Hart, referred to in 1762 by Horace Walpole as 'Draper's old mistress', was Henry Thrale's mistress for a number of years until her common law marriage to the actor Samuel Reddish. She was still in the public eye as late as March 1773, when the *Westminster Magazine* in a section called 'The Court of Cupid' printed the so-called *Memoirs of Miss H--t, alias Mrs R-----h, Mr T----e, and Sir Edward D----g*, inspired by gossip that Polly Hart was to marry Sir Edward Dering, Bt. Nothing came of the rumour.
9. BL: *Gentleman's Magazine*, February 1756.
10. BL: *Town and Country Magazine*, July 1779.
11. Walpole, *Correspondence*, ed. Lewis, Vol. 9, p. 108, to George Montagu, 23 June 1750.
12. *The Times*, 18 January 1787.
13. WA: *Parish Registers: St Martin-in-the-Fields*, Vol. 36.

14. Walpole, *Memoirs of the Reign of George II*, ed. Brooke, Vol. II.
15. BL: AMS 32875 f. 208, Draper to Newcastle, from Charles St, St James's, October 1757.
16. BL: AMS 32875 ff. 435–7, Newcastle to Ligonier, Claremont, 6 November 1757.
17. TNA: PRO: WO 26/23 f. 236.
18. The regiment was initially designated as the 64th Foot, but was redesignated as the 79th Foot in June 1758, by which time it was in India. It was formed by taking the youngest companies of the 4th, 8th, 11th, 12th, 20th, 23rd, 24th, 33rd and 36th Foot regiments. It was disbanded at Chatham in June 1763, before it had finally returned from Manila. It had no connection with the Queen's Own Cameron Highlanders, which was raised as a revived 79th Foot later in the century by Alan Cameron for the Irish Establishment as the 79th (Highland Cameronian Volunteers Regiment of Foot).
19. OIOC: General Letter from E. I. C. London to Fort St George, 23 December 1757.
20. BL: AMS 17493 f196, Calcraft Letters, Calcraft to Burton in New York, 12 November 1757.
21. RA: Cumberland Papers 57/68; Adlercron to Cumberland from Madras, 16 November 1757.
22. TNA: PRO: WO26/23 f339, Orders and Instructions to Lt-Col Draper from Lord Barrington, Secretary at War, 17 December 1757.
23. BL: Burney Catalogue; *Public Advertiser*, 18 December 1757.
24. OIOC: EIC L/Mar 525A, Log of East Indiaman, the *Pitt* (Captain William Wilson), 1757–1760.

CHAPTER FOUR: TO INDIA AND A SIEGE

1. OIOC: L/Mar 525A.
2. TNA: PRO: WO40/1 Letters-In, unnumbered, Draper to Barrington, off Fernando da Loronho, 15 May 1758.
3. BL: Richard Owen Cambridge, *Account of the War in India, 1750–1760*. This 1766 publication contained Lawrence's memoirs of his service in India 'edited from original documents'.
4. OIOC: H95, f. 257, Letter of Henry Vansittart to Adm. Pocock, Madras, 15 December 1758.
5. W. J. Wilson, *History of the Madras Army*, Vol. 1, Chap III.
6. Ibid.
7. Fortescue, *History of the British Army*, Vol. 2.

CHAPTER FIVE: OFFERS AND DEPARTURES

1. BL: Hardwicke Papers AMS 35893 ff. 206–10, Draper to Peirson, Madras, 18 February 1759.
2. General Blakeney had been awarded a Knighthood of the Bath for his brave but unsuccessful defence of Minorca during the French siege of 1756.
3. Ralph Jenison was Master of the Royal Buckhounds at Windsor from 1734 to 1744 and again from 1746 to 1756. At one time he was MP for Newport, Isle of Wight. He was a convivial figure with a wide circle of friends, which included William Draper who followed the Buckhounds from his days at Eton. Jenison retired in 1757 and died in London in May 1758.

4. Major John More was senior captain of the 79th when it first went to India. For a time he commanded the regiment. He was killed in the final assault on Manila in October 1762.
5. TNA: PRO: WO40/1, Letters-In, unnumbered; Draper to Barrington, from Fort St George, 20 February 1759.
6. OIOC: H95, Letter from Draper to Governor and Council at Fort St George, 28 March 1759.
7. OIOC: Orme MSS 293. 17, Draper to officers in the Company's battalion, 13 April 1759.
8. OIOC: H95, Stringer Lawrence to William Pitt, from camp near Madras, 22 February 1759.
9. BL: AMS Egremont Papers 3488 ff. 161–71, Brereton to Holdernesse, undated.
10. OIOC: W2138 Vol. 89, Diary and Consultation Book, Fort St George, Madras 21 April 1759.

CHAPTER SIX: IDEAS FROM A VOYAGE TO CHINA
1. OIOC: L/MAR/B 4D and 4U, Log of *Winchelsea* (Captain Hon. Thomas Howe). The voyage London/Madras/Canton/London lasted from October 1757 to January 1761.
2. H. T. Fry, *Alexander Dalrymple and the Expansion of British Trade.*
3. Ibid.
4. Hosea Ballow Morse, *Chronicles of the East India Company Trading to China,* Vol. 5.
5. BL: William L. Schurz, *The Manila Galleon.*
6. TNA: PRO: 30/47, Draper to Egremont, undated, probably November 1761, 'Reasons and Considerations upon the Enterprise against the Philippines'.
7. BL: AMS 17494 ff. 104–07, Calcraft Letters; Calcraft to Draper, 27 January 1759.
8. Ibid., ff. 134–37, 27 March 1759.
9. OIOC: Letters from Court to Fort William; 1 April 1760.
10. Walpole, *Correspondence*, ed. Lewis, Vol. 9, p. 307. Lewis in a note suggests that Walpole had used the word 'handsomely' as a tribute to Draper for volunteering so soon after his return from India. Yet Draper had been absent for more than a year on the voyage, and needed to get a paid command as soon as possible.
11. BL: Calendar of Home Office Papers, 22 February 1761, 'Col Draper granted his commission as Governor of Forts and Batteries of Yarmouth vice Roger Townshend, dec'd.' Roger Townshend was the uncle of Draper's brother officer, Hon. George Townshend, not his brother Roger, who was killed in action in America at the Battle of Ticonderoga in 1759.
12. OIOC: H 96 ff. 25–31, Letter from Major John Call to Draper, Fort St George, 15 July 1760.

CHAPTER SEVEN: PEACE DELAYED: WAR WIDENED
1. OIOC: OIR 354, 541, Records of Fort St George, Vol. 23, February 1761.
2. H. D. Love, *Vestiges of Old Madras*, Chapter XLIII.
3. Horace Walpole, *Memoirs of the Reign of George II.*
4. Brian Tunstall, *William Pitt, Earl of Chatham*, Chapter XII, p. 295.
5. Ibid. p. 305.

CHAPTER EIGHT: THE MANILA PLAN IS LAUNCHED

1. TNA: PRO: PRO 30/47.
2. 'Rough Sketch of an Expedition to Manila', Rhodes House Library, Oxford, North Papers, Brit. Emp., S.1 *(Documents 2)*.
3. OIOC: B/77, Court Minutes, 30 December 1761 *(Documents 1)*.
4. BL: AMS 32933, Newcastle to Hardwicke, Claremont, 10 January 1762.
5. TNA: PRO; CO77/20, Secret Committee of the EIC to Earl of Egremont, East India House, 14 January 1762 *(Documents 3)*.
6. OIOC: D110, Minutes of Secret Committee, EIC, 16 January 1762.
7. Ibid., 17 January 1762.
8. TNA: PRO: CO77/20, Instructions of George III to Draper, 21 January 1762 *(Documents 5)*.
9. TNA: PRO: CO77/20, Earl of Egremont to Lawrence, 23 January 1762 *(Documents 7)*.
10. TNA: PRO: CO77/20, Earl of Egremont to Secret Committee, EIC, 23 January 1762 *(Documents 8)*.
11. BL: AMS 37836 EIC to Fort St George, 19 February 1762 *(Documents 10)*.
12. TNA: PRO: ADM 2/87, Anson to Captain King of the *Argo*, 25 January 1762.
13. BL: *St James's Chronicle*, 16 January 1762.
14. BL: Ibid., 12 February 1762.
15. BL: Ibid., 21 January 1762.
16. BL: *Public Advertiser*, 28 January 1762.
17. OIOC: E1/44 57A, Draper to EIC, Plymouth, 9 February 1762.
18. TNA: PRO: PRO 30/70 3/115, Draper to William Pitt, Plymouth Sound, 9 February 1762.
19. TNA: PRO: CO 77/20, Draper to War Office, Madeira, 11 March 1762 *(Documents 11)*.

CHAPTER NINE: HUSTLE AND ARGUMENTS

1. TNA: PRO: ADM 1/162 (2), Cornish to Clevland, Madras Roads, 23 July 1762 *(Documents 14)*.
2. TNA: PRO: ADM 1/162 (2), Madras Council to Expedition Planning Group, Fort St George, 10 July 1762 *(Documents 13)*.
3. BL: AMS 35898, Cornish to Anson, 1 November 1762.
4. TNA: PRO: Ibid., note 1.
5. TNA: PRO: WO 1/319, Draper to Secretary at War, Fort St George, 27 July 1762 *(Documents 16)*.
6. OIOC: H77, Draper to Pigot, Madras, 23 July 1762 *(Documents 15)*.
7. OIOC: H77, Cornish and Draper to Pigot and Council, Madras, 28 July 1762 *(Documents 17)*.
8. OIOC: H77, Cornish to Pigot, Admiralty House, Madras, 28 July 1762.
9. OIOC: H77, Cornish and Draper to Pigot and Council, Madras, 31 July 1762 *(Documents 19)*.
10. OIOC: H77, Pigot to Cornish and Draper, Fort St George, 31 July 1762 *(Documents 20)*.
11. OIOC: H77, Cornish and Draper to Pigot and Council, Madras, 31 July 1762 *(Documents 21)*.

12. OIOC: H77, Pigot and Council to Cornish and Draper, Fort St George, 31 July 1762 *(Documents 22)*.

13. OIOC: Letters from Fort St George, 1762, No. 81; Council to Dalrymple in Sooloo, 1 August 1762.

CHAPTER TEN: PRESSURES OF WIDER EVENTS

1. Captain S. W. C. Pack, *Admiral Lord Anson*, pp. 248–52.
2. Rex Whitworth, *William Augustus, Duke of Cumberland*, p. 217.
3. 'Your very obedient servants.' Brian Tunstall, *William Pitt, Earl of Chatham*, p. 328.

CHAPTER ELEVEN: COUP DE MAIN

1. William Nichelson, *A Treatise of Practical Navigation and Seamanship*, p. 277.
2. Rojo to commander of the British squadron, Manila, 22 September 1762 *(Documents 29)*.
3. Cornish and Draper to Spanish authorities at Manila, 22 September 1762 *(Documents 30)*.
4. Rojo to Captain Juan Blanco, 25 September 1762 *(Documents 33)*.
5. Draper to Rojo, Malate, 26 September 1762 *(Documents 35)*.
6. Draper to Rojo, before Manila, 27 September 1762 *(Documents 37)*.
7. Draper to Rojo, 27 September 1762 *(Documents 38)*.
8. Rojo to Draper, 27 September 1762 *(Documents 39)*.
9. Draper to Rojo, before Manila, 28 September 1762 *(Documents 43)*.
10. OIOC: HM76, pp. 55–65, Stevenson's account of the capture, written 10 November 1762 *(Documents 47)*.
11. *London Gazette*, April 1763; *Journal of the Proceedings of His Majesty's forces against Manila*.
12. Ibid.
13. Ibid.
14. Reply of the British commanders to Spanish proposals, 7 October 1762 *(Documents 50)*.
15. Conditions offered to the city of Manila by the British commanders, 6 October 1762 *(Documents 51)*.
16. Proposals Agreed to by the Governor, Audiencia, etc., 6 October 1762 *(Documents 52)*.
17. Draper's Conditions for the surrender of the Philippines, Manila, 30 October 1762 *(Documents 68)*.

CHAPTER TWELVE: FRUSTRATIONS

1. *Annual Register*, 1763. *History of Europe*, Chapter III, p. 14.
2. OIOC: Home Misc. H76, Diary and Consultations of Dawsonne Drake, Manila, September–December 1762, entry for 2 November.
3. Cornish to Clevland, on board the *Norfolk*, Manila Bay, 1 November 1762 *(Documents 69)*.
4. TNA: PRO: WO 1/319 ff. 405–13, Draper to Sec at War, Manila, 2 November 1762.
5. Cornish to Draper, Cavite, 2 November 1762 *(Documents 71)*.

6. TNA: PRO: ADM 1/162 (2) f. 99, Draper to Cornish, 4 November 1762.
7. BL: AMS 34, 686 f. 8, Draper to Lawrence, Manila, 10 November 1762.
8. OIOC: H76, Diary and Consultations of Dawsonne Drake, September–December 1762, entry for 10 November.
9. TNA: PRO: ADM 51/882, Log of *Seahorse*, November 1762–April 1763.

CHAPTER THIRTEEN: QUARRELS IN MANILA
1. OIOC: H77, Drake to Cornish, 16 December 1762.
2. OIOC: H97, Drake to Egremont, 1763.
3. TNA: PRO: CO 77/20 ff. 198–203, Oidores of Manila to King Carlos III (trans.).
4. TNA: PRO: ADM 1/162 (2), ff. 63–6, Cornish to Clevland, off Pulo Timoan, 14 March 1763 *(Documents 96)*.
5. TNA: PRO: WO 1/319 f. 457, Lawrence to Townshend, April 1763.

CHAPTER FOURTEEN: A MUTED WELCOME IN ENGLAND
1. TNA: PRO: CO77/20, Draper to Secretary at War, Pall Mall, 14 April 1763.
2. Earl of Liverpool, *A Collection of Treaties*, Vol. III, p. 174.
3. King's College, Cambridge, Library: Coll. 1. 44.
4. Ibid.
5. BL: AMS 38580 f. 483, Draper to William Draper of Adscomb, Croydon, 7 June 1763.
6. Drummond's Bank: Archives.
7. Nathaniel Wraxall, *Memoirs of My Time*.
8. BL: *Journals of the House of Commons*, Vol. 29, 19 April 1763.
9. BL: *Calendar of Home Office Papers*, 1760–1765, No. 1026, 7 October 1763.

CHAPTER FIFTEEN: INTRUDING REALITIES
1. BL: *Calendar of Home Office Papers*, 1760–1765, No. 1179, 4 January 1764.
2. TNA: PRO: SP94/166, Grimaldi to Rochford, Madrid, March 1764.
3. TNA: PRO: SP94/167, Halifax to Draper, St James's, 3 March 1764.
4. Ibid. Draper to Halifax, March 1764.
5. Ibid. Masserano to Halifax, 23 April 1764.
6. *Grenville Papers*, Vol. 2, Earl of Sandwich to George Grenville, Whitehall, 23 April 1764.
7. Ibid. Duke of Bedford to George Grenville, Bedford House, 25 April 1764.
8. Bedford, *Correspondence*, Vol. 3, Draper to Duke of Bedford, Clifton, 28 April 1764.
9. Walpole, *Correspondence*, ed. Lewis, Vol. XX, Walpole to Mann, Strawberry Hill, 8 June 1764.
10. BL: *Scots Magazine*, August 1764, p. 455.
11. BL: *A Plain Narrative of the Reduction of Manila and the Philippine Islands*, jointly by Cornish and Draper, 1764.
12. Ibid.
13. BL: *Scots Magazine*, June 1764.
14. TNA: PRO: SP94/167 f. 242, Draper to Halifax, London, 1 August 1764.
15. *Colonel Draper's Answer to the Spanish Arguments, addressed to Halifax*, December 1764.

CHAPTER SIXTEEN: MANILA: THE LAST STAGES

1. BL: AMS40759 ff. 89–92, Backhouse to Secretary at War, Manila, 31 January 1764 *(Documents 112)*.
2. OIOC: H 97 *passim*, Dawsonne Drake to Egremont.
3. OIOC: Orme MSS, Vol. 27, Captain Mathew Horne to correspondent in England, Manila, 4 October 1763.
4. OIOC: H 97, Lawrence to Egremont, Fort St George, October 1763.
5. BL: AMS 40759 ff. 92–3, Backhouse to Secretary at War, Manila, 10 February 1764 *(Documents 113)*.
6. BL: AMS 40759 ff. 94–5, Backhouse to Draper, Manila, 10 February 1764 *(Documents 114)*.
7. BL: AMS 40759 ff. 93–4, Draper to Secretary at War, Clifton, 16 August 1764 *(Documents 117)*.
8. *Calendar of Home Office Papers*, 1760–1765, No. 1865, Secretary at War to Mr Secretary Conway 30 July 1765.
9. Ibid.
10. H. B. Morse, *Chronicles of East India Company trading into China*, Vol. 5, pp. 126–7.
11. Ibid.
12. OIOC: Orme MSS 27 f. 137, Mathew Horne to correspondent in England, undated.

CHAPTER SEVENTEEN: THE FALKLANDS LINKAGE

1. TNA: PRO: SP/94, Spain Conway to Lords of Admiralty, 1764.
2. TNA: PRO: SP/94, Spain Conway to Lords of Admiralty, 20 July 1765.
3. TNA: PRO: SP/94, Spain Egmont to Grafton, July 1765.
4. *Correspondence of the Earl of Chatham*, Vol. III, Speech of 14 January 1766.
5. *Grenville Papers*, Vol. 3, Clive to Grenville, Cape of Good Hope, January 1765.
6. BL: *Memoirs of Count Lally* (published Kiernan, London, 1766).
7. Alfred Noyes, *Voltaire*, Chapter XLIII, p. 608.

CHAPTER EIGHTEEN: PUBLIC AND PRIVATE CONCERNS

1. TNA: PRO: SP94/177, Shelburne to Gray, 20 June 1767.
2. BL: *Scots Magazine*, October 1767.
3. BL: Draper's *Plain Narrative*, 1764.
4. BL: Burney, *Public Advertiser*, May 1767.
5. TNA: PRO: SP94/178, Gray to Shelburne, Madrid, 31 December 1767.
6. BL: John Anstey, *Poems and Life of Christopher Anstey*, Anstey to Draper, Trumpington, 24 December 1767.
7. Ibid. Draper to Anstey, Clifton, 9 January 1768.
8. *Correspondence of the Earl of Chatham*, Countess of Chatham to Draper, Hayes, 16 June 1768.
9. Ibid., Draper to Countess of Chatham, Clifton, 19 June 1769.
10. Ibid., Countess of Chatham to Draper, Hayes, 25 June 1768.
11. *Grenville Papers*, Vol. 4, Knox to Grenville, London, 27 September 1768.
12. TNA: PRO: SP94/181, Harris to Weymouth, Aranjuez, 24 April 1769.

CHAPTER NINETEEN: JUNIUS CHALLENGED

1. Junius to *Public Advertiser, Letter I*, 21 January 1769.
2. BL: AMS 40761, Francis Papers: Revd. Francis to his son, Bath, 28 January 1769.
3. Draper to *Public Advertiser, Letter II*, 26 January 1769.
4. BL: AMS 40761, Francis Papers: Revd. Francis to his son, Bath, 5 February 1769.
5. Junius to *Public Advertiser, Letter III*, 7 February 1769.
6. BL: AMS 40761, Francis Papers: Revd. Francis to his son, Bath, 11 February 1769.
7. TNA: PRO: Probate; Wills and Administrations, October 1769.
8. Draper to *Public Advertiser, Letter IV*, 17 February 1769.
9. Junius to *Public Advertiser, Letter V*, 21 February 1769.
10. Draper to *Public Advertiser, Letter VI*, 27 February 1769.
11. Junius to *Public Advertiser, Letter VII*, 3 March 1769.
12. Draper to *Public Advertiser*, 1 May 1769, Clifton, 24 April 1769.

CHAPTER TWENTY: JUNIUS REVISITED

1. Draper to *Public Advertiser, Letter XXIV*, 14 September 1769.
2. Junius to *Public Advertiser, Letter XXV*, 25 September 1769.
3. Draper to *Public Advertiser, Letter XXVI*, 7 October 1769.
4. Junius to *Public Advertiser, Letter XXVII*, 13 October 1769.
5. L. D. Campbell, *Miscellaneous Works of Hugh Boyd*.
6. BL: AMS 5808 Cole MSS f. 227.
7. BL: *Catalogue of Political and Personal Satires*, 4283n.
8. BL: HMC Townshend MSS, Mrs Orme to Lady Townshend, Clyst, Devon, 28 October 1769.

CHAPTER TWENTY-ONE: AMERICAN CONNECTIONS

1. *Memoirs of Sir Philip Francis*, MacKrabie to Francis, Philadelphia, March 1770.
2. Parish Registers, Trinity Church, Wall Street, 13 October 1770.
3. OIOC: B86 East India Company Court Minutes, 6 February 1771.
4. BL: Barrington Letter Books, Barrington to Draper, Cavendish Square, 25 May 1772.
5. BL: Burney, *Public Advertiser*, 23 June 1772.
6. MCC Archives: *The Laws of Cricket, revised at the Star and Garter, Pall Mall 25 February 1774*.
7. Horace Walpole, *Correspondence*, ed. Lewis, Vol. 39, p. 197.
8. *Thoughts of a Traveller on our American Disputes*, 1774, Lenox Library, New York 4781.
9. *Papers of Benjamin Franklin*, Vol. 22, Benjamin Franklin to Jonathan Shipley, 7 July 1775.

CHAPTER TWENTY-TWO: DOMESTIC GENEROSITIES

1. *Correspondence of King George III*, ed. Fortescue, Vol. III, Letter 1986, 5 April 1777.
2. BL: AMS 32875 f. 112, Eliza Draper to John Wilkes, 22 March 1778.

3. *Memoirs of Sir Philip Francis*, Chapter VII, p. 226.

CHAPTER TWENTY-THREE: FINAL CALL TO ARMS
1. BL: Catalogue of Political and Personal Satires, No. 5591, and *Town and Country Magazine*, Vol. XI, p. 345, 1 August 1779.
2. BL: AMS 38307 f. 180, Jenkinson to Draper, War Office, 29 May 1780.
3. Mahon, *Life of James Murray*, Chapter XVIII, pp. 402–4.
4. TNA: PRO CO 174/41, Minorca correspondence between Draper and Murray.
5. Beatson, *Naval and Military Memoirs*, Vol. 6.
6. BL: AMS 38217 f. 299, Draper to Jenkinson, Minorca, 5 February 1782.
7. Walpole, *Correspondence*, ed. Lewis, Vol. 25, pp. 263–4.
8. Ministere des Affaires Etrangeres, Paris: Correspondence Politique/Angleterre, Vol. 536. ff. 276–7.
9. *Correspondence of King George III*, ed. Fortescue, Vol. V, Letter 3631, 5 April 1782.

CHAPTER TWENTY-FOUR: COURT MARTIAL
1. William L. Clements Library, University of Michigan: Draper to Lord Sydney, Secretary at War, Bath, 14 May 1782.
2. Walpole, *Correspondence*, ed. Lewis, Vol. 25, pp. 308–9.
3. Ibid. p. 342.
4. TNA: PRO: WO 71/100, Court Martial, 1782.
5. Walpole, *Correspondence*, ed. Lewis, Vol. 25, pp. 361–2.
6. BL: *Observations on the Hon. Lieutenant-General Murray's Defence by Sir William Draper*, 1783.

CHAPTER TWENTY-FIVE: THE CHIMERA RENEWED
1. William L. Clements Library, University of Michigan: Draper to Sydney, Brompton Row, 15 March 1784.
2. Ibid., Draper to Sydney, Bath Hotel, Arlington Street, 28 March 1784.
3. Ibid., Draper to Sydney, Brompton Row, 3 September 1784.
4. TNA: PRO: Prob 11/365, Will of Anna Susannah Gore, 1793.
5. Southampton University: *Wellington Papers* WP1/6, Colonel Arthur Wellesley to Lord Mornington, Fort William, 17 April 1797.
6. *Gentleman's Magazine*, Vol. 69, 1799.

RESEARCH
SOURCES

DOCUMENTARY SOURCES
British Library
    Egerton MSS 3488
    Barrington Papers HA174/1026/36
Additional Manuscript Collections
    5808 Cole MSS
    9242 Coxe transcripts
    17493–17496 Calcraft Letters
    19298 Dalrymple
    Plan for conquest of Southern Philippine Islands
    28060–067 Leeds Papers
    29111 Warren Hastings to Court of EIC
    29133–94 Warren Hastings – General Correspondence
    30875 John Wilkes – General Correspondence
    328753, 32919, 32933 Newcastle Papers
    33765 Geographical Collection of Alexander Dalrymple
    33963 Miscellaneous Original Letters (D)
    34686 Palk Papers
    35893, 35898, 35917, 35918, Hardwicke Papers
    37836 Robinson Papers
    38200, 38211, 38212, 38217, 38305–7, 38465, 38580, Liverpool Papers
    40756–65 Francis Papers
    45429–31 Anderson Papers
    62551 Miscellaneous Letters and Papers
Historical Manuscripts Commission Reports; Journals of the House of Commons;
    British Library; Oriental and India Office Collections
Classes
    B: Minutes of East India Company Directors and Proprietors; 1599–1858; 77–98
    D: Minutes and Memoranda of the General Committee; 1700–1858; 22, 110
    E: General & Miscellaneous Correspondence, E1/4; E1/44, E1/45, E/1/49,
    E/4/862
    H: Home Miscellaneous Series incl H76, H77, H91, H95, H96, H97, H98
    L/MAR/A–C Marine Records 1700–1879; Log of *Pitt* 1757–60, L/MAR/B 4d &
    4U Log of *Winchelsea*
    L/P & S EIC Political and Secret Department Records; N: Returns of Baptisms/
    marriages/burials
    MSS EUR 657/1, D1018/1–2; Orme MSS Vols. 27, 293

Z/E/434 & 435 Index Madras Despatches 1753–83
Letters to and from Fort St George, Madras; OIR 345. 541
Records of Fort St George; Diary & Consultation Book OIR 354. 541
The National Archives: Public Record Office
Admiralty Papers
ADM 1 Admiralty In-Letters: 1/162 East Indies; ADM 1/1494 Brereton
ADM 2 Admiralty Out-Letters; 2/85–87
ADM 51 Ships Logs; 51/58 Log of *Argo*, 51/643 *Norfolk*, 51/882 *Seahorse*
Calendar of Home Office Papers
Calendar of State Papers
Chatham Papers PRO 30/8
Colonial Office Papers
CO 77/20 relating to Manila expedition
CO 174/12–14 Minorca 1765–85
State Papers
SP78: Vols. 269–76, Corresp. London/Paris 1760s
SP94: Vols. 165–84, Corresp. London/Madrid 1760s
SP105: 288, Corresp. London/Florence 1781–1782
Treasury Papers
TI 223/25, TI 379 67–70, TI 381/34, TI 382/45, TI 388/86, TI 466, TI 472/235–36, TI 480/130
War Office Papers
WO 1 Secretary at War: Letters-In; WO 4 Secretary at War: Letters-Out; WO 5
Marching & Militia Orders; WO 24 Establishments; WO 25 Registers Various/
Commission Books; WO 26 Warrants, Regulations and Precedents; WO 40,
40/1 Unnumbered In-Letters and Reports; WO 45 Ordnance Office and Office
of C-in-C; WO 47 Board of Ordnance Minutes; WO 55 Ordnance Office;
Miscellaneous Entry Books; WO 64 and 65 Army Lists; WO 71 Judge- Advocate
General's Office Proceedings 71/100 Court Martial 1782
Wills and Probates
Group Probate/Wills
and Administrations – Probate 31
King's College, Cambridge
Corresp. Draper/College 1763
Anthony Allen 'Skeleton of College Members' 1750
Bodleian Library
MSS 25428, 24432 Anstey Letters
County Record Offices
Dorset: Calcraft Papers D/RWR
East Yorkshire: Draper family of Beswick
East Sussex: Murray family correspondence
Somerset: Gore family correspondence
Marylebone Cricket Club Archives
National Army Museum
Adlercron Journal: NAM 8707–48–1
Royal Archives, Windsor
Cumberland Papers

University of Hull
    Hotham Papers
William L. Clements Library, University of Michigan
    Draper-Sydney corresp. 1782 & 1784
University of Southampton
    Wellington Papers
City of Westminster Archives
    Rate Books
    Parish Registers of St Martin-in-the-Fields/St James's/Marylebone
Bristol
Bristol Record Office
    Parish Registers of Bristol: 18th Century
    Corresp. Edward Gore of Kiddington and Sir John Smyth of Barrow Court
    Somerset
Bristol Central Library
Bristol Poll Books
Felix Farley's Bristol Journal
Sketchley's Bristol Directories
Society of Merchant Venturers
    Hall Books 1760–1790

GENERAL REFERENCE
American Dictionary of National Biography
Biographical Dictionary of Actors and Actresses
Canadian Dictionary of National Biography
Complete Peerage
New Oxford Dictionary of National Biography
Journals of the House of Commons
Victoria County Histories

Contemporary Publications
    European Magazine
    The Gentleman's Magazine
    London Gazette
    London Magazine
    Scots Magazine
    The Annual Register 1760–1800
    Town and Country
    Westminster Magazine

Newspapers, incl. *Cambridge Chronicle, Bath Journal, The Public Advertiser, Felix Farley's Bristol Journal, London Chronicle, The Times, St James's Chronicle*

Almon, John, *Anecdotes of the Life of Rt. Hon. William Pitt*, London, 1810
— *Biographical and Political Anecdotes*, London, 1797
Anstey, Christopher, *New Bath Guide*, London, 1766

Barrétt, William, *History and Antiquities of Bristol*, Bristol, 1789

Beatson, Robert, *Naval and Military Memoirs of Great Britain, 1727–1797*, Vols. II & III, London, 1803–1804

Boyd, Hugh, *Indian Observer*, Calcutta, 1795

Cambridge, Richard Owen, *Account of the War in India 1750–60*, Dublin, 1766

Carracioli, Charles, *Life of Robert, Lord Clive*, London, 1775

Charnock, John, *Biographia Navalis*, Vols. 5 & 6, London, 1799

Cornish, Samuel, and William Draper, *A Plain Narrative of the Reduction of Manila and the Philippine Islands*, London, 1764

Dalrymple, Alexander, *Oriental Repertory*, London, 1792

Draper, William, *Colonel Draper's answer to the Spanish arguments ... in a letter addressed to the Earl of Halifax*, London, 1764

— —, *Thoughts of a Traveller upon our American Disputes*, London, 1774

— —, *Observations on the Hon. Lieutenant-General Murray's Defence*, London, 1784

Draper, William Henry, *Morning Walk*, London, 1750

Entick, Revd. John, *General History of the Late War*, London, 1764

Gurney, M., *The Sentence of the Court martial ... held at the Horse Guards*, London, 1783

Lally Tollendall, Comte Arthur de, *Memoirs*, trans., London, 1766

Liverpool, Earl of, *A Collection of Treaties*, London, 1785

Nichelson, William, *Treatise of Practical Navigation*, London, 1796

— —, *New Directory for the East Indies*, London, 1774

— —, *Sundry Remarks and Observations in a Voyage to the East Indies*, London, 1773

Orme, Robert, *History of Military Transactions in Indoostan*, London, 1803

Thicknesse, Philip, *Memoirs and Anecdotes*, Dublin, 1790

— —, *New Prose Bath Guide*, London, 1778

SELECT
BIBLIOGRAPHY

Adamson, Donald, and Peter Beauclerk Dewar, *The House of Nell Gwynn*, London, 1974

Albemarle, Earl of, *Memoirs of the Marquis of Rockingham*, London, 1852

Anderson, Fred, *Crucible of War: The Seven Years War and the Fate of the British Empire in British North America*, London, 2000

Anderson, Philip, *The English in Western India*, London, 1856

Anstey, Christopher, *The New Bath Guide*, ed. Gavin Turner, Bristol, 1994

– –, *An Election Ball*, ed. Gavin Turner, Bristol, 1994

Anstey, John, *Poetical Works of Christopher Anstey*, London, 1808

Ayling, Stanley, *George III*, London, 1976

Barrington, Shute, *The Political Life of Viscount Barrington*, London, 1814

Begbie, P. J., *History of the Services of the Madras Artillery*, 2 Vols., Madras, 1852

Bence-Jones, Mark, *Clive of India*, London, 1974

Bessborough, Earl of, and A. Aspinall (eds.), *Lady Bessborough and Her Family Circle*, London, 1940

Biddulph, J., *Stringer Lawrence*, London, 1901

Blair, Emma H., and James Robertson (eds.), *The Philippine Islands (Vol. 49)*, Cleveland, 1903–1909

Bolitho, Hector, and Derek Peel, *Drummonds of Charing Cross*, London, 1967

Bourke, Hon. Algernon, *History of White's*, London, 1892

Brown, Peter Douglas, *William Pitt, Earl of Chatham*, London, 1978

Burford, E. J., *Royal St James's*, London, 1988

Campbell, Lawrence D., *Miscellaneous Works of Hugh Boyd*, 2 Vols., London, 1800

Cannon, John (ed.), *The Letters of Junius*, Oxford, 1978

Cash, Arthur H., *Laurence Sterne: The Later Years*, London, 1984

Charteris, Hon. Evan, *William Augustus, Duke of Cumberland*, 2 Vols., London, 1913 and 1925

Chaudhuri, Nirad C., *Clive of India*, London, 1975

Chenevix-Trench, Charles, *George II*, London, 1973

Chesterfield, Earl of, *Letters of the 4th Earl of Chesterfield*, ed. B. Dobree, 6 Vols., London, 1932

Clifford, James, *Hester Lynch Piozzi*, London, 1941

Clowes, William L., *History of the Royal Navy*, London, 1890–1895

Corbett, Julian S., *England in The Seven Years War*, London, 1907

Cross, Wibur J., *The Life and Times of Laurence Sterne*, New Haven, 1929

Cushner, Nicholas C. (ed.), *Documents Illustrating the British Conquest of Manila 1762–63* (Camden 4th Series, Vol. 8), London, 1971

De Lancey, Lady, *A Week at Waterloo in June 1815*, ed. B. R. Ward, London, 1906

de la Noy, Michael, *The King Who Never Was*, London, 1996

Dodington, G. Bubb, J. Carswell, and L. A. Dralle (eds.), *Political Journal of George Bubb Dodington*, Oxford, 1965

Duffy, Christopher, *The Military Experience in the Age of Reason*, London, 1987

Edwardes, Michael, *The Nabobs at Home*, London, 1991

Ehrman, John, *The Younger Pitt: The Years of Acclaim*, London, 1969

Egerton, Hugh (ed.), *Royal Commission on Losses and Services of American Loyalists*, Oxford, 1915

Everett, C. W. (ed.), *The Letters of Junius*, London, 1928

Fitzmaurice, E. G. P., *Life of William, Earl of Shelburne*, 3 Vols., London, 1875–1876

Flick, Alexander C., *Loyalism in New York during the American Revolution*, New York, 1901

Forbes, Arthur, *History of the Army Ordnance Services*, 3 Vols., London, 1922

Forbes, James, *Oriental Memoirs*, London, 1812

Foreman, Amanda, *Georgiana, Duchess of Devonshire*, London, 1998

Fortescue, Hon. Sir John, *History of the British Army*, Vols. 2 and 3, London, 1910

— —, *Correspondence of King George III: 1760–1783*, London, 1928

Francis, Beata and Eliza Keary (eds.), *Letters of Sir Philip Francis*, 2 Vols., London, 1901

Fry, Howard T., *Alexander Dalrymple and the Expansion of British Trade*, Toronto, 1970

Gadd, David, *Georgian Summer: Bath in the Eighteenth Century*, Bradford-on-Avon, 1977

George, Dorothy M., *Catalogue of Political and Personal Satires in the British Museum*, Vol. V, London, 1978

— —, *London Life in the Eighteenth Century*, London, 1925

Gleig, Revd. G. R., *Life of Clive*, London, 1907

Goebel, Julius, *The Struggle for the Falkland Islands*, Yale University, 1929, rev. 1982

Gregg, Edward, *Queen Anne*, London, 1950

Grenville, George, *The Grenville Papers*, ed. W. J. Smith, 4 Vols., London, 1853

— —, *Additional Grenville Papers*, ed. J. R. G. Tomlinson, London, 1962

Gurney, Lt-Col. Russell, *History of the Northamptonshire Regiment*, London, 1935

Guy, Alan J., *Oeconomy and Discipline*, London, 1985

— — (ed.), *Col. Samuel Bagshawe and the Army of George II, 1731–62*, London, 1990

Hamilton, Sir Frederick, *History of the Grenadier Guards*, London, 1872

Hamont, Tibulle, *La fin d'un empire Francais aux Indes*, Paris, 1897

Harcourt, E. W. (ed.), *The Harcourt Papers*, 19 Vols., London, 1880–1905

Harlow, Vincent T., *The Founding of the Second British Empire*, Vol. 1, London, 1952

Haswell, Jock, *The British Army: A Concise History*, London, 1974

Hayter, Tony (ed.), *An Eighteenth Century Secretary at War*, London, 1988

Hayward, A., *Autobiography and Letters of Mrs Piozzi*, 2 Vols., London, 1861

Hotblack, Kate, *Chatham's Colonial Policy*, London, 1917

Hough, Richard, *Captain Cook*, London, 1994

Jenkinson, Charles, *The Jenkinson Papers 1760–66*, ed. N. S. Jucker, London, 1949

Johnson, Curt, *Battles of the American Revolution*, Maidenhead, 1975

Jones, Thomas, *History of New York during the Revolutionary Wars*, ed. E. de Lancey, New York, 1879

Keay, John, *The Honourable Company: A History of the East India Company*, London, 1991

Kelch, Ray A., *Newcastle: A Duke without Money*, London, 1974

Kerr, S. P., *George Selwyn and the Wits*, London, 1909

Kimball, Gertrude S. (ed.), *Correspondence of William Pitt to Governors in America*, London, 1906

Kincaid, Dennis, *British Social Life in India 1608–1937*, London, 1973

Lawford, James P., *Britain's Army in India*, London, 1978

Lawson, Philip, *The East India Company*, London, 1992

Lennox, C. H. Gordon, Earl of March, *A Duke and his Friends*, 2 Vols., London, 1911

Lindsay, Jack, *Thomas Gainsborough: His Life and Art*, London, 1981

Lillywhite, Bryant, *London Coffee Houses*, London, 1963

Little, D. and G. M. Kahrl, (eds.), *Letters of David Garrick*, 3 Vols., Oxford, 1963

Longford, Elizabeth, *Wellington: The Years of the Sword*, London, 1969

Love, H. D., *Vestiges of Old Madras 1640–1800*, 4 Vols., London, 1913

Maclachlan, Archibald, *William Augustus, Duke of Cumberland*, London, 1876

MacMillan, Dougald (ed.), *Drury Lane Calendar 1747–76*, Oxford, 1938

Mahon, R. H., *Life of Lieutenant-General Hon. James Murray*, London, 1921

Malmesbury, 3rd Earl of, *Diaries and Letters of 1st Earl of Malmesbury and Friends*, 2 Vols., London, 1870

Manners, Walter Evelyn, *Life of the Marquis of Granby*, London, 1899

Marshall, Dorothy, *18th Century England*, London, 1962

Marshall, P. J., *East India Fortunes*, London, 1976

Martelli, George, *Jemmy Twitcher*, Oxford, 1962

Morris, Christopher, *King's College: A Short History*, Cambridge, 1988

Morse, Hosea Ballow, *Chronicles of the East India Company trading to China*, 5 Vols., Oxford, 1926–1929

Mowll, Timothy, *Horace Walpole: The Great Outsider*, London, 1996

Namier, Sir Lewis, and John Brooke, *Charles Townshend*, London, 1964

— —, *History of Parliament: House of Commons 1764–90*, London, 1964

Nelson, Paul David, *William Tryon and the Course of Empire*, North Carolina, 1990

Norton, Mary Beth, *The British Americans: Loyalist Exiles in England 1774–1789*, London, 1974

Noyes, Alfred, *Voltaire*, London, 1936

Owen, John B., *The Eighteenth Century 1714–1815*, London, 1974

Pack, S. W. G., *Admiral Lord Anson*, London, 1960

Parkes, Joseph and Herman Merivale, *Memoirs of Sir Philip Francis*, 2 Vols., London, 1867

Parry, John H., *The Spanish Seaborne Empire*, London, 1966

Petrie, Sir Charles, *King Charles III of Spain*, London, 1971

Phillips, Hugh, *Mid-Georgian London*, London, 1964

Plumb, J. H., *England in the 18th Century*, London, 1950

— —, *Chatham*, London, 1953

Pocock, Tom, *Battle for Empire*, London, 1998

Powell, William C., *Christopher Anstey: Bath Laureate*, Philadelphia, 1944

Quennell, Peter, *Memoirs of William Hickey*, London, 1960

Reid, Stuart, *Like Hungry Wolves: Culloden Moor April 1746*, London, 1944

Rodger, N. A. M., *The Insatiable Earl: Life of John Montagu 4th Earl of Sandwich*, London, 1993

Rogers, H. C. B., *The British Army of the 18th Century*, London, 1977

Roscoe, E. S., and Helen Clergue, *George Selwyn: His Letters and Life*, London, 1899

Russell, Lord John (ed.), *Correspondence of John, Fourth Duke of Bedford*, 3 Vols., London, 1864

Schurz, William L., *The Manila Galleon*, New York, 1959

Schwartz, Richard B., *Daily Life in Johnson's London*, Wisconsin, 1983

Sedgwick, Romney (ed.), *Lord Hervey's Memoirs*, London, 1952

Sheppard, E. W., *Coote Bahadur*, London, 1956

Sherrard, O. A., *Pitt and the Seven Years War*, London, 1955

Sherson, Erroll, *The Lively Lady Townshend and her Friends*, London, 1926

Spear, Percival, *The Nabobs*, London, 1932

Stephens, Henry (ed.), *The Pacific Ocean in History*, San Francisco, 1917

Sutherland, Dame Lucy, *The East India Company in Eighteenth Century Politics*, Oxford, 1952

Taylor, W. S., and J. H. Pringle, *Correspondence of the Earl of Chatham*, 4 Vols., London, 1838–1840

Thomas, Peter D. G., *John Wilkes: A Friend to Liberty*, Oxford, 1996

Thrale, Hester, *Thraliana: The Diary of Mrs Thrale, later Mrs Piozzi*, ed. K. C. Balderston, Oxford, 1942

Tillyard, Stella, *Aristocrats: Caroline, Emily, Louisa and Sarah Lennox 1740–1832*, London, 1994

Townshend, C. V. F., *Military Life of Field-Marshal George, 1st Marquess Townshend*, London, 1901

Tracy, Nicholas, *Manila Ransomed*, Exeter, 1995

Tunstall, Brian, *William Pitt, Earl of Chatham*, London, 1938

Turner, E. S., *Gallant Gentlemen: A Portrait of the British Officer*, London, 1956

Valentine, Alan, *The British Establishment 1760–1784*, Oxford, 1970

van der Kiste, John, *King George II and Queen Caroline*, Stroud, 1997

van Schaak, Henry, *Memoirs*, New York, 1892

Villiers, Marjorie, *The Grand Whiggery*, London, 1939

Vulliamy, C. E., *Mrs Thrale of Streatham*, London, 1936

Wade, John, *Junius*, London, 1850

Wake, Joan, *The Brudenells of Deene*, London, 1953

Walpole, Horace, *Correspondence*, ed. Wilmarth S. Lewis, 48 Vols., New Haven, Connecticut, 1937–1983

— —, *Memoirs of the Reign of George II*, ed. J. Brooke, New Haven, 1983

— —, *Memoirs of the Reign of George III*, ed. G. F. R. Barker, London, 1894

— —, *Last Memoirs of the Reign of George III*, ed. D. Le Marchant, London, 1846

Ward, George A. (ed.), *Journal and Letters of the late Samuel Curwen*, New York, 1845

Warner, Oliver, *The British Navy*, London, 1975

White, R. J., *The Age of George III*, London, 1968

Whitworth, Rex, *Field-Marshal Earl Ligonier*, Oxford, 1958

— —, *William Augustus, Duke of Cumberland*, London, 1992

Williamson, Victor, *Memorials of Brooks's*, London, 1906

Willson, Beckles, *The Life and Letters of James Wolfe*, London, 1907

Wilson, W. J., *History of the Madras Army*, London, 1882

Wraxall, Nathaniel, *Historical and Posthumous Memoirs*, ed. H. B. Wheatley, London, 1884

Wright, A., and W. L. Sclater, *Sterne's Eliza*, London, 1923

Wylly, H. C., *Life of Eyre Coote*, London, 1922

BRISTOL

Cave, Charles, *A History of Banking in Bristol*, Bristol, 1899

Collard, Jane, David Ogden, Roger Burgess, *A History of Bristol Cathedral School*, Bristol, 1992

Jones, Donald, *History of Clifton*, Chichester, 1992

Latimer, John, *Annals of Bristol in the 18th Century*, 3 Vols., Frome, 1893

McGrath, Patrick, *Bristol in the 18th Century*, Newton Abbott, 1972

—, *History of the Merchant Venturers of Bristol*, Bristol, 1975

Morgan, E. T., *History of Bristol Cathedral School*, Bristol, 1913

Nicholls, J. F., and John Taylor, *Bristol Past and Present*, 3 Vols., Bristol, 1882

SPORTING

Bowen, Rowland, *Cricket: a History of its Growth*, London, 1970

Buckley, George B., *Fresh Light on 18th Century Cricket*, Birmingham, 1935

Gordon, Ross, *A History of Cricket*, London, 1972

Hare, J. P., *History of the Royal Buckhounds*, London, 1895

Marshall, John, *The Duke Who Was Cricket*, London, 1961

McCausland, Hugh, *Old Sporting*, London, 1948

Mortimer, Roger, *The Jockey Club*, London, 1958

Reynard, Frank H., *Hunting Notes from Holderness*, London, 1914

Waghorn, H. T., *Cricket Scores from 1730–1774*, London, 1899

THESES OR PUBLISHED ARTICLES

Hayes, J. W., 'Lieutenant-Colonel and Major-Commandants of the Seven Years War', *Journal of Society for Army Historical Research*, Vol. 36, 1958

Leebrick, Karl C., 'Troubles of an English Governor of the Philippine Islands', in H. M. Stephens and H. E. Bolton (eds.), *The Pacific Ocean in History*, San Francisco, 1917

McGrath, Patrick, and John Cannon (eds.), *Essays in Bristol and Gloucestershire History*, Chapter 9, 'The American Loyalists'

Middleton, Richard, 'Pitt, Anson and the Admiralty, 1756–1761', *History*, Vol. IV, 1970

Savage, W. R., *The West Country and the American Mainland Colonies 1763–1783*, Ox. B. Lit Thesis, 1952

Sibley, N. W., 'The Story of the Manila Ransom', *Journal of Comparative Legislation and International Law*, 1925

Thornton, A. P., 'The British in Manila, 1762–1764', *History Today*, Vol. 7, 1957

Tracy, Nicholas, *Vice-Admiral Sir Samuel Cornish and The Conquest of Manila 1762*, M. Phil. diss., University of Southampton, 1967

INDEX